D0554374

Flying Freestyle

Flying Freestyle

An RAF Fast Jet Pilot's Story

Jerry Pook MBE DFC

Pen & Sword
AVIATION

To Lena and Karen

First published in Great Britain in 2009 by
Pen & Sword Aviation
an imprint of
Pen & Sword Books Ltd
47 Church Street
Barnsley
South Yorkshire
S70 2AS

Copyright © Jerry Pook, 2009
ISBN 978 184415 824 9

The right of Jerry Pook to be identified as Author of this Work has
been asserted by him in accordance with the Copyright, Designs and Patents
Act 1988.

A CIP catalogue record for this book is
available from the British Library
All rights reserved. No part of this book may be reproduced or transmitted
in any form or by any means, electronic or mechanical including photocopy-
ing, recording or by any information storage and retrieval system, without
permission from the Publisher in writing.

Typeset in Sabon by
Lamorna Publishing Services

Pen & Sword Books Ltd. incorporates the imprints of Pen & Sword
Aviation, Pen & Sword Maritime, Pen & Sword Military, Remember When
Publications, Wharncliffe Local History, Pen & Sword Select, Pen & Sword
Military Classics and Leo Cooper.

Printed in the UK by the MPG Books Group

For a complete list of Pen & Sword titles please contact
PEN & SWORD BOOKS LIMITED
47 Church Street, Barnsley, South Yorkshire, S70 2AS, England
E-mail: enquiries@pen-and-sword.co.uk
Website: www.pen-and-sword.co.uk

Contents

Foreword

by Air Vice-Marshal R.D. Elder CBE FRAeS RAF

I first met Jerry Pook at the Royal Air Force College Cranwell in 1965, almost immediately after arriving there myself as a fresh-faced aspirant Flight Cadet. Amongst my recollections of those frantic early days of cadet life, was the close 'attention' meted out to us by the Senior Entry, and being strongly impressed by this dapper and energetic Under Officer – who at that time seemed impossibly senior to me – and who was to win the coveted Flying Prize on graduation. Unbeknown to us then, our paths were to cross many times in our later careers: on Hunters, in the Cold War Recce world and on Tornados and it soon became apparent that his innate skill and fierce, unbridled enthusiasm for flying would take him on to greater things in the air. Jerry also seemed to possess that indefinable lucky streak, so essential for survival in those accident-prone days, when we lost many colleagues in flying accidents.

Jerry was, and is (!), one of life's natural rebels, and even during early training, he made no secret that he would never aspire to high rank or administrative responsibility. His great talent is in the skies as a gifted airman and leader. In Bahrain, I flew with him as 'chase' pilot for his Fighter Recce sorties; during the Cold War we were contemporaries in the Ground Attack and Recce world in RAF Germany, and in the late 1970s we were both Flight Commanders at sister Recce stations in NATO, Jerry flying RF 104G Starfighters at RNLAF Volkel and I just 20 miles away over the border in West Germany, flying Jaguars. At the time we were all considerably impressed not only with Jerry's flying skills, but also his command of the Dutch language when dealing with his 'fire-cracker' pilots!

Allied to his sustained professionalism, Jerry deployed a caustic wit and laconic sense of humour which enabled him to find entertainment in the most trying circumstances – an essential requirement on exercise and in war. His professional talents (and sense of humour) were tested to the limit in the Falklands War where he was awarded the Distinguished Flying Cross for demonstrating outstanding courage and leadership in the air. Later on at RAF Cottesmore, where I was his Station Commander, he was awarded the MBE, for his excellent work training flying instructors of the 3 nations. who contributed to the famous Trinational Tornado training Establishment.

Ron Elder

Preface

The RAF I joined in the early 60s still retained many aspects of the Second World War – inspired professionalism and determination to achieve the operational task. Flying accidents were frequent, particularly in single-seat fíghters. As an example, just ten years previously, at the end of the massive expansion caused by the Korean War, the RAF had lost nearly 500 aircraft in one year's peacetime training. In the early 60s the service was losing, on average, fifty to sixty pilots killed each year – in peacetime. These facts were well known to all of us aspirant pilots. In the main they caused no second thoughts or fears of mortality – rather they were seen as an exclusive and stimulating cachet to the overwhelmingly thrilling prospect of military flying. There were no non-volunteers among us.

This is unashamedly a story about flying and the sheer lust to get into the air at all costs. It is about everything to do with becoming a military flying professional and the adventures, sacrifíces and heartaches involved. It is about surviving the risks through sheer luck, guile and maybe some animal self-preservation instinct on my part. If my success was also due to any special flying skíll then that was also good fortune on my part. Many of my colleagues and friends were killed in flying accidents. Of my Cranwell Entry of about forty pilots who graduated in 1966, seven were killed in flying accidents, three of them while flying Lightnings.

By the end of my service flying career I had flown some 5,500 hours on the Jet Provost, Gnat, Hunter, F104G Starfíghter, Harrier and Tornado. I had also been an instructor on several of these types. I flew for twenty-eight years non-stop, without a Staff or Ground Tour. I flew overseas tours of duty in the Persian Gulf, West Germany and Belize. The majority of my flying took place during the Cold

War, which was treated very much as a 'Hot War' by our commanders. I also flew low level ground attack and recce missions during the Falklands War.

Looking through my flying log books I can find only about eight complete months during that twenty-eight year period when I did not fly at all, most of those periods being taken up by various Ground School courses on new aircraft types.

This is not a career officer's story and it is written from the point of view of a relatively junior pilot. I joined the RAF to see the world from a single-seat fighter cockpit, not to become an air marshal. A squadron commander whose opinion I valued, once told me that loyalty was something you owed to your subordinates as a bound duty, while getting it in return only if you had earned it.

I started writing this story shortly after completing my *Falklands Diary*, having discovered an enjoyment of writing for its own sake. I have concentrated on the flying, and there is scant attention to the domestic details of my life, for which I apologize to my loved ones, who may be disappointed not to find more reference to them. I hope this will not be seen as a sign of my indifference, rather as an indication of my total enthusiasm and absorption in the business of flying aeroplanes from an early age until the sad day in 1992 when I was stopped permanently from flying military aeroplanes because of ill health.

Jerry Pook
2008

The views and opinions expressed in this book are those of the author alone and should not be taken to represent those of HMG, MOD, the RAF or any government agency.

Chapter 1

Beginnings

30 May 1982. About 4 kilometres short of the target things began to happen very fast. I could see the target area clearly (the saddle of Mount Harriet) and realized that it was unoccupied, i.e. no helicopters were visible on the ground. At the same moment we crossed a dirt road on which several military vehicles were stopped. Within a couple of seconds I felt a significant 'thump' in the airframe somewhere behind me. I knew I had been hit. Having seen no tracer or SAMs, I assumed it was small-calibre stuff. JR, my wingman, had seen the vehicles and observed the hit on me. He transmitted straight away: 'Jerry, you're leaking fuel!'

This was a considerable understatement as I immediately began to generate a substantial 'contrail' of fuel which, of course, I could not see. A quick glance in the cockpit showed nothing amiss and a glance ahead confirmed that our planned target area was bare of activity. All of the above happened within the space of about ten seconds. Before reaching the landing zone, I decided to turn hard left immediately and try an opportunity attack on the artillery position which lay only a few seconds flying time to the west, before setting course for home with my punctured jet. I crossed over JR in the turn, calling my intentions on the radio. (JR did not hear this as my radio was packing up again.) I rolled out on a south-westerly heading and looked right to the saddle of Wall Mountain, where the artillery position was located. Within a few seconds I heard a garbled call from JR, who I picked up about a mile to my right, heading towards me in a dive onto the target, which I now saw clearly. Instinctively I hauled around to the right at full power on to the target, simultaneously calling JR to break out left after my attack, which was almost head-on to his. By chance we had achieved the perfect coordinated attack. I dimly remember JR flashing past me as I rolled out and fired my rockets from close range, aiming low to allow for the reduced gravity drop. (Naturally, peacetime firing ranges were only of academic interest with targets that shot back.) The first rockets were exploding amongst the gun positions before the last had left the pod After the attack, a hard right turn left me running out at maximum speed to the south-east. I could no longer see JR, who was almost back in position on my right, strafing the road as we passed to keep heads down. Barely two minutes had elapsed since I had been hit and now I settled down to check a few things. By now one of my two hydraulic systems had failed and, as I pulled up into the climb, several unanswered calls to JR demonstrated that my radios had packed up for good. The final twenty minutes of my sortie were to be flown in silence. In the climb through cloud I checked fuel again; before the hit I had over 4,500lb of fuel and, as previous small calibre hits had caused leaks from one side only, I was still confident that I could get back to the ship.

At 10,000 feet I pulled the handle. My first Harrier ejection was extremely violent and I clearly remember my head being forced down between my knees by the 3,000lb thrust of the rocket seat. After this the relief of hanging in the harness was overwhelming...

I dropped the PSP at what I estimated to be about 200 feet and immediately smashed into a large piece of the South Atlantic which rose to meet me. Now the panic really started. I was unable to release my parachute and straight away I was off, being dragged by the strong wind on a wild rollercoaster ride from wave to wave. Luckily I was dragged on my back or I would have drowned very quickly. However, try as I might I was unable to get enough purchase to release my parachute with my rapidly freezing fingers. I could not see what I was doing because of the bulk of my lifejacket and the Browning pistol stowed underneath. At last my chute collapsed, allowing me to pull in my life raft pack and inflate it, although I was still unable to release the parachute harness. A Lynx was already hovering overhead, but I realized that I had to get into the life raft first in order to get rid of my parachute. Although I should have waited for the life raft to harden up a bit, the urge to get out of the water was too strong. With all my remaining strength I managed to haul myself aboard, helped by the fact that the life raft was travelling steeply downhill as I entered. Temporarily safe in the wildly rocking life raft, I sprawled face down for several minutes, not daring to move in case I fell out. I knew that I would never be able to climb back in again should I capsize.

This and many more adventures are described in *RAF Harrier Ground Attack Falklands*, also published by Pen & Sword, but I'm getting ahead of my story...

With Hitler's war just about wrapped up and the Japanese war in its final stages I was born in a nursing home in Teignmouth, a sleepy little haven on the sheltered south-east coast of Devon. My mother, Pam, had spent most of the war living either in Dawlish or in various 'digs' around the country while Dad was at sea with the Royal Navy. Dad had joined the 'Andrew' (a lower-deck term for the RN) as a writer in 1923, reaching the rank of petty officer at the outbreak of war while serving aboard the battlecruiser HMS *Repulse*. He had left the *Repulse* before her ill-fated voyage to the Far East and spent a couple of years aboard the heavy cruiser HMS *Norfolk*. In her he had taken part in nine Russian convoys, including the infamous PQ17, had chased the *Bismarck* and been shelled by her, and had witnessed the apocalyptic demise of the German raider at close range. After some brief shore postings in the UK Dad embarked for the Far East for a posting to HMS *Maidstone*, our largest Submarine Depot ship, then very active in the final stages of the Pacific war. Fortunately for us all, he finally arrived in Manila with the war just about over, to return safely home after many more adventures at the end of 1945.

My elder brother Robin and I were blissfully happy growing up in a small south Devon seaside town. We didn't need much to keep us happy. There was little vehicle traffic to speak of, and we often played football in the street. School seemed to be a minor irrelevance whose only purpose was to interrupt play, and I have few memories of what went on within the walls of Dawlish Infant and Junior schools. I passed my early years in the sleepy seaside town in a hazy remembered glow of childhood happiness. To us children there seemed to be no end to our secure and peaceful existence. Even the outbreak of the Korean War affected us little. It all seemed so remote from our lifestyle.

With the Korean war in full swing Dad had been in contact with some of his old Naval pals and was hankering after a return to the 'Andrew'. Eventually he was offered a job in the Reserve Fleet at Devonport, serving aboard HMS *Berry Head*. He commuted daily to and from Plymouth by train for a while but eventually there came the momentous announcement that we were moving to Plymouth to live. Mum had already taken us on a few visits to the big city and Robin and I were overwhelmed at the sheer size and busyness of it after our sheltered years in Dawlish. I remember exciting shopping trips to the bomb-devastated city, with the pre-war big stores such as Dingle's and John Yeo's housed in temporary Nissen huts amidst the rubble of the old city centre. In January 1954 the move was made and while Mum and Dad looked for a house to buy we took a rented house at 20 Winston Avenue, right next to North Road railway station. Robin and I were enrolled at the Public Primary school in North Road itself, a grim Victorian institution just a few minutes' walk from home. Straight away we discovered that life in the big city was going to be different. Although this was by no means the toughest district, the streetwise working-class kids at Public Primary gave me, in particular, a hard time. Bullying was the order of the day, and I was usually the target of one or other bully in the playground. Although fairly weedy in body, I was doing well academically and was regarded, unfairly, as a bit of a swot. This was the beginning of my lifelong hatred of bullies.

At play in the local area life was one continuous adventure. At this time the city was still recovering from the devastation of the Luftwaffe air raids and there was evidence of recent apocalyptic destruction around every corner. This had a powerful influence on me, both at the time and in my future years, giving me a rather fatalistic attitude to life. Somehow the destruction and chaos of war never seemed far away.

A striking contrast between the old and the new Plymouth, the partly-completed blocks of the modern city centre development gleamed futuristically white amongst a sea of ruined buildings, temporary Nissen huts and bombed sites. These latter were the source of almost unlimited adventure and excitement for the small gang with whom Robin and I associated in the North Road district. The further you moved away from the city centre the fewer were the gaps in the once-grand stone terraces. However, there were still plenty enough 'Luftwaffe car parks' to provide ad hoc sports pitches and ready-built adventure playgrounds. On each side there would be severely damaged houses in some danger of collapse. Only the most paltry and ineffective measures had been taken to keep out marauding gangs of kids – i.e. us. The authorities were still snowed under with the gigantic task of re-housing the thousands of families made homeless during the war years. Vast estates of 'prefabs' were still being built as a stop-gap measure until the impoverished local economy recovered sufficiently to allow the building of new housing estates. To our delight many of these bombed houses still had panes of glass intact. With a home-made catapult or a handful of stones we did not shirk our self-appointed task of smashing every remaining pane of glass we could find. After all, we reasoned, the whole lot was going to be demolished anyway, wasn't it?

Of even greater excitement, and even more dangerous, were the tunnelling expeditions into the semi-collapsed basements of bombed buildings. The greatest challenge was for a group of us to find a relatively unexplored ruin and, in an inside corner safe from the prying eyes of the local police, to dig as far as we could into the rubble-filled cellars. Sometimes we would break through walls from one cellar to the next and explore with the dim light of a torch. The aim was to find some untouched items of bric-a-brac or, far more valuable, a piece of wartime ordnance or shrapnel to take home and keep in secret. The whole exercise was quite ludicrously dangerous for a bunch of young children, (this being the main attraction) and I still marvel at how we survived without being buried alive or brained by falling rubble. When not vandalizing bombed-out buildings the most common team sport was the game of 'King', for which you needed just an old tennis ball, a bombed site, and a gang of enthusiastic kids. We would draw lots for who was to start as 'King', who would then be given the ball while the rest of us fled a suitable distance away. King's task was to hit us (preferably as hard as possible) with the ball; those who were hit then being required to join with King in clobbering the remaining players until all had been hit, the last man hit being the winner.

The normality of being close to destruction and weapons of war spread its influence to children's play, young lads being particularly keen to get hold of mislaid items of ammunition (of which there was a lot lying about, particularly on the Dartmoor gunnery ranges). These were then dismantled for their explosive content, to make lethally-dangerous fireworks. Many youths of the period had mutilated hands, missing fingers and thumbs from the unexpected detonation of items of live ammunition being played with.

There were regular visits to Gran and Granfer's cottage in Morchard Bishop, a tiny, primitive farming hamlet in the wilds of north Devon. Granfer was a farm labourer, working mostly with horses and other livestock near the village. The train and bus journey seemed to be to the ends of the earth for one so unused to travel as I was. All of my Devon uncles were ex-wartime servicemen, none of them commissioned. Uncles Alan and John were ex-Army, Ken and

Wally ex-Navy and Reg ex-RAF. All I ever wanted to talk about was the services, and what had happened to them in the war. Granfer had been wounded twice while serving as a farrier in the Devonshire Regiment in the First World War. He would never talk of his experiences but eventually I managed to persuade him to show me the bullet wound in his arm.

In this gentle pre-television, pre-space travel era, home entertainment was simple. We didn't have a lot in the way of toys but there were Jennings and William books and the radio and we would sit for hours listening to Dick Barton, Journey into Space and the Goon Show. *Eagle* was the favourite comic by far, and very good value for money in those days, with excellent artwork and stories of derring-do in space. I was desperately in love with Wendy of the Peter Pan series, mainly because she was always whizzing about in the air with Tinkerbell. I started to have more and more realistic dreams about flying, in which I would hurl myself off a high building and just zoom around like a bird. The space stories of Dan Dare were just about the last word in excitement and there would be a mad rush to grab the comic and catch up with the latest serial when it came through the letterbox on a Saturday morning.

As we grew more adventurous we explored more of the city and were taken on summer boat trips across Plymouth Sound to the lovely beaches of Bovisand, Cawsand and Kingsand. Even better were the long day trips to the endless golden beaches of Whitsand bay, just across the River Tamar. Our favourite destination was Treganhawk beach, after a bus ride to Stonehouse, a trip on the Turnchapel ferry across the River Tamar to Millbrook, and then another journey through the impossibly narrow lanes of Cornwall on an antique little bus, before the final long walk down the cliff path to the beach. At the same time we were introduced to the delights of Dartmoor, by bus to Yelverton followed by long walks into the moors for picnics and epic climbs to the tops of the famous Dartmoor Tors. In the city the reconstruction of Plymouth city centre was almost complete and we felt the first swelling of civic pride in the smart new shopping areas and broad arcades. As well as the beach trips in summer there were regular trips to the unheated Hoe swimming pool or to Mount Wise baths, and the regular Saturday morning cinema show at the Odeon. The old Odeon cinema was at the civilized end of Union Street, (still a notorious 'red light' area) and there was pandemonium as hundreds of young hooligans shouted and fought and threw ice cream, gobstoppers (partly sucked) and any other missile which came to hand. On walking home I was always mildly surprised to realize that no child had actually been killed or maimed during the performance. There was still desperate poverty in many parts of the city, and the children from these areas were ferociously aggressive towards anyone of a different social class.

From Plymouth Hoe I loved to watch the RAF's Sunderland flying boats making their majestic take-off and landing runs across the Sound. Additionally, with Dad now permanently based in Devonport dockyard, there were regular trips for us boys to see the sights of the yard and go aboard various warships, both on private visits with Dad and during Plymouth Navy Days. I recall going aboard HMS *Vanguard* in dry dock, the Navy's last and prettiest battleship, already destined for the scrapyard. Moored alongside Dad's base ship, HMS *Berry Head*, was HMS *Roberts*, a 16-inch gun monitor used for shelling shore targets in the Second World War. In one of the turrets Dad showed me the workings of the gigantic breech in which it would be quite possible to hold a small children's party. I had always been impressed by his stories of serving in the gun turrets of various warships – his usual post at action stations. At various dumps around the yard there were more sad reminders of the once-grand scale of our naval power: dozens of large-calibre gun barrels were piled up in corners like so many rusty drainpipes awaiting disposal, each set of barrels the poignant reminder of yet another fine warship which had disappeared in the holocaust of scrapping which had followed the end of the Korean War. On several occasions Dad took us to see his brother, then serving aboard the Light Fleet carrier HMS *Ocean*, just returned from seeing action in the Korean War. Uncle Ken, a radiographer in the sick bay, showed us round and on one magical occasion I was allowed to sit in the cockpit of a Fleet Air Arm fighter parked in her cavernous hangar deck. Until then I had been determined to join the Seaman Branch of the RN , but this first insight into the wonders of a fighter aeroplane had me hooked straight away. I had never been close to any aircraft before and to me the sleek, shiny fuselage and tiny cockpit were pure science fiction, straight out of a Dan Dare story. A seed was planted and from that moment on I was overwhelmed by the burning ambition to fly jet fighters.

In early 1955 Mum and Dad bought a terrace house in Barn Park Road, Peverell, right next to Central Park. I was already used to

playing in this splendid park which occupied a hilly site not far away
in the northern suburbs. Offering a huge play area, the park was just
like a large slice of the open countryside a few yards from our new
doorstep. Across the allotments just 100 yards from our house lay
the old disused Peverell reservoirs, now empty and overgrown with
trees. This was another ready-made adventure playground, the floors
of the various basins being several feet deep in rich silt which
supported a jungle of luxuriant undergrowth. This was ideal for
various adventure games, to the despair of Mum when we came
home covered in mud from the more swampy areas. Our local
Peverell 'gang' would spend hours roaming the park and looking for
trees to climb out of sight of the ever-vigilant park keepers. These
formidable guardians of public property would relentlessly pursue
and wallop any child caught breaking the byelaws, or being cheeky
for that matter. We had great respect for them. Another favourite
sport (also strictly forbidden in the park) was the downhill racing of
home-built 'carts' which were lashed up from bits of old prams.
There were plenty of steep footpaths down which we would career
out of control, scattering innocent pedestrians and piling up in a
heap on the grass. With no television there was no incentive to stay
at home, indeed most parents were only too glad to have the dirty
feet of their offspring out of the house for as much of the day as
possible. This in contrast to the modern-day obsession with the
ludicrous concept of 'quality time' with offspring. At this time a
child's definition of 'quality time' would have been time spent
entirely removed from the influence of any adult – parent or
otherwise.

   Time at home was usually spent reading, listening to the radio or
doing homework. Favourite radio shows were *The Goons* (Still an
all-time favourite: I've got all the BBC tapes), *Journey Into Space* and
Dan Dare on Radio Luxembourg. I was still fascinated by the Navy
and my favourite fallback for reading consisted of Dad's two copies
of the official RN Manual of Seamanship, which I read again and
again. One copy was from pre-war days and the other post-war. I
was fascinated by the details of knot tying, damage control, slinging
loads, signalling, boat handling and other hows and whys of good
seamanship. As a family we never missed a Plymouth Navy Days and
I was in heaven wandering about the warships, dry docks and heavy
machinery of Devonport Dockyard. In those days the Navy was not
at all shy in letting off quite large explosive charges to simulate depth
charge attacks and torpedo impacts in the huge Number 1 Basin

where all the action took place. I was gun shy at this time and it was a constant source of shame to me, particularly after listening to Dad's tales of sneaking out on deck during firing of HMS *Repulse*'s 14-inch guns (this was a foolish bravado – he confirmed that the concussion had knocked him flat). At the end of each display day huge crowds would gather at the playing fields for the Marines' Sunset Ceremony, where hundreds of Marines and a full Marine Band would display for the spectators. Dad would never miss it and it always brought a lump to the throat as the *Last Post* played and the ensign was lowered.

Although Robin and I were sorry to leave the bombed sites and more central location of Winston Avenue, plans were already laid to get us both into Plymouth College, a minor Public School nearer to our new home. I arrived at Plymouth College with the intake of new boys in September 1956, to be placed in the 'A' set because of my scholarship results. There was a lot of snobbery at the school and an additional area of difficulty resulted from my generally 'weedy' stature. It was soon obvious that I would never succeed at 'blood sports' (such as rugby) which were held in such high esteem throughout the school. Plymouth College had an enviable sporting record and fielded a large number of teams in all the usual sports. If you were not in a school team you were a nobody and your chances of becoming a prefect were slim. Apart from a fitful start at the newly-introduced game of squash, I was a complete duffer at sports until I reached the Sixth Form. Naturally enough, the many social snobs in my year were joined by the 'macho' sporting snobs in looking down on us 'rabbits' as a lower form of life. Discipline was rigidly enforced by the masters and senior prefects by use of the cane or more subtle forms of GBH. After a painful initial introduction to the system I worked out that only the less intelligent boys were getting beaten regularly. From then on, by means of guile and a certain amount of fast thinking when required, I managed to maintain a low profile, to pass relatively unscathed through the school years.

As I had no bike I walked the half-mile to school each day along Peverell Park road. This meant I had to pass the newsagent's shop which was a regular hang-out for some rather unpleasant local yobs. One in particular, a part-time garage mechanic, took an instant dislike to me and began to give me verbal abuse every time I walked by. He was a couple of years older than me, a fair bit bigger, and I didn't fancy my chances against him one little bit. As he grew more aggressive I realized that I would have to do something about it.

Hoping to avoid a beating-up, I never responded to the taunts I received but I refused to change my route to school to avoid the newsagent's shop. I joined the small group taking boxing lessons after school. The instructor was a wonderful ex-Navy boxer who now ran a pub, giving lessons to schools just for the love of it. In spite of his working-class and lower-deck background he was a natural gentleman, always polite and considerate with everyone he met. He taught us the old-fashioned skills and etiquette of the sport, plus some useful tips on techniques to use in a real-life brawl.

Unfortunately, no amount of exercise could make up for my generally feeble frame in such a physical sport. Additionally, I suffered from an over-developed hooter which could not take punishment. In my first serious bout during the boxing contest I ended up bleeding all over the place after the lightest blow to the face. This was a serious embarrassment and put an end to my attempts to become a boxer. However, I reckoned I had learned enough in those few months to have a chance of defending myself against the lout who was becoming more aggressive by the day. By now he, along with some of his mates – he would never act on his own – would regularly intercept me and drag me around the corner of the shop into a lane where I would be given a bit of a 'roughing up' and general abuse about being a 'college boy'. I would just stand there and take the punishment in silence, trying not to give any sign of emotion to satisfy these scumbags I hated so much. I would stumble home in tears of anger and frustration that I was being picked on by these cowards. Eventually the day arrived when I had to go for it.

They had given me a particularly rough time, punching me about the body and banging my head against the wall in the alley. On arriving home I changed into old clothes and gym shoes and walked back to the newsagent's. I knew that the lout was usually there on his own later on in the day. Sure enough he was, and I went straight up to him and challenged him to come round the corner and 'sort it out one-to-one'. He refused. He wanted me to wait around for a bit. I knew his mates would be back soon, and he was too much of a coward to risk it on his own. I realized that I couldn't win against these scum and walked home with a bitter heart. Strangely, the harassment stopped from that moment and I was left in peace on the way to school. I have hated bullies with a passion since that time, and I have always reacted very strongly to anyone who has attempted to bully me either physically or mentally. Unfortunately, this was to make life difficult for me at times during my RAF career later on.

My enthusiasm for flying was growing all the time and I was doing all the 'right' things for a lad with an overwhelming ambition to fly in the RAF. (My initial preference had been to join the Fleet Air Arm, but Dad had talked me out of that. He could see that I was determined to fly and that there would be far better opportunities for a long flying career in the RAF rather than in the Navy). By now I had built just about every KeilCraft model I could afford, including a Jetex-powered Javelin which made just one glorious high-speed flight before smashing into the trees. I had read and reread all the *Biggles* books, plus anything else I could get hold of in the library with the remotest reference to flying. (I had read *The Dam Busters* half a dozen times, although my ambition was to be a single seat fighter pilot – I had always been very independent and fancied the idea of making my own decisions all the time).

In the fourth year, aged fourteen, I joined the RAF CCF Section and went on as many courses and camps as I could. Annual camps were to Gaydon, Shawbury, Horsham St Faith and Wyton, and I went on courses to RAF stations Compton Basset (Radio School), Mountbatten and St Eval near Newquay, the latter a weekend gliding course where I gained my A and B licences in one glorious day's gliding in the summer of '61, achieving over twenty launches before sundown in the old wood-and-fabric Sedburgh and Kirby Cadet. My first gliding licence was signed by Lord Brabazon, one of Britain's pioneer pilots. This first taste of solo flying was a precious experience, although the ultimate thrill was my first powered flight in a Hunting Percival Provost at Shawbury. To a young cadet the machine looked enormous as I struggled up into the side-by-side cockpit. The big 550 hp Alvis radial thundered into life with a crash of the starter cartridge and we were off, taxiing at breakneck speed. After a very snappy take-off my pilot stood the machine on its ear just after lift-off and we exited stage left from the airfield, seemingly clipping the tops off a few low trees at the boundary. Then we were straight into aerobatics over the glorious sun-dappled Shropshire countryside, my head spinning from the intoxication of the g forces and violent manoeuvring. I didn't feel queasy at all, just completely harmonized with the machine and the tumbling sun and sky which revolved gracefully around me. Now I had no choice – I knew that this was what I wanted to do for ever. The feeling that the air was my element and natural home was to remain with me as a permanent subdued longing for the rest of my flying career.

Back at school to my surprise I found that I was prepared to accept more and more responsibility in the school CCF, and by the end of schooldays I had reached the rank of Cadet Flight Sergeant in charge of the RAF Section. The cadet camp at RAF Horsham St Faith convinced me that I wanted to fly the Hawker Hunter. This was my first close- up view of the Hunter, and we spent hours sitting in the cockpit and crawling over the beautifully-proportioned airframe. One day we visited RAF Coltishall, then home to the RAF's famous Air Fighting Development Squadron, plus a couple of the newly-formed Lightning squadrons. The armourers had laid on a demonstration of the 30-mm Aden cannon, at that time the RAF's primary airborne cannon armament. Our group of nervous cadets stood in a half circle just a few yards away from the gun which was mounted on a fixed cradle and pointing into an enormous stop-butt some fifty yards away. The compressed air lines and electrical leads were connected and the armourer cocked in an ammunition belt which was yards long. The sergeant warned us that 'this would be a bit noisy' and reached for the firing button. We pressed our hands over our ears and leant forward into the fierce muzzle blast as the gun hammered out a stream of ball ammunition at twenty rounds per second into the stop-butt. After a few seconds the firing stopped, leaving us literally stunned in a cloud of cordite fumes. The dispersal behind the gun was littered with scores of gleaming shell cases. The power of the weapon was awesome and our daily contact with the RAF's front-line fighters reinforced my determination to get into the single seat fighter business any way that I could.

In the Sixth Form I teamed up with various layabouts a little older than me who were heavily into guitars, Bob Dylan, 12-bar blues and rock 'n roll. We played and sang Bob Dylan and blues stuff and a friend taught me to play some Merle Travis picks and rhythm guitar on a tatty old steel-string which I had traded for my much-loved bike, although I was never much good at it. I deeply regretted not making more effort to get into the choir in the early school years, as most of the local rock group singers were ex-choirboys. (In those days you actually had to have a good singing voice to be accepted as a group singer).

In spite of being permanently skint, my social life in Plymouth seemed to get better and better as we entered the permissive '60s. You didn't need much cash to enjoy yourself. Favourite hang-outs included El Sombrero, a coffee bar in the old Drake's Circus; La Roca, another coffee bar on Mutley Plain, handy for a clandestine cough and a drag during school lunch break; The Minerva, a famous old pub on the Barbican for Saturday night drinking; plus any number of superb country pubs out of town on Dartmoor. A friend was often able to borrow his father's Wolseley 444 in which a regular team of us would roar out of town on drinking sprees, accompanied by various girl friends. Drinking and driving was very much the norm, and I am amazed that we survived without major accidents as we reeled along the narrow Devon lanes. Parties and drinking expeditions seemed never-ending. A typical Saturday night out would start in El Sombrero to meet some girls, continue to the Minerva for as much cheap beer as we could drink, and we would then wind up scrounging drunken sailors' pass-out tickets from the YMCA so we could get in free for the last half of the jazz. Kenny Ball, Alex Welsh, Ken Colyer and many other high-class bands would play every Saturday night at the YM. The dance for jazz was called the Stomp, a laid-back, jive-like hop which was done on the 'on' beat. A party at someone's house merely required a gallon of sweet and a gallon of rough cider for sustenance. With some gin or wine for the girls and a few Buddy Holly and Elvis records you were set up for a good time. We would all sing along with the Bob Dylan stuff, believing every word he wrote, while my best friend's party piece was a hilarious version of Coleridge's *Rime of the Ancient Mariner* sung as a 12-bar shout blues, which would get us in fits on the floor.

In 1961 I went to the Aircrew Selection Centre at the famous RAF Hornchurch to do the medicals and interviews for an RAF Scholarship (for Cranwell Cadet entrance). Throughout the interviews and rigorous testing I was uncomfortably aware of my perceived lack of 'officer-like' qualities. I knew already that I had no wish to be a great leader of men – I just wanted to enjoy the flying and see the world from a single-seat fighter cockpit. I was mildly surprised that they accepted me, as I felt sure all along that the grim-faced selection board officers could see what I really was. I was also awarded a Flying Scholarship, and in the summer holidays of 1962 I reported to Plymouth Flying Club, Roborough, to begin flying the Tiger Moth in order to gain a Private Pilot's Licence (PPL). These free scholarships were intended to convince schoolboys that their future lay in flying as an RAF career. Some forty-five years later an RAF colleague told me that in fact I had been sent to Cranwell by the Aircrew Selection people as a 'Training Risk'; apparently I had not done well enough in the essential Flying Aptitude tests. It was their policy to occasionally send a 'training risk' on through the system, to see if they failed, thereby validating their selection procedures. I was to prove them wrong in my case.

My first instructor was a hard-faced and unsympathetic type who gave precious little praise for anything. Roborough was then a tiny grass airfield on a hilltop, and I was not doing too well during my initial circuit-bashing sessions. My instructor was unremittingly critical and scathing about my ability; he seemed to have a down on all students, and I wished fervently for a transfer to one of the other instructors, with whom my fellow students got on well. Grimly I pressed on and was grudgingly sent solo. My confidence improved and I relaxed and flew better on solos and on duals with the other instructors. However, I was convinced at this stage that I was not a natural pilot, and would have to work hard in future to succeed in the RAF. This first experience of learning to fly in the simple, old-world Tiger Moth (without radio) coloured my views on flying and instructing later on. I had learned that a bad-tempered or poor instructor could destroy the ability of the best of students. More importantly, I had learned the hard lesson that flying ability was never a natural 'gift' to anyone. The only way to success and survival was constant hard work and regular critical analysis of one's own technique and attitude to flying. Without this the dread disease of complacency lurked ready to kill at a moment's notice. The RAF I was about to join had a tremendously high accident rate. Aircrew funerals were almost as routine as parades.

The Tiger Moth was a splendid old machine on which to learn to fly. The reassuring wood and fabric construction left you in intimate contact with the airflow in a way that is lost in more modern machines. After a few hours' practice the pilot could judge airspeed just from the sound and feel of the airflow and the response of the controls, the most perfect and natural way to fly and enjoy flight. We were not taught aerobatics as such: they were not part of the PPL syllabus. However, I recall a terrifying moment when my instructor demonstrated an impromptu slow roll. The old 'Sutton' seat harness was not particularly efficient and as we rolled upside down my body slid about a foot higher in the seat towards the ground some 3,000 feetbelow. As I hung half-out of the machine I thought my last moment had come; with no parachute I gripped the leather coaming in terror until positive g forces returned me to my seat. During solo circuits my favourite manoeuvre was the steep sideslip on finals to achieve an accurate touchdown. The Tiger was perfect for this, the technique being to over-bank a lot into the finals turn, at the same time applying top rudder to keep the nose up. Glidepath could be adjusted at will merely by varying the amount of rudder and bank. You aimed just short of the boundary fence and then smoothly straightened out the sideslip and levelled the wings at the very last moment to make a three-pointer at the beginning of the grass strip. For maximum effect the idea was to make a tight final turn and get impossibly high and then make a sideslip with full top rudder, the aircraft appearing to stand on its ear as you dropped like a stone. Very satisfying if done correctly.

The culmination of the Flying Scholarship was the solo landaway sortie, which I flew to Weston-super-Mare. With no radio or radio aids the whole thing was 'map and stopwatch' navigation throughout. The plan was to refuel and have lunch at Weston, then fly back via Exeter where I was to do one 'touch and go' before returning to Roborough. The day was bright but cool and I soon began to feel the cold at 2,000 feet over Dartmoor. We borrowed ancient canvas 'Sidcot' suits for long flights, but we had no adequate gloves or boots and the thin RAF cloth helmets left your head very cold. We appreciated the hardiness and endurance of the old open-cockpit pilots of the past, who thought nothing of a climb above 20,000 feet where the air temperature could be 40 degrees Centigrade below zero. This, combined with the freezing 100mph air blast, would soon chill the best-protected aviator to the marrow.

I found Weston without much problem and enjoyed the slow glide down into the balmy, warm air near the ground. Weston was a huge grass airfield and I touched down so far from the pumps that I actually got airborne again while taxiing in. (This was fairly normal procedure, although strictly forbidden. A fellow cadet had enraged our chief instructor when he had the cheek to claim an extra five minute flight in his log book from the touchdown point to the refuelling pumps!) I took a leisurely lunch in the club canteen with a fellow cadet aviator who had landed after me, and we boasted about our exploits as if we had flown solo across Africa. En route to Exeter my troubles began. There was a lot more cloud about and I soon became uncertain of position and began to scan the ground anxiously for anything recognizable long after I should have seen Exeter. Eventually I recognized the town of Newton Abbot, some fifteen miles south-west of Exeter. I turned around in a hurry and raced back there to do my landing. By now I was uncomfortably aware that I had wasted far too much time at Weston, and it was getting noticeably late in the day. Sure enough, Exeter was suspiciously deserted as I rolled across the grass and turned ready for take-off again. A flashing light from ATC signalled me to taxi into dispersal. The airfield was closed and I was ordered to shut down and return to Plymouth in ignominy by train. I repeated the landaway successfully and became the proud possessor of a Private Pilot's licence at the age of seventeen. I had never driven a car or ridden so much as a moped.

In the Sixth Form I was very happy with my chosen science special-ization subjects of maths, physics and chemistry. I needed 2 'A' levels to get into Cranwell, and I achieved this with maths and physics. So ended my schooldays. On reflection it was a glorious carefree time, suffused with the permanent golden glow of summer and edged with the cool ultramarine of the south Devon sea, fading away to the misty slate blue of Dartmoor. For me the best of times in Plymouth was forever captured by Procol Harum's *Whiter Shade of Pale*, dancing with the girls in the dusty heat of the early evening at the Green Lanterns Club, then a drinking club on the Barbican.

After the bitterly cold winter of 1962-63 I lazed through the last beautiful West Country summer of my schooldays. From my brother I had learned roughly what to expect at Cranwell, (he was just finishing his first year at Sandhurst). I knew it was going to be a hard slog, so I was determined to enjoy myself as much as possible. At the beginning of the long summer holidays I was at a party and intro-duced myself to a lanky, blond-haired lad who from a distance looked a bit like Steve McQueen. He was from Devonport High School, and I found that he was joining Cranwell at the same time. I discovered that we had similar tastes in girls, beer and, more impor-tantly, that he was a keen spear fisherman (I had taken up the sport in my early teens). We became inseparable friends immediately and within a few days we were on joint spear fishing expeditions.

At the beginning of September my friend and I hitch-hiked to Farnborough to watch the International Air Display. We were in heaven, overwhelmed by the majestic thrill of it all. The thunderous crackle of the fast jets was music to our ears, two hopefuls on the threshold of the great adventure of joining the RAF to fly.

Chapter 2

Cranwell

On 9 September 1963 we were on our way, with RAF rail warrants, to Grantham via London. Stepping off at the grimy Lincolnshire station the temperature was degrees cooler than the balmy West Country air we had forsaken. A cold easterly wind cut across the platform, an ominous portent of the three freezing winters to come. This was the furthest north I had ever been, and we tried to guess the thoughts of the grim-faced NCOs who were herding us along with dozens of other anxious-looking youths towards the drab RAF coaches outside the station. We all wore hats, which at that time were compulsory. After a shortish bus journey, the hangars of RAF Cranwell and the imposing façade of the Royal Air Force College appeared on the horizon. This was my first sight of Lincolnshire and I was impressed by the endless vistas of flat terrain, unhindered by the customary tall roadside hedges of the West Country. We stared in awe at the magnificent college buildings and imposing entrance; however, such grand accommodation was not intended for our lowly life form for a long time. The coaches turned away, down among the narrow roads and austere huts of the South Brick Lines, our home for the next six months.

In the Junior Mess we were introduced to our flight commander, an ex-Hunter pilot; and the NCOs of 'A' Squadron who were to give us intensive drill and discipline for the next six months. Our intake, No. 89 Entry, comprised some eighty cadets divided among the four College Squadrons, from A to D. The majority were pilot cadets but there were also navigator, equipment and regiment cadets as well. Dick, our live-in cadet mentor in Hut 146 was a tall, handsome youth who looked impossibly 'steely' and smart when he greeted us in his epauletted Number One uniform and fashionably 'bashed' hat which sloped down, SS-style, from the peak . The cap was kept stuffed in a flying boot for months in order to achieve this effect. To us bewildered recruits he was the epitome of what we wished to become as soon as was humanly possible. Our mentor's bawdy stories and caustic sense of humour were to sustain us well during those early dark days when we were literally run off our feet and totally bamboozled by the sheer volume of things to learn. One ominous comment from our mentor did not go down well on our first night in the hut. 'Is there anyone here who could have got into university instead of this place?' he said.

Along with a couple of others I stuck my hand up.

'You guys have really screwed up, then' he continued, dragging our morale several notches lower. 'You realize that the RAF is giving all the good jobs to the 'Green Shieldies' from now on?'

This was the first time I had heard the term. 'Green Shield Stamps' commission was a slang reference to the ease of joining and the accelerated promotion offered to those who joined after a university degree. This was all news to us. Our mentor went on: 'There's no kudos in going through this place any more: they won't even guarantee you promotion to squadron leader these days. Didn't anyone tell you that before?'

He feigned amusement when we shook our heads. We were hopelessly naive. My natural rebellious instincts were reawakened and this did not bode well for my future career, such as it was to be. In the long run this early disappointment was probably no bad thing. Our mentor gave us a word or two about the college 'wheels', or senior officers. The commandant was a famous wartime pilot as was the assistant commandant. The wing commander in charge of cadets was a V-bomber pilot with little sense of humour. Our 'A' Squadron commander was also ex V-force. These college staff officers in general seemed to us hard-faced and unsympathetic in their attitude to us lowly cadets:

From *The Mint* by T.E. Lawrence, (reference Wing Commander Bonham-Carter, Commandant at the RAF's recruit training depot at Uxbridge, 1922.)

His character was compounded of the corruption of courage, endurance, firmness and strength: he had no consideration for anyone not commissioned, no mercy (though all troops abundantly need mercy every day) and no fellowship. He leaned only to the military side of the Air Force, and had no inkling that its men were not amenable to such methods.

The Senior Entry were described to us in lurid detail by our mentor, with emphasis on their sadistic tendencies during their regular 'crowing' sessions in the South Brick Lines. He explained 'crowing':

> You lot are all crows, OK? That is, until the next Junior Entry arrives to take over in six months time. Until then you get the full benefit of the attention of the Senior Entry any time they want a bit of fun.

We were to expect being woken up in the middle of the night at any time, to be subjected to various humiliating rituals and punishments at the whim of these characters. I felt my hackles rise as Dick described some of the things that had happened to him when his Entry had been crowed. Some of the silly charades and exercises sounded innocuous enough – just healthy schoolboy ragging. However, according to our mentor there were one or two hard characters around who took a real pleasure out of tormenting the weakest looking cadets. Crowing involved being made to hang upside-down from beams, recite obscene poems, run around the huts with a rifle above the head, being doused with icy cold water in the shower etc., etc. Like anyone else I had a deep objection to being pushed around, and this is what crowing was all about. I determined to resist as much as was possible and not allow myself to be picked on. Later on when crowing was in full swing I adopted an attitude of contempt and sullen defiance with anyone who tried anything on me, to the point of outright mutiny. I soon gained a reputation as a bit of a maverick. It was easy to recognize the hard characters: from their tone of voice and facial expression you could tell that they wanted to see you crumble. In this case I would answer back in contempt, refusing to be in any way deferential or give any sign of submission. If ordered to do anything I would carry out the order in quick time like an automaton, at all times keeping a dead-pan expression and trying to avoid betraying any emotion or fatigue – no outward sign other than a deep dislike and contempt for the person giving the order. After a while I found this technique quite effective and I was more or less left alone, even by the toughest individuals. The key to this performance was adrenalin. Anticipating a hard time from some particularly unpleasant individual, I would inwardly screw myself up to a peak of aggression, letting it flow inside me in a controlled and directed manner to keep up the resistance to my would-be tormentor. I was to find this technique very useful later in life in dealing with occasionally unpleasant senior officers, and, more important, it enabled me to develop a very hard-nosed and phlegmatic attitude to the extreme pressures of Service flying later on.

As I gained confidence in my 'resistance to interrogation' technique I would deliberately goad the senior cadets who attempted to 'crow' us, so that they would make a point of trying to pick on me. The senior cadets seemed to have everything on their side: they were older, much more experienced in the college, and they had rank and authority on their side. As the Junior Entry we were the lowest form of life, supposed to be subservient and instantly obedient, but still I found it was possible to gain a moral victory by controlled defiance and insolent repartee, thereby embarrassing the senior cadet in front of his compatriots. This was immature bravado on my part, but I had always had an aversion to being ordered about and inwardly I was relieved to discover that I could take these people on and gain some kind of victory in front of my fellow cadets. After regarding myself as a hopeless physical 'weed' for so long, it was a refreshing development. I realized for the first time that such unpleasant characters could be taken on and defeated in the absence of mere physical strength, that mental agility and resilience under pressure were of infinitely greater importance. (This lesson applied equally well to combat flying, as I was to discover later on.) I became grimly determined that I was never ever going to be pushed around again, by anyone at any time no matter how superior in rank they were.

The thirty or so accommodation huts of the South Brick Lines were uniformly drab and austere. Heated by an ancient coke stove, each hut contained half a dozen steel bedsteads, to each of which was attached the Lee Enfield No. 4 rifle issued to each cadet on the first day. For the next couple of years this rifle was our personal responsibility, and woe betide anyone who lost or damaged one. At nights it was kept chained to the bed with an issue padlock. The walls of the huts gleamed with clean paint and we had the luxury of our own showers and toilet just inside the entrance. However, the crowning glory of each hut was the floor. This was covered throughout with gleaming brown linoleum which had been polished to a luxurious sheen by generations of cadets. We soon learned the importance of maintaining this gloss: on daily inspections the slightest untoward mark would call forth the wrath of the inspecting officer or senior cadet, followed by instant retribution in the form of restrictions or punishments for the offending cadets. We soon got used to gliding around the hut on homemade bumpers made of discarded pieces of

RAF blanket. This was just the beginning of the 'Bull' to which we were subject for the next three years. For inspections all bedding and issue clothing and kit had to be laid out to a precise pattern on an immaculately made-up bed, at the foot of which each cadet stood stiffly to attention. There was an endless amount of cleaning and polishing and changing of the various uniforms issued over the next few days. We spent hours of each day parading and marching to and from the vast East Camp stores where we stood in patient lines to draw clothing and kit and be measured for uniforms and, joy of joys, flying clothing!

There was almost no free time and we were not allowed off camp for the first eight weeks. Apart from the Junior Mess, the only escape from the constant routine of drill, inspections, lectures and cross-country running was to play sport on a Saturday or Wednesday afternoon. On arrival our mentor had introduced us to the 'A' Squadron Junior Mess batman, an extremely funny, gangling individual who bore little resemblance to our mental picture of what a batman should be. We discovered to our delight that this character was a true eccentric, more of a reprobate elder brother than batman, with a wicked sense of humour and an attitude towards the college authorities exactly in line with our own. He was unapologetically cheeky with us cadets and although he did his own work with the minimum of fuss he was constantly taking the mickey and chiding us tongue-in-cheek for our failures in 'bulling' the hut and cleaning our kit. We all grew to love and appreciate our batman, as generations of cadets had done before, and he remained a great friend and confidante for years afterwards.

During the attestation ceremony, held on the first day after arrival, I self-consciously declared myself an atheist, thus causing some raised eyebrows and muttering amongst the officers in charge. After some delay I was duly sworn in via a solemn affirmation instead of the customary religious mumbo-jumbo. Only one other cadet deviated in this way; he declared himself an agnostic. We fondly imagined that our declaration would relieve us of the tedium of church parade. Some hopes. The college authorities made us attend every church parade for the next three years. While the rest of the cadets sat comfortably in church we had to remain guarding the rifles in a freezing hut, to march back with the squadron after the service.

Under the strict eye of our drill sergeant parade ground drill became almost enjoyable for me. I discovered to my surprise that I had a bit of a talent for it and was eventually awarded the prize for smartest cadet at the end of our initial training. I found marching to the excellent college band most enjoyable – especially after standing still in the freezing wind for an hour. Early morning parade practise in winter was tough. We were not allowed to wear greatcoats, and the simple remedy for anyone who looked to be suffering from cold was a couple of circuits of the frosty parade ground with the rifle above the head. To get some 'crack' out of our rifles when they were struck on parade we would secretly cut down the woodwork under the swivels and other metalwork in order to make them rattle a bit more. Naturally this was strictly forbidden, but we did it just the same because it gave our drill squad just a bit extra 'snap' and an edge over the other squadrons. Slowly and steadily, unbeknown to us, we were learning the value of teamwork, mutual trust and individual sacrifice for the good of the organization. We were a fairly disparate bunch of lads, all individualists who wanted to do things our own way. The very nature of the tough RAF aircrew selection process had ensured this, and now the Service was moulding us into a team and bending us to its traditions by means of stealthy and unrelenting indoctrination both on and off parade.

Fortunately we were confined to camp for this period, as most of us were totally broke. Our RAF pay was £16 per month, before deductions for mess bills, breakages etc. My best friend and I were saving frantically to buy a car. Owning a car was the only means of socializing off-camp. However, nothing was going to stop us having a good time on our first Saturday night 'launch' to Grantham. (The nearest town, Sleaford, was off-limits because of a series of drunken 'incidents' caused by cadets). Dressed in jackets and ties and wearing the regulation hats we all piled into a decrepit hired minibus and set off for town and a good time. We spent the evening reeling hatless from pub to pub and generally making an exhibition of ourselves in front of the long-suffering locals. A recommended watering-hole was the Regency bar in the High St, which was full of fluffy WRAF recruits, just let out from their initial training camp at RAF Spitalgate. Like us they were undergoing a pretty tough regime and were also a little homesick. Most of us cadets saw no problems in socializing with these girls; soon we learnt that the RAF was very much against any fraternization between potential officers and 'Other Ranks' – that dreaded term – indeed our squadron commander was totally against 'public demonstrations of affection' (called PDAs), either in or out of uniform. At the end of a riotous evening we piled into the minibus in order of incapacitation, the comatose lying sardine-fashion on the floor, while those still capable of movement sprawled on top and sang all the way back to Cranwell. Outside our huts we fell out of the transport, hastily donning crumpled hats, jackets and ties when they could be found. The duty cadet abandoned attempts to inspect us and ordered us to bed in disgust, accompanied by dire threats of reporting us all to the flight commander for being improperly dressed. There were to be a lot more launches like this in the months to come.

My friend and I were both pretty rebellious at heart. We were proud of our basic Janner (West Country) origins, and were determined not to be overawed by what we saw as the rather overblown pomp and seriousness of RAF officer cadet training. Sharing his hut next door to mine was another burly Janner from Newton Abbott, who had just completed a gruelling three years of apprentice training at RAF Halton before being selected for Cranwell. The three of us made a noisy trio, prone to singing the 'Oggie Song' at the drop of a hat. In addition we began to develop a private joke language between the three of us and a few other like-minded eccentrics on 89 entry. Communication was in the form of Goon-like grunts added on to sentences at random and accompanied by manic facial expressions in the middle of a perfectly normal conversation. The rules of the game meant that you had to reply in kind as soon as it was started. Those of us in the know would soon be reduced to helpless giggling when any one of us started off – this was the main aim of the exercise, especially in the middle of some important occasion such as a speech by a senior officer or an important drill parade. After a while we only needed to suspect that one of us was going to start it and we would be helpless with mirth.

This was all gloriously infantile and quite a serious embarrassment at times later on. However, it was fun and we could turn a boring or unpleasant situation into a farce at the drop of a hat. Our wacky group of 'grunters' comprised the hard-core 'Janner Faction' plus many other characters of 89A. As far as the rest of the college was concerned we were all several pages short of a checklist. To our delight our batman joined in the 'grunting' with total enthusiasm, taking great delight in embarrassing us cadets when we were trying to keep a straight face with visitors or in the middle of a Dinner Night when he was waiting at table.

Soon there was one good piece of news: hats were no longer compulsory. We lit a bonfire and burned most of them. The career officers hung on to theirs.

After the initial few days of hectic indoctrination and kitting-out all of 89 entry were divided up into the various academic sets in which we were to be instructed for the next three years. The authorities committed us to an average of eight hours of academic and military studies lectures every day for most of our non-flying time at college. This was a pretty daunting prospect – especially as we knew already that there would be no academic qualification of any sort awarded to the vast majority of cadets after all that work. For a small group of us things were to be different. Anyone who had sufficiently good 'A' level results (I had done pretty well in maths and physics), was placed (without choice) in one of the specialist sets. The C stream was for the 'arty farties' who could study for an external arts degree. I was placed in the B stream to study maths, aerodynamics, electronics and thermodynamics in order to qualify for Associate Fellowship of the Royal Aeronautical Society (AFRAes) – the equivalent of a science degree. This was regarded as the thing to do for science-orientated officer cadets. I soon discovered that the B Stream was no easy option. We all had to do lots of heavy maths to get in trim for the awesome stuff involved in aerodynamic theory. This was to be my downfall some eighteen months later at the half-way examinations. Unfortunately my brain just wasn't up to the maths and in particular the speed at which it was put over by our maths lecturer, a dour, grim-faced Yorkshire man with little sympathy for anyone who was struggling. Aerodynamics was given by another squadron leader, a more sympathetic character, although shy and withdrawn by nature. The other lecturers were all career RAF education officers, quite senior in rank. This was a major drawback to the system.

With me in the B Stream of 89 Entry there were just four other students. Our normal daily routine would start with about forty-five minutes drill practice at 0700, followed by a quick change and form up into academic sets with our RAF issue Navbags (rather like a canvas attaché case), to march off to the Whittle Hall for lectures starting at 0800. All the rest of 89 entry were in the various A sets, in which they continued to study for the rest of their time at college.

The one thing you could not get away from at Cranwell was the thrilling aura of flying, present every minute of the day. As we sat in our lectures Chipmunks buzzed to and from the North Airfield and we could hear the constant whistle of jet engines and the roar of the Jet Provosts climbing away into the blue from the South Airfield. We were literally surrounded by aviation which everyone else was enjoying. We ached to get into a cockpit and get on with the real business as far as we were concerned. The thought that we would have to wait another eighteen months before we got into a jet cockpit was like a constant physical pain, a denial of our prime reason for being alive. Amongst us cadets skill at flying was prized above everything else, and we soon got to hear of which characters were the 'aces' of the more senior entries already busy with flying training. As each Senior Entry graduated the majority of us were only interested in the winner of the Flying Prize, the best pilot of the entry. These cadets were our real heroes, the original 'right stuff'. At the same time we listened avidly to stories of recently-graduated cadets who had moved on to the fighter pilot's Valhalla – 4 FTS at RAF Valley.

My friend and I weren't interested in any other advanced FTS, for us it was to be fighters or nothing. Just to add to our frustration the Senior Entry cadets would often drop in to 'crow' us on their way back from Jet Provost night flying. The Jet Provost flight line was just a couple of hundred yards from our huts and we could smell the hot jet fuel wafting in on the evening breeze. Standing stiffly to attention we would seethe with jealousy at their casually-worn flying boots and they would do their best to demoralize us by saying that we would never make it through the training, that we would be chopped and thrown out after just a few hours flying. Almost as bad was the threat that we would end up as V-Bomber co-pilots, in our view the worst option for any student pilot with spirit and a bit of flying skill. At this period of RAF training over two thirds of all graduates from basic flying training were being posted to non-fighter advanced training, i.e. to the large bomber and transport fleets. Only the most talented and determined had a chance of getting to RAF Valley to fly the Gnat, the brand-new advanced trainer of our dreams and an aeroplane custom-built for extreme flying to the limits.

January 1964 was the start of flying training for 89 Entry! Admittedly, it was only Chipmunk flying, and we were only at Flights for half a day a week; but it was a start. My instructor was a splendid old (he must have been at least forty) Second World War bomber pilot with a kindly and relaxed style of instruction. The Chipmunk was a splendid step forward from the Tiger Moth, very good for aeros and 'flick' manoeuvres. We also spent a lot of time practising forced landings in farmers' fields – still regarded as an essential skill for all single-engine pilots. Take-off and landing from the enormous North airfield, (once the largest area of unfenced grassland in England) was easy, although we took pride in side slipping and judging use of flaps to make a spot landing right next to the touchdown marker boards. The flying was very different from the free and easy Tiger Moth club flying. This was properly-conducted RAF training. We wore parachutes, used correct radio procedures and were subject to all the usual RAF rules and disciplines. However, enjoyable though it was we knew that the pitifully few hours allocated were to be spread out tantalizingly over the next eighteen months or so, just to keep up our interest in flying while awaiting our delayed jet training.

Now in our second term the whole of 89 entry began fitness and leadership training in earnest. We started cross-country running in our combat boots to build up stamina and there were several 3-day exercises in the Peak District, freezing under canvas in preparation for the big survival exercise to be held in the Troodos mountains of Cyprus in spring. I was looking forward to the challenge of this as my brother had been on the same exercise the previous year as a guest cadet from RMA Sandhurst. As expected, he had impressed the hell out of the RAF staff, always marching into checkpoints immaculate and cool after the most arduous exercise in company with Cranwell cadets of 87 Entry. He told me how he had done it. According to him the secret weapon was a comb, which he used to smarten himself up just before arriving at a checkpoint. This was sheer modesty on his part: in fact he was supremely fit and the RMA cadet training – physically even tougher than ours – had prepared him superbly for the exercise. I was determined to do as well as possible after his example. However, a sunny trip to Cyprus was not on the cards for 89 Entry. Following the lousy run of our luck we were told that the Cyprus exercise was cancelled because of some political unrest in the area.

Hence, in early March the whole of 89 entry were on a train through the snow-covered Cairngorms to alight at the freezing hell of Dalwhinnie railway station. We completed our journey to Laggan Bridge by truck and were then sent up into the hills to pitch two-man tents and dig latrines for our two week stay in glorious Scotland. Sharing two-man tents I have never been so cold, hungry or exhausted as I was then. We operated in sections of seven cadets and marched further and further each day, through the snow-covered hills and glens, to build up our fitness for the ultimate test: the three-day Escape and Evasion exercise. At the end of each day's march – wet, cold, exhausted and hungry – we were put through a series of initiative tests and leadership exercises: the usual Boy Scout stuff of building bridges with a few poles and bits of string, etc. etc. The aim of all this was simply to put us under so much physical and mental stress that the weaker ones would crack. Quite a few did, and were put on light duties with various injuries. My brother's advice had been quite clear on this: 'Whatever you do, don't give up and don't go sick – that's what the staff are waiting for. Just try to stick it out without complaining.'

All of our section managed it – just. At the end of the exercise we piled wearily into the train back to Lincolnshire, exhausted yet strangely satisfied that we had taken all that they could throw at us. We had all been to the far limits of our physical and mental endurance, and it was very satisfying to know that we could take that much and still keep functioning.

My car made a big difference to our social life back at Cranwell. There were regular runs to Grantham and Lincoln at weekends, plus occasional forays to Nottingham or Retford, where there were yet more teachers' training colleges. Other members of the entry had a weird and wonderful variety of vehicles: one character had a Second World War ambulance, while another drove in style in a Rolls Royce hearse. With no MOT test to bother us, anything on wheels was useable as a means of transport. We were even given a road safety ticking off by the Chief Constable of Lincoln . He said that the Lincoln police could put up with our crazy vehicles being driven overloaded at speed around the city – but could we please not do it so often while roaring drunk! The teacher's training college at Lincoln soon became a favourite destination and we had a lot of good times there with the girls, jiving to some splendid rock and roll bands and getting drunk across the road at the Skylark pub. Back at college we were now having regular Dinner Nights in the Junior Mess, practising for the full-blown events of the Senior College. The staff took this social aspect of RAF officer life very seriously and there were many rules of etiquette to be learned when we paraded at table dressed in stiff wing collars and our best uniforms. With my lack of social graces I did not look forward to this aspect of college life one bit, but I soon discovered that there was a wealth of useful advice available from other cadets on how to behave and eat properly.

Once the meal and 'speechifying' was complete we then got stuck into Mess games. After the first such dinner one of our pilots was crippled for life in a game of Mess rugby – that was the end of his flying career. I was terrified that I might lose my flying medical category through injury and remained a wimp at all these events throughout my RAF career. I left the physical side of the drunken shenanigans to the sporting 'hearties': my interest was more in plotting various pranks to irritate the staff. Once out of the Mess we would go on rampages through the South Brick lines, raiding and ransacking the huts of any cadets foolish enough to go to bed early. There were other stunts. On one occasion about forty of us got hold of an old Hawker Hunter fighter which was parked about 100 yards away and manhandled it round on to the parade square. In the morning it was a splendid sight with its nose buried deep into the entrance foyer of the Junior Mess. I can't recall any severe punishment being handed out for this kind of thing; I think the staff regarded it as normal development activity for officer cadets. It was not unusual for cadets to hijack fire vehicles, senior officers' staff cars etc., and go on driving sprees around the base. In this we were merely following the distinguished traditions of various RAF heroes of the 50s, in which one of the most notable exploits was to steal a train in Germany after a Dinner night. The miscreant was also our hero for another famous incident when he was flying the Fighter Reconnaissance Swift in Germany. He wanted a picture of himself flying upside down at low level over the River Weser, a perfectly reasonable aspiration for a young RAF pilot at this period. His wingman, a young pilot officer, got in position to take the picture as his leader rolled upside down. However, the wingman saw immediately that the aeroplane had caught fire at the back end. This was not at all uncommon with the Swift. He shouted frantically:

'I say old man, you're on fire!'

'I know – take the fucking picture!'

This with a certain amount of urgency in the voice!

One day the whole college was given a briefing on the TSR-2, potentially the most important aircraft project for the RAF since the Second World War. The head of the British Aircraft Corporation gave us a stunning presentation on the capabilities of the machine and current progress with the test flying. To our dismay he warned us that the TSR-2 project was under threat and could be cancelled.

At Cranwell punishments were called 'strikers'. On strikers you were confined to camp and had to parade three times a day to be inspected and given drill by the duty senior cadet who would look out for the minutest flaw in your turnout and drill. The big problem with 'strikers' was that you could end up being charged again and again by senior cadets for minor infringements of the restrictions, thus keeping you on punishment for weeks on end. I used my well-developed 'resistance to interrogation' techniques to the full in order to fight back. One particular senior cadet – a muscular knucklehead who spent a lot of time shouting at full volume – was known as 'The Head Boy' by many of us who were unimpressed by his gung-ho sporting prowess and free-and-easy relationship with college staff officers. He was my Senior Under Officer and I had to get applications for weekend leave approved by him personally. He took an instant dislike to me because of my growing reputation as a maverick who refused to be browbeaten either by him or by his fellow senior entry cadets. He sent back my application forms time after time with 'Untidy – Resubmit' scrawled on them. My handwriting had always been crablike and there was nothing I could do about it. This was a result of high blood pressure and a constant dose of the 'shakes', which I had managed to conceal from the medics so far.

The Easter break seemed all too short, barely enough time to get round old haunts and renew old acquaintances back in Plymouth. By now it was becoming obvious to my friend and I that we were steadily growing apart from our old school buddies, which was a sad but inevitable consequence of the vast differences between Cranwell and university life. Back at college there was bad news. One of our entry had been killed in a road accident just a few miles south of Cranwell while driving back from leave. This was our first full military funeral. The whole entry was drilled for days in the complicated procedures for the funeral, which was held in Cranwell village churchyard on a beautiful spring morning. There were to be many more funerals for 89 entry before my time in the RAF was over.

In the autumn term Chipmunk flying continued at a painfully slow pace. I had soloed after five hours in the 'Chippy', but our continuity was so poor that we needed a dual check before each solo thereafter. Since January I had flown just sixteen hours. Meanwhile the constant aroma of hot jet fuel and the roar of jets overhead reminded us of just what we were missing. By now we had moved up to the senior college, to live in single rooms in the 'A' Squadron wing.

The academics in the 'B' Stream continued at a gruelling pace, and I felt that I was slowly losing it, particularly with maths. The relentless progression of imaginary numbers, Fourier analysis, Lorenz transforms, set theory etc. left me further and further behind. From contacts with more senior cadets doing the AFRAeS course I knew that the final eighteen months would be even harder, with little time for a social life. I was enjoying the social life so much that this was a daunting prospect. At the end of term we had the AFRAeS Part 1 exam and my results were indifferent. At the beginning of the spring term I was offered the choice of withdrawing, and I took it with some relief. We were due to start jet training in the summer, and I wanted to concentrate full time on flying. I was put in the A1 academic set and we soon began lectures on RAF specialist equipment which we would be using later on, such as RADAR, TACAN, VOR etc. This was much more interesting: the lecturers were all regular RAF Technical (Engineer) officers, with a practical approach and relaxed style of instruction. At last we felt we had a glimpse of what the RAF was really about. There was a term of workshop practice when we were given basic training in workshop techniques by RAF instructors. We learned how to file flat, use a lathe, spin metal, plus many other useful skills.

I was heavily into swimming and represented the college at breast stroke and water polo. I was also playing some squash, occasionally for the college and was beginning to get seriously fit. I had joined the college sub aqua club and did my sea qualification as a BSAC diver. We had already been on some field trips to dive in various gravel pits, plus a visit to Anglesey for some sea diving.

At Anglesey we stayed in the officers' mess of RAF Valley and stood open-mouthed in wonder at the speed and agility of the Gnat trainers whistling about the Welsh skies. We also caught sight of a five-ship formation of yellow-painted Gnats manoeuvring in the high blue above Valley. These were the famous 'Yellowjacks', distinguished forerunners of the Red Arrows. I also went on some rock-climbing weekends in Snowdonia, which were marvellous sport. Unfortunately, there was so much choice of activities that you couldn't possibly do everything.

There were also many weekend runs to London, to meet up with old school pals and another old acquaintance from Plymouth, then at LSE, who claimed close links backstage with the Rolling Stones. The students were a wild bunch, tending to anarchist politics, but not taking life too seriously. The mob lived in various seedy mews flats where you could turn up and doss down at any time.

At Easter I went on a trip on an Oberon-class submarine, HMS *Opportune*, from Portland RN base. All of 89 had to go on one kind of boat or another and as I was interested in the history of the submarine service I chose this trip. *Opportune* was a conventional (diesel-electric) boat with minimal space for the crew. I bunked in the so-called wardroom, a cupboard about 6 feet square with a dining table occupying most of the floor space. There were six bunks distributed about the walls. Seven ship's officers occupied this space. There was just room for all of us to sit down around the table. At sea we were 'hot bunking' and it was not unusual at breakfast to have someone's sweaty foot beside your plate as he got out of his bunk. We spent the first six hours or so on the surface after sailing from Portland. It was pretty rough and I annoyed the officer of the watch by 'chundering' into wind from the conning tower – a typical landlubber's blunder. Diving was much more relaxed and I enjoyed the peaceful cruising about submerged while we took part in exercises against surface ships. Torpedo attacks were reruns of Second World War films, the skipper hanging on to the periscope and shouting orders to the crew. I had a go at handling the hydroplanes. Although there was an antique-looking autopilot, the crew spent a lot of time manually handling the boat: for practice, I was told. A pretty sweaty lifestyle really. The ablutions consisted of one tiny basin just large enough to wash your hands.

On board *Opportune* I finished reading *Stranger to the Ground* by Richard Bach, who had been a USAF F84 Thunderstreak fighter pilot in the '50s. The book was a lyrical firsthand account of the routine of single-seat fighter flying in NATO. Bach was a natural fighter pilot and a good writer – a combination as rare as hen's teeth. The book had totally captured my imagination, summing up the glories of flying and the animal thrill of air-to-ground weapon firing and air combat. Apart from Bach, only Gavin Lyall has ever satisfied me as an aviation writer.

After the Easter break we flew our last Chipmunk sorties and began Ground School for our Jet Provost flying training. With excitement rising to fever pitch amongst 89 Entry pilots, we reported to Flights at the beginning of July.

Chapter 3

Jet Training

At last we had started! My flying instructor was an extremely laid back ex-Canberra man whose father was an air marshal. He was a first-class instructor, calm and courteous at all times, and yet prepared to let me stick my neck out when necessary – especially if he thought I was about to make a fool of myself and would thereby learn a valuable lesson. I had the great fortune to stay with him for most of our twelve months of jet training. On 6 July we took off for my first familiarization sortie in the Jet Provost Mk4, quite a hot ship even by present-day standards. The newish Mk4 was a higher-powered version of the distinctly sluggish Mk3, much faster and capable of climbing to 35,000ft. It could do 330 knots flat out and the limit was 400kt in a dive. I felt immediately at home with jet flying. Overall performance was comparable to a late mark Spitfire, according to our ex-Spitfire instructors. The Jet Provost was amazingly quiet and smooth in the cockpit and, although straight-forward to fly and land, it was quite a challenge to fly accurately at all times. My instructor kept me hard at it and never let me accept second best performance. He was always encouraging when I did well, and never got angry if I screwed anything up – more likely he would laugh like a drain. The college Jet Provost squadrons were split evenly between Mk3s and Mk4s, and the policy was for student pilots to start flying either on the 3 or the 4 and continue on that mark until after first solo, when they were given a conversion trip on to the other mark, which was a large step forward or a step back, depending on which mark you started on. This was real flying! The Mk4 was brilliant for aerobatics and I was soon learning all kinds of exotic stunts, including flick manoeuvres (in which the aeroplane is put into the beginnings of a spin and then immediately recovered). We really piled on the pressure and got in a lot of flying in July and

August. By the end of the summer term I had flown thirty-two hours in the Jet Provost and was already doing solo navigation and aerobatics. The instructors were a great bunch, many of them master pilots and flight sergeants with Second World War flying experience. We were introduced to the honourable RAF tradition of 'minimum bullshit'. Basically, shouting off about your own ability was regarded as the worst thing you could do and was quickly stamped on by relentless piss-taking by everyone else, both fellow students and instructors alike.

It seemed to us that the RAF was overpopulated with bomber pilots and 'truckies' (transport pilots) and there were not many ex-fighter pilots as instructors in basic flying training. The ones that we did have seemed surprisingly modest and retiring, both on the ground and in the air, and it was only when they took control of the aircraft that you could see the punchy, cavalier flying style and lightning-fast decision making in action. This is not to run down the genuine talents of many of the non-fighter instructors, who could often fly just as accurately. However, those instructors were noticeably slower in the way they went about the whole business of flying. To me it was immediately apparent that the fighter pilots were capable of doing everything much faster than the others – without any reduction in their standards of accuracy. This fact was hoisted aboard rapidly by those of us aspiring to be fighter pilots. My friend and I started practising with a bit of extra pace added on to everything we did; invariably this led to some mistakes, but we stuck with it and took pride in our ability to get a ripple on and get airborne quicker than anyone else. I had always had hyperactive tendencies, and managed to get a 'buzz' out of doing things fast. To us the fighter pilot instructors were gods whose every word was taken as the only true gospel. They were also meticulous about being on time for anything to do with flying: briefings, take-off times, time-on-target etc. Being late for such important things was regarded as a 'spastic' tendency, to be avoided at all costs. At the same time it was regarded as 'not cool' to show that you had actually made an effort to be on time. Turning up sweaty and breathless was not on. I discovered that being on time was really just an attitude of mind which could be turned into a game: once you were determined to avoid being late, it became easier and easier to be aware of exactly how much time you had available before the next event. Like 'smooth' flying (see page 39), many pilots never really cracked this problem throughout their flying careers.

There was a grim practical necessity for fast reactions when flying jet fighters, where a problem could become desperate in an extremely short time. In many emergency situations there were just two kinds of pilot – the quick and the dead.

The ultimate 'spasticity' was to get over-excited about *any* drama to do with flying. Real pilots – especially fighter pilots – stayed cool *no matter what happened*. We learned that the bigger the drama the more you should try to control your emotions and not get worked up about it. This was the only way to stay in control of the situation, to maintain the capacity to think coolly and rationally under any pressure. Even when you knew you'd had it – that you were going to die – there was no point in getting bunched. The attitude was: 'That just means you're going to die all tensed up!'

Our favourite apocryphal tale was of the fighter pilot who, supposedly diving out of control and too late to eject, called laconically on the radio: 'I think I'll buy this farm.[1] (i.e the farm he could see directly beneath him.) 'Buying the farm' was the standard American expression for dying. In the RAF it was normally 'spearing in', 'getting creamed', or 'tent pegging'.

Shouting and screaming on the radio just because you had an emergency was the ultimate sin in our book, in total contrast to the accepted media portrayal of pilots in action. I realized now that most of the films and dramas supposedly portraying military pilot behaviour were a sham. In these, all pilots – especially fighter pilots – were roaring testosterone freaks with grossly inflated egos in permanent competition with their comrades, just like the infantile morons portrayed in *Top Gun*. This kind of behaviour was deplored in real RAF squadrons. In the air you did your best to remain polite, restrained and courteous at all times on the radio, using the absolute minimum number of words necessary to get the message across:

Only Spastics and Actors scream on the radio.

On the ground anyone with special flying talent just shut up about it and let the facts speak for themselves. There was always genuine sympathy for those who couldn't 'hack' it – after all it could be you having problems next. The basic philosophy was: 'You're only as good as your last sortie, and don't bullshit about it because the next one might be a bad one.'

It might also be your last one – no matter how good you were even the best pilot could be wiped out by an unfortunate combination of circumstances. To stay alive you needed to anticipate those situations, and you needed luck – lots of it. Our instructors reminded us of the old RAF adage that new pilots began their careers with two large bags. One bag was full of luck and the other – empty at first – was there to hold your flying experience as you gained it. All pilots hoped that their bag of luck would last out long enough to get some experience in the bag.

As with our Chipmunk flying there was constant emphasis on the importance of learning Visual Attitude Flying, with minimum use of the flight instruments. This was standard RAF flying instructional policy, and over the years of peace and war it had produced the high standard of pilots that the RAF needed for military flying duties. Basically, you were taught to judge aircraft performance in all manoeuvres merely by assessing the visual picture you could see out of the windscreen. Use of the flight instruments – particularly the artificial horizon – was not permitted for visual flying, apart from the briefest check when you occasionally looked around the cockpit. Having learnt to fly this way the pilot was able to spend the majority of his time carrying out all-important lookout, which for any fighter pilot meant the difference between life and death. This flying technique was difficult to learn and was in direct contrast to the way in which many civilian pilots were taught to fly, by 'cheating' and using the artificial horizon and other flight instruments most of the time – in effect instrument flying even in good weather. By that method you could certainly learn to fly with accuracy and give an impression of a competent pilot, but your lookout was appallingly bad, with poor appreciation of what was going on outside the cockpit. This was not a problem for potential airline pilots, who could rely permanently on air traffic controllers to tell them where to go and keep them clear of other aircraft.

I soon found myself itching to step up the pace of learning, as I had done during my later Tiger Moth flying. I was never satisfied with learning how to do a particular exercise simply by the book – I always wanted to try it out under more difficult circumstances. Unfortunately I suffered from a dangerously low boredom threshold. Suppose I could just hack a particular aerobatic manoeuvre at a certain speed: I would try to go one step further and start the manoeuvre 10 knots slower. (Starting off slower meant that you ran out of speed sooner and were more likely to stall or spin out.) An instrument flying exercise on full panel soon became boring: I would want to try it as soon as possible on limited panel, (with the artificial horizon covered up) just to see if I could hack it. Practiced forced landings getting easy? I wanted to try them out at night. Close

formation getting mundane? I was only interested in flying
formation in cloud, the thicker the better. I was desperate to try
formation aeros or night formation, both of which were achieved on
my instructor's tour. This was to become a continuous theme of my
flying career on subsequent aeroplanes. I always wanted to do the
difficult things, just to see if I could cope. I would never walk away
from any challenge in the air, no matter how difficult.

The end of the summer term was the start of a busy time for 89
Entry. We travelled en masse to RAF Lyneham to be flown to Paris
for the first stage of our NATO visit. After a few days of bliss in Paris
we emplaned for RAF Wildenrath in Germany, most of us nursing
heavy hangovers. Wildenrath was a Canberra tactical nuclear
bomber base, running at a peak of tension and preparedness during
the Cold War, which was still very much a 'hot' war as far as NATO
was concerned. We were fascinated to see a couple of visiting
German Air Force RF84s flown by a couple of NCO pilots.
Although we still had many warrant officer and flight sergeant pilots
instructing at Cranwell, the RAF had none on front-line aircraft.

I managed to scrounge a trip in a Canberra T4. The heat was
intense as we whistled through the German terrain at low level at
what seemed like a tremendous speed, this being my first real taste
of low flying. This was the life, I thought, but I didn't think much of
the Canberra after handling the controls and flying a couple of
circuits back at Wildenrath. It was definitely a bomber and very
heavy on the ailerons at high speed. The cockpit was also a bit of a
shambles, and very uncomfortable with two people.

Next, on the vast tank ranges of Bergen-Hohne we camped out
with the army and had huge fun learning to drive tanks and scout
cars. I ended up attached to a Guards company defending a trench
in the middle of nowhere against a full-scale infantry battalion attack
in the middle of the night. Amazingly, none of us was killed or
maimed, and after a sobering visit to the site of Belsen concentration
camp and yet another exhausting farewell party, we embarked, heads
throbbing, for UK and some summer leave, feeling that we had
found out all we needed to know about NATO and the Cold War.

After a few days in Plymouth I was in my car en route for Penzance
and the Scilly Isles, as part of a college diving expedition to search
for the wreck of the *Association*, Admiral Sir Cloudesley Shovell's
flagship, which had foundered in the eighteenth century, reputedly

with a treasure in gold on board. In St Mary's we stayed at the Customs House. The diving was as good as you could get anywhere in UK in warm, crystal-clear water. Social life was idyllic. We had a large contingent of 89 Entry, plus a young airman photographer who later became very famous as a TV documentary film cameraman. We spent most nights in the delightful Mermaid pub on the harbour front.

The final year at Cranwell flew by. To my amazement I was promoted to Under Officer and moved into the UO's flat. Jet Provost flying just got better and better as it went along. I enjoyed every aspect of the training and tried to get solos as often as possible in the JP4 to practise my aeros sequence. Although I enjoyed the duals I was happier and more confident when flying alone. My instructor had shown me how to do various 'flick' manoeuvres, including the porteous loop (basically a loop with a flick roll thrown in at the top). He gave instructions with a nod and a wink that I was not to do it solo, but of course I did. Sure enough eventually it went wrong on a brilliant morning when I was practising solo aeros a shade lower than I should have been. (There were strict minimum height limits for aerobatics.) I ended up in a fully-developed spin at 3,000 feet overhead Bardney sugar beet factory, a favourite location for aeros. I managed to recover quite low down after expending a fair amount of adrenalin. I had nearly become a statistic: if I hadn't recovered I would have been too ashamed to eject and save myself. Anyway, at 3,000 feet I was already 2,000 feet below the mandatory ejection height for a spin.

 Instrument flying was a real challenge and I got stuck into it with enthusiasm. In contrast to the violent manoeuvring of aeros, instrument flying required the lightest touch on the stick, combined with fast reactions to fly the increasingly demanding exercises in and out of cloud. Now that we could fly on instruments we could practise flameout spirals, controlled by ATC; a means of gliding back down through cloud to land after your engine had failed. Basically you homed overhead base and then, when the controller got a short trace on the CADF tube,[2] you started the glide spiral down, the controller checking on each 90 degrees of turn that he still had an overhead indication. (If not you rolled out and steered direct for base.) Breaking out below cloud, you made a dirty dart for a glide landing on the nearest runway.

On instrument flying training missions we wore the I/F blind flying visor, like a set of blinkers attached to our helmets which cut off all vision of the outside world. My instructor showed me how to fly really smoothly at all times on instruments: 'Just imagine you've got an egg balanced on top of the stick and you don't want it to fall off.'

He told me there were basically just two kinds of pilot: the smooth flyers and the 'stick stirrers', who kept the stick constantly moving in the mistaken belief that they could somehow average out their errors and 'nudge' the aircraft in approximately the right direction. Such people never grew out of the habit, which grew worse when their flying came under pressure. They usually ended up flying bombers: the ones who did get on to fighters found a lot of difficulties later on with precision exercises like weapon firing. My instructor encouraged me as I developed my instrument flying technique and was always setting me challenges which were just beyond my capability. One I never quite hacked during basic training was to do a full 360 degree steep turn (60 degree angle of bank), on instruments while keeping the needle of the vertical speed indicator permanently within the black of the zero on the gauge. Some instructors would do it as a party piece. (Much later on I taught myself the trick and was able to do it even on limited panel I/F, when the artificial horizon was covered up and you only had the turn needle to judge bank angle).

As a follow-on to the egg-balancing I/F technique my instructor encouraged me to fly smoothly during all types of flying – formation, circuits and even aeros, where he encouraged me to make smooth and progressive applications of the stick even during the most violent manoeuvres. This was machine empathy, in which you showed maximum consideration for the stresses you were putting on the aircraft at all times.[3] I got a lot of satisfaction from using this technique, and I determined to use it for all my future flying. Another trick was the 'stick-fixed landing', practised in smooth air conditions when you tried to fly a whole final turn and touchdown without noticeably moving the stick. (No cheating on the trimmers.) I also tried to cultivate this technique as much as possible, moving the stick the absolute minimum required to achieve the desired flight path. For many pilots these techniques became a permanent philosophy which could be applied to every aircraft they flew subsequently. They could be applied to the use of any machine, including driving a car.

Later on, low flying training began in earnest and we were shown how to navigate and handle the aeroplane at what was supposed to be 250 feet above ground level. The thrill of low level, whistling through the treetops and zooming down valleys with the wingtip close to the ground was just overwhelming and we did as much of it as we could get away with. We also trained at high altitude, climbing up to the deep blue stratosphere at 35,000 feet for handling exercises. (The RAF still did a lot of training at high altitude because of the continuing Cold War threat of the huge Soviet bomber fleet). In spite of full cockpit heating from take-off the Jet Provost's canopy would be freezing over at this height and would not clear until you descended to low level again. We were only allowed to spend a maximum of thirty minutes above 30,000 feet but within a few years such high level flying without pressurization was banned anyway, because of the serious risks of decompression sickness.[4]

Night flying was another source of thrills and new risks to take. From the air the night landscape of the east Midlands was a magical fairyland of lights, the cockpit a cosy reassuring cocoon with the instrument panel glowing dimly in the red internal lighting. This was before the explosion of 'light pollution' which was already beginning with the construction of ever more motorways and bypasses, all garishly over-illuminated with sodium lights. In the mid 1960s towns and cities still stood out as individual splashes of light, with extensive dark areas in between. By the 1990s these dark areas had shrunk dramatically and there was enough reflected artificial light to see your cockpit instruments clearly just about anywhere in the south of England. For night flying at Cranwell we had red lights in crew rooms and the line hut to acclimatize pilot's eyes to the darkness. There were no dazzling stadium lights illuminating the aircraft flight line: you had to find your aircraft with a torch and taxiing out was done in almost pitch darkness. By the time you were airborne your eyes were fully dark-adapted and you could literally see in the dark. Soon the stadium lights were to be introduced everywhere, on the engineers' insistence, to assist with ground servicing procedures. The flight line was lit up like daylight and you were airborne at least fifteen minutes before your eyes became night-adapted.

Aerobatics were pretty routine at night (although strictly forbidden). During solos it was important to switch off your navigation lights before aeros if you were anywhere near the airfield. If not, the duty instructor could soon spot which students were doing illegal aeros. I can clearly recall doing slow rolls at 1,500 feet over the middle of Nottingham on a night solo sortie.

This period of basic jet training was the most precious time of my life
so far. I felt that all of my schoolboy dreams and aspirations about
flying were being realized and were turning out even better than I
had dared to imagine. I felt totally and blissfully immersed in the
exhilarating process of learning new flying skills, taking calculated
risks and just enjoying being a creature of the air. I just couldn't get
enough of it and longed to be airborne again and trying something
new, as soon as I was back on the ground. I was self-confident and
had no fear of any new task in the air. To me everything was a
challenge to be met head on: somehow I would succeed and get the
hang of it quickly. There was vast experience amongst our instructors, and we hung on their every word. One constant theme which
came up from the ex-fighter instructors was the exhortation to 'be an
all-rounder' – to try and raise your standard at all kinds of flying.
There were always plenty of prima donnas and specialists who could
do one or two things particularly well, but the pilot who could turn
his hand to anything was worth much more and gained infinitely
more satisfaction from his flying. I took this completely to heart and
from then on strove to improve the things I was worst at in the air,
to try to bring up my overall standard as high as possible. This meant
constant and realistic self-analysis and self-criticism in the air.

For a long time we had been planning a sub-aqua expedition to the
Maldive Islands during the Easter break, which promised to be a trip
to paradise. However, in line with 89 Entry's lousy run of luck the
trip was cancelled at the last minute because of local unrest.
Hurriedly we tried to get on to alternative 'jollys' and I managed to
get myself on to a rock climbing expedition to – of all places –
Gibraltar. The small group of us included several 88 and 89 Entry
stalwarts. We hitched a free lift in an Argosy transport from RAF
Lyneham, then the RAF's major air trooping terminal and gateway
to the world. (There was still a lot of the world left to see in those
days, with RAF stations located on every continent.) The Armstrong
Whitworth Argosy was a medium range transport known variously
within the RAF as 'The Whistling Wheelbarrow', the 'Whistling Tit'
or – my favourite – 'The Armlong Woolworth Allsoggy' in deference
to its slow and meandering flight characteristics. Gibraltar was a
splendid place for a bunch of young lads on the loose: we didn't do
a lot of climbing but got to see most of the pubs and clubs and even
scraped together enough money for a night at the casino. We went
over the border to Spain, and some of us took a boat trip for a couple

of days to Tangiers, the ancient ferry chasing schools of porpoises through the impossibly blue waters of the Straits. Tangiers was hot, dusty and exciting, and we spent most of the time drinking cheap cassis and ouzo in the bars. On the return flight to UK I spent a lot of time in the cockpit of the Argosy and even handled the controls for a bit. Transport flying was stupefyingly boring and I hoped desperately that I wasn't going to end up flying one of these heaps.

Back at Cranwell there was more bad news for 89 Entry. We had been looking forward for months to the visit to the USAF Academy at Colorado Springs, by all accounts the most popular visit for any Cranwell cadet. Once again 89's run of bad luck continued, and we were told that the trip was cancelled because of a lack of air transport to get us there. By now the natives were revolting somewhere else in the world. Instead we were tasked with a continuity drill demonstration, to be given to a bunch of senior officers at RAF White Waltham. As part compensation for loss of the USA trip, we were told at short notice that we would be going to the Cafe de Paris in London to escort the Miss World contestants at a dinner dance after the competition. This was more like it! Dressed to the 9s in our dinner jackets and drenched in the world's known reserves of aftershave we bussed into London to meet up with the girls who were all feeling a bit let down after the excitement of the competition. To avoid arguments, names had been drawn at random to match cadets with each contestant. I drew Miss Malaysia, a petite and surprisingly homely lass. The girls were pretty stand-offish at first, and most of us were a bit embarrassed, but after a few drinks things warmed up a lot and we all had a good time in spite of the ever-vigilant chaperones, on the alert for the slightest bit of hanky-panky.

My first taste of formation flying came the morning after my twenty-first birthday. I had made the traditional attempt to drink twenty-one pints of beer during the evening and had failed miserably, collapsing in a stupor at about 4 a.m. after a mere dozen or so. Some cadets had actually managed it. One cadet who did so was a splendid source of entertainment for all of us: I have never met anyone before or since so determined to have a good time regardless of the consequences.[5] I reported to flights at 0800 for my first formation dual with my instructor. I was still feeling very much the worse for wear.

'I'm sorry Sir, I'm still airborne', I said. 'It was my 21st last night,' I added feebly.

'I know, I was there.' said my instructor. (I hadn't noticed at the time).

'How do you feel?' he continued.

'Not too bad.'

'Let's give it a shot then.'

It was the most wonderfully smooth first formation he had seen, until I started to feel better just before landing.

Close formation flying was wonderful fun, especially the tail chase manoeuvring when the leader broke away and we had to chase him all over the sky. Near the end of the course we were briefed for our solo land-away sorties, which both my friend and I planned to make to RAF Valley in Anglesey. There were strict warnings against any hooliganism en route. By chance we took off within a few minutes of each other. We had secretly planned to join up and go in formation, but we cocked up the join-up and arrived at Valley about five minutes apart. My friend's break into the circuit was pretty low, but mine was outside all the limits and I had orders to report to the duty instructor as soon as I touched down. We were asked sternly if we had come across in formation, which I was able to deny truthfully, but there was no escaping the low break atrocity. Back at Cranwell the chief flying instructor grounded us both after the most blistering bollocking imaginable. My friend and I were quaking in our shoes in case we were to be chopped, but we lived to fly again. I was one of the four finalists for the end-of-course Aerobatics Trophy; however, during the fly-off my final manoeuvre, (a negative-g push-out to level flight) went a bit wrong and I ended up disqualified for going below the minimum height. At the end of the course I was delighted to discover that I had won the Flying Prize as best overall pilot on 89. In my final interview the commandant congratulated me but added a stern warning that many previous winners of the prize had been killed in flying accidents due simply to overconfidence. I took this at face value and privately determined not to join the casualty list that I knew we had to face in our future flying careers. My friend and I were ecstatic to discover that we were both posted to No. 28 Course at RAF Valley in September.

 The formalities and social events concluding our three years of hard grind passed by in a whirl. Our passing out parade, on which I was Parade Adjutant because of the flying prize, took place on an incredibly hot day. During the evening we graduates kept fingering the microscopically thin pilot officer's stripe which seemed scant reward for our three years' hard grind as flight cadets. However, the real prize for all of us was the pilots' and navigators' wings, and for a lucky few pilots the prospect of advanced flying training at RAF Valley.

What had three years of Cranwell training done for me? In retrospect not a lot. On the plus side I was pretty slick at rifle and sword drill and could stand smartly on parade for hours in all weathers without fainting. I had gained some fantastic friends and we had suffered many privations and disappointments together, learning just how far we could push ourselves in extreme conditions of stress. I had learned to resist bullies in all circumstances and fight back effectively. But I was a young man keen to conquer the world as soon as possible, and Cranwell had taken up a large chunk of my formative years. If I had gone direct entry into the RAF, I would by now be flying operationally on my first squadron. Instead I was soon to discover that I would have to face several more years of personal frustration and disillusionment before I would finally step into my own single-seat fighter cockpit.

Shortly after the end of term my friend and I were on the way to Gosport, Hampshire, to join *Lady Corrine*, a lovely old wooden ketch belonging to the RAF's Offshore Sailing organization. We had an idyllic week's sailing with a hard-nosed but fair skipper. He was an instructor at Cranwell, as were some others in the crew. We got as far as Brixham after some exciting sailing in Lyme Bay. Straight after the sailing I managed to fix up a lift to Cyprus with another cadet, who was due to go with us to RAF Valley in October. This would be my first trip to a hot climate. After a night departure from Lyneham we were ecstatic when we woke up in the Argosy in the early morning over the remote Greek islands, which lay like sunbaked dust patches floating in a calm sea, the colour of deepest ultramarine. The September heat was intense and a wall of humidity took our breath away as we stepped out of the Argosy on to the sunbaked pan at RAF Akrotiri. This was what we had joined up for. After booking into the Mess we went straight to the sea at the boundary of the enormous base and plunged into the warm, crystal-clear water. After the cold waters of the Devon coast it was sheer luxury to stay in the water for hours and swim through the coral-strewn reefs and caves underwater. The colours of the fish were unbelievable and we were to spend many hours diving and baking in the sun right on base at Akrotiri. Downtown in Limassol we strolled in wonder through the dusty, sun-baked streets, drank our fill of Keo beer and ouzo and marvelled at the variety of nationalities present.

Fortunately the island was going through one of its rare periods of calm after years of fierce EOKA violence directed mainly against the occupying British.

In the mid 1960s Akrotiri was one of the largest and busiest stations in the RAF. On base was the Middle East Air Force Canberra Wing, plus two Vulcan squadrons and 70 Squadron, a Hastings transport outfit. After a couple of days exploring the local area I hitched a lift to RAF El Adem in Libya, where an ex-89 entry colleague was on holiday at home with his father, a flight lieutenant. This was my first trip in the venerable Hastings, a sort of four-engined Dakota which had once been the RAF's primary long-range transport in a more leisurely era. Formalities before departure were absolutely minimal on this cargo flight: I was the only passenger and had the free run of the cabin and cockpit. After the long, leisurely climb to cruising altitude an RAF en route navigation chart was ceremonially unfolded and clipped over the windscreen to shield us from the blinding sunlight. The crew had done this twice-weekly 'milk-run' dozens of times. We drifted lazily through the heat haze of the eastern Med, the wings flexing and dipping gently in the soft air currents as we floated through endless fields of fluffy cumulus clouds. I spent a lot of time on the flight deck, the two pilots being quite happy to let me sit in one of the pilot's seats for most of the time. Most of the flight was carried out on autopilot, except when I expressed an interest in flying it myself. The whole tempo of the flight (like most RAF air transport operations in hot climates) was, to me, one of laid-back boredom, the fierce blinding glare outside contrasting strongly with the delicious cool of the cockpit and cabin at cruising altitude. The big Hercules radial engines droned comfortingly along, seemingly capable of running for ever. Far out to port in the haze lay the thin, sandy line of the north African coast, pointing us unerringly towards the remote coastal town of Tobruk, outside which lay the RAF's last base in Africa.

From the air the famous town and port area gleamed white in the searing sunlight, the whitewashed buildings a jumble of sugar cubes scattered on a hillside. El Adem was literally a desert airstrip, seemingly just a few prefabricated single-storey buildings scattered around the heat soaked concrete expanse of the aircraft parking area. My colleague met me and whisked me off to the bar for the first of many marathon drinking sessions, followed by a run back to his parents' married quarter in the town. We went back to the bar in the evening where we met some Hunter pilots out from the UK on a 'ranger' and recce for a forthcoming armament practice camp. Making use of the vast desert bombing ranges nearby, a lot of RAF squadrons flew out to El Adem for weapon training. We listened avidly to tales of what the Hunter guys got up to, both in the air and on the ground, where there was a lot of drinking and good-natured rioting – to the disgust and fury of the staid 'truckies' who formed the majority of the base staff. I spent a week at El Adem and Tobruk and was completely captivated by this first-ever taste of the romance and excitement of the desert and the Arab township. We visited the souk and spent a lot of time lounging about at the officers' beach club in town, swimming in the crystal-clear water of the harbour. There were expeditions out into the desert in borrowed RAF Land Rovers, including a magical picnic at the spectacular beach at Bardia with a friendly bunch of WAAFs. I left El Adem reluctantly, and returned to Cyprus for a few more days of sun-drenched idleness before my colleague and I had to return to UK. After this glorious introduction to hot climates the thought of a posting to fly the Hunter somewhere hot was now almost too exciting to contemplate.

By the end of September the excitement of advanced flying training on the Gnat drove all other thoughts from our minds as my friend and I made the long trek up through Wales to RAF Valley, the last outpost of civilization at the westernmost tip of Anglesey.

Notes
1. Like many apocryphal flying stories, this one is illogical: no sane pilot would waste time pressing the radio transmit button when he could be pulling the ejection seat handle. Similarly, no pilot would fail to try to eject, even if he knew there was no chance of survival.
2. CADF: this was a development of a Second World War homing aid, ground-based equipment which could tell the direction of an aircraft relative to base pretty accurately. It could also tell when you were directly overhead base. Unlike radar, it continued to work well in really heavy weather.
3. The 'stick stirrers' often had little feel for machine empathy. Perversely, for many of them it was a source of pride how much they could bang the aircraft about in flight – they equated this with a 'fighter pilot mentality', in the mistaken belief that it would guarantee them a posting to fighters.
4. Decompression sickness or 'bends' resulted from staying too long in the extremely low pressures at high altitude. This, along with oxygen system failures had been the cause of many deaths of

solo high-flying pilots during the '50s.

5. This cadet was a good aviator and was posted to a Lightning Squadron. Sadly he didn't last long: he died after carrying out a reheat rotation take-off, for which a cameraman was positioned near the end of the runway. Apparently there was a technical problem with the aircraft and by all accounts it was a spectacular manoeuvre: for some reason the pilot ejected too late from the departure and spin which followed. In the next few years three more pilots of 89 Entry were to die in Lightning accidents.

Chapter 4

Advanced Training

RAF Valley was a bleak, windswept outpost whose prefabricated buildings were scattered about the rock-strewn dunes on the western tip of Anglesey. The Mess was a nondescript modern building, although comfortable enough for us students. The bar was enormous, which was handy because we were to spend a lot of time in there. We met up with the non-Cranwell members of 28 Course, the infamous ex-university 'Green Shieldies', about whom we had heard so much at Cranwell. I was amazed to see that all of these characters were of flying officer rank, and had been drawing officer's pay for most of their time at university. Compared with us they were affluent, although they had spent only a third as much time as us in the RAF. Several of them were still whingeing about their Jet Provost training, complaining about the 'juvenile' discipline and petty restrictions of the RAF. My hackles rose on hearing this: with all their extra pay and rank they still weren't satisfied with their lot. For us ex-Cranwell cadets it was sheer joy to be let loose on a real RAF station and be allowed out whenever we wanted. However, we put our prejudices aside and discovered that in the main they were a fun-loving bunch, just as eager to fly the Gnat as we were. A particularly good character was a mad Scotsman with a first in aerodynamics, whose sense of humour gelled with ours; we soon recruited him as an honorary 'grunter'. We found that social life off base was almost non-existent, except for the occasional party at married students' rented accommodation. The local Welsh were fairly hostile to the English. In Holyhead the shopkeepers were surly and unhelpful as soon as they heard an English accent. Not only did they object to the aircraft noise but this area was a hotbed of Welsh nationalism.

Ground school for the Folland Gnat T1 was short but intense. For its day it was a very advanced aeroplane. The cockpit was a dream, pretty cramped but with a splendid view all round. The machine was tiny, the cockpit so close to the ground that the ground crew standing alongside could speak face-to-face with the pilot. The primary flight instrument display was the OR946 system as used in the Lightning, with a large roller-blind attitude indicator next to a combined offset TACAN (Tactical Air Navigator – a navigation aid) and ILS (Instrument Landing System) display for navigation. There was a Zero Reader Flight Director which could be linked to ILS for automatic localizer and glidepath acquisition – pretty advanced stuff in comparison to the Jet Provost, and far more advanced than the Hawk, the Gnat's eventual replacement in the next decade. At the end of Ground School we were sent on the inevitable 3-day survival exercise in north Wales, living for the last forty-eight hours on the contents of the Gnat ejection-seat survival pack and sleeping – or more accurately freezing – under a parachute. On the last night the staff generously threw us a scrawny, unplucked chicken to cook. As the bird slowly burned away on our camp fire someone's transistor radio was broadcasting the news of an appalling landslide disaster at a south Wales village called Aberfan.

My regular Gnat instructor was to be an exceptional 'Creamy' (first tour) instructor, a laconic and bookish honours graduate in aerodynamics who had started life as an RAF engineer. He was modest, dryly amusing and a brilliant flyer. This was the first time we had really taken note of the 'Creamy' phenomenon. Basically, the RAF was always short of good instructors and selected good aviators were being sent direct to Central Flying School at the end of their Advanced Training, to do a thirty-month stint as instructors before being given the posting of their choice (within reason). Although the latter prospect was tempting, my friend and I were not interested in wasting any more time in Flying Training Command. At this time the Labour Government was already making noises about withdrawal from the Far East and all the other interesting overseas areas. The DFGA Hunter Squadron in Hong Kong – every pilot's dream posting – had just folded up, and a date had been set for final withdrawal from the Far East. Time was running out fast. We just wanted to get on with it and get to RAF Chivenor as fast as possible to become ground attack pilots before all the exciting postings dried up.

The Gnat was a totally exhilarating machine to fly. With 4,500lb thrust from the Bristol Siddeley Orpheus engine it had very snappy acceleration and was capable of nearly 600 knots at low level. Its main attraction was the extremely high rate of roll of 250 degrees per second (The Red Arrows had the aileron stops taken out and could achieve 400 degrees per sec in their 'Twinkle Roll' manoeuvre). Compared with the Jet Provost the hydraulic powered controls were extremely responsive, requiring only the lightest touch on the stick to manoeuvre. Best of all, it felt like a single-seat fighter. You sat suspended above the landscape like a god, with the world manoeuvring about you at the lightest touch on the stick. Your instructor was unobtrusive, just a quiet voice on the intercom. Everything in the aeroplane was done at a fighter-like pace. Because you sat so close to the ground, take-offs and landings – even taxiing – proceeded at incredible speed. The final approach speed was in the range 150-170 knots, and you had to calculate it – and fly it – to the nearest knot, depending on fuel weight. Flying in mechanical mode was a real challenge, the controls becoming as heavy as lead as the instructor turned off the 3,000lb hydraulic pressure by means of a lever in his cockpit. This was usually done at the top of a loop, when you had just a few seconds to carry out the correct emergency (STUPRE) drill:

GNAT HYDRAULIC FAILURE DRILL – STUPRE DRILL

SPEED -	CORRECT SPEED RANGE
TRIM -	HANDS-OFF
UNLOCK -	ELEVATOR
POWER -	OFF
RAISE -	GUARD ON STANDBY TRIM
EXHAUST-	HYDRAULIC POWER

There had been several fatal accidents in the Gnat because pilots had failed to carry out this drill correctly.[1] It was burned into our memories in letters of fire and I can clearly remember it forty years later. For normal flying the Gnat had a fully-powered slab tailplane like all modern fighters. However, after hydraulic failure or engine failure the tailplane would 'freeze' and you were left with only the electric standby trim control (which moved too slowly for effective handling) and the puny little elevators, which had to be unlocked for this purpose.

Most of the instructors at Valley were ex-fighter or ex-Canberra pilots and so there was a vast expertise on low-level and operational fighter flying. Things were done at a much faster pace than Jet Provost flying. We learned how to cut corners during sortie preparation in order to get airborne as fast as possible. Navigation planning became much more complex as we did more HI-LO and HI-LO-HI profiles, with part of the route flown at high altitude. My mental dead reckoning (MDR) improved in leaps and bounds as we applied 'fudge factors' and 'seaman's eye' techniques to speed up planning. As an example, during Jet Provost flying the high altitude portion of the trip would be planned with much laborious use of the famous Dalton computer, which gave very accurate courses and timings after applying the forecast met wind at the planned flying altitude. This took far too long for fighter planning. Met winds were never that accurate anyway, and you could achieve perfectly satisfactory results by using the famous 1 in 60 rule after a rudimentary maximum drift calculation. This was a simple application of a basic scientific principle of experimental measurements. This principle stated that there was no point in measuring any one parameter of an experiment to an order of accuracy greater than the other parameters – you were just wasting your time. 'Measuring it with a micrometer and then hitting it with a sledgehammer' was the common expression for this error.

At Valley there was also an extremely practical approach to the plethora of rules and regulations surrounding flying, and particularly low flying. We were expected to 'interpret' the rules with common sense in a way which enabled us to carry out our task quickly and efficiently. Any tedious restrictions which slowed things down were quietly ignored. However, irresponsible flying and flagrant hooliganism were not tolerated: we were expected to work hard, learn fast and behave as grown-ups at all times. Beat-ups and other forms of showing off were looked down upon by the more professional operators. The key to really rapid response was 'multi-tasking' both in the air and during planning on the ground. If you could do a couple of tasks at the same time then you had an immediate advantage over others. Even more important was the ability to divorce your concentration from the task in hand and think ahead to anticipate what was going to happen next. Many students just could not do this effectively, and were always being caught out because they weren't able to estimate how any given situation was going to develop. The 'chop' rate at Valley was pretty high; a lot of students never completed the course and were sent to RAF Oakington to continue training on the Varsity.[2]

Sorties in the Gnat were action-packed. A standard general handling sortie would be as follows: First, an instrument departure using the TACAN departure procedure to send you off on an accurate track into the upper air. This had to be flown exactly on the radial and at an accurate 360kt climbing speed. After just a few minutes of climbing through cloud you were in the deep blue at 40,000 feet and ready for a supersonic run over the sea to practise high-Mach number handling. From this height on a clear day you could see 100 miles or more to the east coast of England. To the north the peaks of the Lake District were hazy blue shadows, seemingly just a few miles away, the Isle of Man a sand-coloured leaf floating just offshore in Morecambe Bay. Lower down we would carry out some steep turns, followed by maximum rate turns, winding up to a breathtaking 7g in a descending spiral, your body organs crushing down into the ejection seat while the vice-like grip of your anti-g trousers tried to force some blood back up to your brain. Then we zoom climbed again for some stalling. We slowed down to minimum control speed and recovered as she fell away into an incipient spin. (Fully-developed spinning was prohibited: it was far too unpredictable to be safe.) Aeros next – loops, slow rolls, point rolls, Cuban 8s, Lazy 8s, Vertical 8s – everything to be entered at the correct speed and height and all linked together as smoothly as possible to practise our sequence for the end-of-course competition. At the top of the last loop the inevitable hydraulic failure warning came on as our instructor pulled the throttle to idle and switched off the hydraulics. 'Simulated engine failure,' he said helpfully, having made sure that we were pointing straight at the biggest cloud he could find.

'Into the STUPRE drill; easy really, can't understand why they make so much fuss about it – CHRIST these controls are heavy!'

And then a sweaty glide back towards base for a flameout spiral down through the cloud, engine idling, (same as the Jet Provost procedure), followed by a glide landing on whichever runway we saw when we popped out underneath. And then circuits. Too busy at Valley, so off down the road to Mona, our relief landing ground, via a complicated set of departure and recovery procedures. We whistled round the circuit at impossible speeds, coping with the inevitable screaming crosswind which made us over-bank to 80 degrees to get round finals. Normal circuits, manual circuits, flapless circuits; get the speed right, get the touchdown right, all pounding the runway in tandem with other sweating students. As always my instructor took over now and then to demonstrate a circuit, just to avoid getting bored and to give me a bit of a rest. His flying was immaculate, as always, quite sick-making to see the precision of it. We students knew just how much more difficult it was to fly from the back seat with severely restricted forward view. At Valley I discovered for the first time that I began to stammer a bit under pressure. It became a sure indicator that I was working almost to capacity, and I had to make a conscious effort to steady up and keep a grip. Whatever the pressure, never let it show through on the radio. Stay cool: keep your voice low-pitched, calm and slightly bored:

Only actors scream on the radio.

Night flying would involve a similar profile, with less general handling. Naturally, there would be a lot more as we flew in quite dirty weather conditions. The many all-weather pilots on the staff would think nothing of doing night circuits in heavy rain under a 400 feet cloud base with poor visibility underneath. By far the most difficult exercises were manual circuits on standby instruments. With the splendid attitude indicator and electric altimeter completely covered up we had only the tiny standby artificial horizon and, worst of all, the horrible little standby altimeter, hidden behind your left knee. On this single-pointer instrument the difference between 1,000 feet and zero feet was represented by a needle movement of just two or three millimetres. In the poor light in that corner of the cockpit it was very difficult to read with any accuracy. On my final night check I ended up flying downwind at 400 feet instead of 1,000 feet, trying to read this wretched instrument in the dark and wrestling with manual control.

Don't complain: if you can't take a joke you shouldn't have joined.

Low flying in Wales was epic. We were shown how to 'seaman's eye' our position on the half million scale low flying chart, and find our way back to Valley from anywhere in north Wales without using a map. Valley was always at the receiving end of the worst of the Atlantic weather systems, which often left the whole area covered in low cloud with rain underneath. Conditions could be lethal in the valleys, with cloud forming an unbroken ceiling covering the hills on either side. Then it was like flying in a tunnel, with the ground rushing by at 700 feet per second. We were shown 'slot flying' or 'letterboxing', letterboxes being the narrow slots between cloud and lower ground between peaks. The secret of getting through safely was to aim your pink body as close as possible to the ground in the slot. If you chickened out and flew too high you ran the risk of losing contact with the ground and being forced into an emergency pull-up. In that case any attempt to dive down out of cloud to regain contact was lethally dangerous, and had been the cause of fatal accidents over the years. Because of the hard training the RAF was still suffering weather-related fatal accidents.

There was a lot of low flying in the Advanced Flying Training syllabus and the end of most sorties involved a bit of free navigation followed by a 'white-knuckle ride' down the Nant Ffrancon (A5) Pass in Snowdonia (at this time still a two-way system: eventually, after concerns about near head-on collisions the valleys of Snowdonia were made into a one-way system). Half way down the pass you overflew Llyn Ogwen, a dark, forbidding stretch of water below the famous peak Tryfan. At this point the valley turned over 60 degrees to starboard and dropped several hundred feet. My instructor showed me how to make the standard 'racing turn' to get around the bend and into the pass down to Bethesda at maximum speed without going above 250 feet. Low over Llyn Ogwen you put on full power and pulled up to aim just below the dark peak of Tryfan on the left. Just before you reached the rock face – and before you could see around the bend – you rolled almost inverted and pulled 6g to turn right and down into the next part of the valley, which was still obscured by the rocky wall on the opposite side. If you judged it right the last stretch of the valley would appear upside down in the top of the windscreen. You could now roll completely inverted to make a hard pull down into the last stretch of the valley. Very satisfying if done accurately, and very spectacular to see from the ground on the A5 at the bend, the aircraft trailing thick vapour trails from each wingtip as it passed around the corner almost upside down. Rock climbers hanging on to Tryfan by their fingernails were not usually impressed.

Valley was also home to Fighter Command's Missile Practice Camp, and we had a series of visits from Javelin and Lightning squadrons. They came to fire off their annual allocation of missiles on the range in Cardigan Bay. At one time we had a whole Javelin squadron for several weeks, just returned from 'guarding' Zambia against the Hunters of the Smith regime in Rhodesia. Although we were jealous of their exploits, detached to darkest Africa, none of us was impressed with the Javelin, an inadequate fighter and a typical

post-war compromise of procurement and design. We soon became
sick of the peculiar moaning resonance of their Sapphire engines, and
were glad when they finally departed, soon to be disbanded and their
aircraft scrapped. The Lightnings were hardly more capable as
fighters, limited to a ludicrously short range and seriously deficient
in weapons. They looked prettier though, and gave a cracking air
display.

I had continued to play squash and was in the station team. Matches
were few and far between because of the vast road distances between
us and other RAF stations. However, on one occasion the team piled
into an ancient Anson transport (of the Northern Communications
Squadron), to fly to St Mawgan in Cornwall for a match. I felt privileged to fly in an aeroplane with such a distinguished service record.
We dropped into Topcliffe in Yorkshire on the way back and
continued after dark to Valley, the ancient Master Navigator demonstrating the Second World War-vintage GEE navigation kit to me en
route.

At Valley we had the RAF Helicopter Search and Rescue training
squadron and a fellow squash player, was kind enough to give me
quite a few dual trips in the Whirlwind 10. This was great sport and
a total contrast with Gnat flying, although demanding a lot of concentration. Eventually he let me fly the machine during drum
winching exercises, with a trainee winchman hanging on the wire. I
also flew some splendid mountain exercises, taking the machine into
and out of some impossibly small landing sites on top of mountains
in Snowdonia. He was an excellent instructor and was quite fearless
about letting me do a lot of the landings and take-offs, although I
wasn't a bona fide helicopter student. Mountain flying could be
extremely dangerous, especially in the strong winds we often
suffered in that area. On several occasions my instructor demonstrated the engine failure procedure after lift-off from a precipitous
mountainside landing site, no bigger than a table top. For a single-
engined helicopter this procedure was vitally important and was
practised often. I was sitting in the cabin doorway for the first one
and my instructor told me to 'hang on tight'. As soon as we cleared
the edge of the site he dropped the collective control lever to the floor
and stood the machine on its nose to 'Taxi down the mountainside',
in helicopter parlance. After a stunning white-knuckle ride straight
down between the boulders at 100 knots plus, we had built up
enough airspeed and rotor r.p.m. to carry out a safe engine-off

landing, way down in the valley below. Eventually my instructor let me have a go at one myself.

My Gnat instructor had his own private aeroplane, a single-engined Beagle Airedale, and one weekend he flew three of us students across to Dublin to see the sights. The four of us climbed into our immersion suits and donned RAF lifejackets for the short hop across the cold and forbidding Irish sea. After landing at Dublin International we strolled into Passenger Arrivals and amazed onlookers by stripping off the immersion suits to emerge, Bond-like, in dapper civilian clothes. One of our student colleagues – an ace guitarist, bon viveur and professional Irishman – was an expert on the drinking environs of the city; more importantly he knew where you could take an English accent without getting a knife stuck between your shoulder blades. The weekend passed by in a haze of draught Guinness, quaffed in wonderfully atmospheric pubs. By Sunday afternoon we had had enough and staggered back into the Airedale for the flight home, satisfied that we had found out all we needed to know about Dublin, Guinness and the Irish.

We finished the Gnat course and I was awarded the overall Flying Prize once again, although I was miffed at losing out to a good friend in the aerobatics competition. This pilot was a delightful character, one of the world's true gentlemen, who had been an exceptionally popular member of 89 Entry at Cranwell. His brother was in the same regiment as my brother. Before the end of course excitement rose to fever pitch as we discovered that there were no less than 4 Hunter DF/GA (Day Fighter/Ground Attack) slots available at Chivenor for the 15 of us still on No. 28 course. My friend and I had already made ourselves absolutely clear that DF/GA was the only thing we wanted and my instructor told me that everything looked good for me to get the posting. Having won the Flying Prize I thought I was home and dry but then – disaster...

The squadron boss called me in and told me I was posted immediately as a 'Creamy' to CFS, along with three other members of my course. I was devastated and felt completely betrayed by the system. Having worked so hard to come out on top to guarantee the Hunter posting, to be told that I was being selected for CFS entirely against my will was almost too much to bear. With deep irony he told me that I had to go to CFS 'because they desperately needed good young pilots as instructors'.[3] Had I not done so well my chances of going to CFS would have been minimal. I listened in misery as I heard the names of the students who had been given the Hunter postings for which I had worked so hard for the last four years. I was disgusted and protested to anyone who would listen, wrote to staff officers, etc., but it was no good: I was stuck with another three years in Training Command, after which I would be lucky if there were any decent overseas postings left. We were sent home for a short leave and then I returned to Valley for a few 'refresher' sorties before setting off for CFS in mid-March 1967.

Notes
1. If not trimmed correctly when all hydraulic power was exhausted, it was impossible to land the aircraft – there was not enough control authority left on the back-up elevators and electric standby trim.
2. The Vickers Varsity was the RAF's multi-engined trainer. A large, powerful twin-engined aircraft, it was powered by two Bristol Hercules engines. I had a go at flying one much later: it seemed enormous from the cockpit.
3. This at a time when the RAF's training system was entering its largest 'glut output' period for decades. Graduates from AFS were having to wait nearly two years before a slot was available at OCUs. The RAF was still operating seven Flying Training Schools – a huge overcapacity for the rapidly-reducing size of our front-line force.

Chapter 5

Central Flying School

RAF Little Rissington in the Cotswolds was the home of the RAF's Central Flying School, its oldest and most famous establishment which had existed in various locations since before the First World War. This was a pity because as far as I was concerned it was a complete dead loss, and I lost no time in making it clear that I didn't want to be there. In this I was not alone: none of us 'Creamies' from Valley was impressed with the ethos and traditions of the place. As far as we were concerned it was a poor substitute for being on an operational squadron. The sole aim of the place was to inculcate the good old RAF traditions of high-quality flying instruction in new flying instructors from all over the globe. Many years later I came to appreciate the training I received there on Number 238 course, in spite of my ungrateful attitude at the time. There were students from all over the place, from every type of RAF background, plus Royal Navy pilots and a lot of foreigners; Arabs, Lebanese, Malaysian and African.

Ironically, 'Rissy' was probably the most attractive of all RAF flying stations. Sitting on a hill just above the pretty tourist trap of Bourton-on-the-Water, its three short runways were draped carelessly across a hilltop, presenting a stimulating challenge to the embryo instructor trying to demonstrate and teach landing techniques in the prevailing downdraughts and tricky crosswinds. The basic aeroplane for instructor practice was the Jet Provost, with a small flight of Varsities for instructors destined for that aeroplane. There was a separate Chipmunk training flight. Of more interest to me was the Gnat training flight, based ten miles down the road at the famous RAF Kemble, home of the Red Arrows. As I was forced to waste the next few years in Flying Training Command I rashly assumed that I would be able to become a Gnat instructor – I had no wish to go

back to the Jet Provost again. However, continuing our run of bad
luck we were told, to our disgust, that Gnat flying was definitely
'out' for us Creamies. Valley was having some problems with their
Creamies and didn't want any more for the present. Bloody marvellous, I thought. We were amazed at the low level of knowledge of the
majority of students. Traditionally, a certain amount of ignorance of
the subject mattered little in the old CFS tradition of the jobbing
instructor, who was supposed to be able to teach others anything he
could do himself in an aeroplane. QFIs (Qualified Flying Instructors)
had always worked on the well known doctor's principle – 'See one,
Do one, Teach one.' If this led to a little 'flannelling' around the
subject on the ground – then so be it. What counted was ability to
instruct in the air.

Eventually I came to appreciate the wisdom of this philosophy, and
the way in which graduates of CFS had produced the quality of pilots
that the RAF needed over the years of peace and war. However, for
the moment I was still an all-out rebel, petulantly refusing to see any
merit in what I was to be trained for. In ground school I could still
remember a lot of my aerodynamics and thermodynamics stuff and
our aerodynamics graduate knew it all backwards. We realized that
we would have to introduce the concept of 'negative learning' to
make sure we didn't suffer the indignity of winning the Ground
School Examination prize. To achieve this aim we spent time in the
bar reciting the *wrong* answers to various aerodynamic questions, to
the total bewilderment of the more serious-minded students. The
flying phase of the CFS course promised to be unspeakably tedious.
After a few 'refresher' sorties to improve our flying we started the
cycle of dual, mutual and give-back to learn the instructional aspects
of the whole of the 120 hour basic training syllabus. In the duals a
CFS instructor would show you the standard CFS way to instruct the
various exercises. In the mutuals (more of these later), we were sent
airborne with another luckless student of our own course, ostensibly
to practise these sequences again – some hopes! Finally, on the
dreaded 'give-back' sorties you flew again with your CFS instructor
with him acting as student to give it all back again and demonstrate
that you had learned something. Most of the CFS instructors seemed
a drab and pedantic lot: they took great delight in simulating the
most awkward, stupid and perverse student type, in order to make
our practice instruction sessions as difficult as possible. Very fortunately, I was allocated a Canadian ex-Sabre pilot as instructor. His
laconic sense of humour and spirited flying kept me sane for the

course. He was a short, punchy, bullet-headed fighter pilot who kept me in check but allowed me just enough rope to burn off my frustration at being confined to instruction when he could see that I desperately wanted to be a fighter pilot.

Straight away on the 'mutual' sorties we were let loose on our own in the airspace over Gloucestershire. A typical 'mutual' sortie profile would be as follows: After take-off we would spend no more than ten minutes 'practising' the instructional sequences for which we had been authorized. Everything would be done inverted, just for fun. For example, if I was demonstrating how to do a level 30 degree banked turn then I would demonstrate and 'patter'[1] an outside turn, rolling the aircraft on its back to achieve the turn. Of course, while inverted the controls worked the opposite way, so we were continuing our philosophy of 'negative learning' to avoid doing well on the course. All of this was accompanied by infantile giggling and 'grunting' to liven up the patter a bit. Then for a while we would try out wacky aerobatic manoeuvres on each other, doing our best to make the other one ill. We would soon tire of this and so the hunt for a worthy opponent would start in earnest.

The airspace over the Vale of Evesham would be full of Jet Provosts, Varsities, Chipmunks and Gnats going through the same routines, some with staff instructors on board and some, like us, 'mutuals' out for a bit of fun. We would edge closer to any other Jet Provost we found and see if he wanted to play. A sudden hard turn towards us and the game was 'ON'.[2] Now began a wild, tumbling air combat with each aircraft trying desperately to get close on the tail of the other. We Creamies had no specific training in this; we taught ourselves how to fly the tactics and manoeuvres gleaned from listening to the ex-fighter pilots bragging in the bar. We learned fast and got better; like rookie Battle of Britain pilots thrown up against Me109s, we either won or got massacred. You learned a lot from either experience and no one was firing live ammunition. Some of these combats went on for a punishing half an hour or more, (the Jet Provost used very little fuel), and then we would creep guiltily back to Rissy to land on the fumes in the tank. We were pulling up to 6g for a lot of the time without benefit of a 'g' suit, or turning desperately at minimum speed, the aircraft barely under control. Any tactic was allowed, many combats ending up with a chase around the woods and hills of the Cotswolds at low level. We dived in and out of cloud willy-nilly to gain a tactical advantage and came so close that we could see right into each other's cockpits. We survived, and learned a lot. In later years on fighters I was able to remember many of the techniques I taught myself at CFS: they stood me in good stead on faster aircraft when I eventually became an air combat instructor. Because the Jet Provost could turn so rapidly you got through a hell of a lot of fighter manoeuvring in a short time. The one big danger in these illicit 'bounce' sorties was to pick on the more powerful JP4 if you were flying a JP3. You couldn't identify the mark for certain until you got within about 30 yards.

Air combat was always a sweaty, dirty, heaving sport. You pulled and rolled and grunted viciously as the g forces came on and off and your opponent whirled and danced around you. There was a lot of 'patter', much of it obscene, especially if there was someone else in the aircraft with you offering, not always welcome, advice:

'PULL, Jerry, PULL, for Christ's sake!'

'I am, I am – it's 6 already!' (6g was the limit for the Jet Provost)

'SHIT, this bloke's good! He MUST be in a 4!' (i.e. a JP4)

'I think it must be the instructor – he took off just behind us'

'No it can't be – that's not his helmet'

'CHRIST, Jerry, NOT SO FUCKING CLOSE!'

'Oops! Sorry mate, reversing left, he's getting close – let's try a flick roll'

'JESUS CHRIST, JERRY!'

'Hang on, HANG ON – he's going in front! – Claiming a Kill!'

'Let's get out of here!'

Sometimes in desperation you would hand over control to your partner, to see if he could sort it out. The prospect of being 'jumped' or 'bounced' by any other aircraft in the sky did wonders for our lookout. Many times I pleaded with my instructor to teach me some proper air combat techniques but, true professional that he was, he always refused.

'You're here to be an instructor, Jerry: just accept it,' was all he would say, tongue planted firmly in cheek. He knew what the Creamies got up to when we were airborne on our own.

With low flying we had to be a bit more careful. Unauthorized low flying was the number one crime in the RAF, so you had to wait until you were actually authorized for low level before we could let rip a bit over the Cotswolds. However, each return to Rissy could legitimately involve a run-in-and-break before landing. Traditionally this was carried out fairly low over the airfield, and we Creamies would make a point of breaking as low as we could right outside the office window of the Chief Instructor. He was a real gent of the old school, always polite and calm and considerate towards us layabouts who were showing so little gratitude for the excellent training we were being given. Like many of the staff he realized how frustrated we were and allowed us some latitude to burn off our energies. Every now and then he would ring up our long-suffering squadron commander and ask him to tell the Creamies to 'Tone it down a bit' after some particularly exuberant behaviour in the circuit. At weekends you could 'borrow' a Jet Provost to fly home just about whenever you wanted, and I staged through Exeter airport many times. Often I could get a lift onwards to Plymouth with an ex-89 Entry colleague now on a holding posting flying Chipmunks at Exeter. He was waiting for the Canberra OCU and soon achieved his aim of a posting to 39 Squadron in Malta, the dream posting of the Canberra world. Unfortunately he didn't survive for long. After an engine failure he crashed on finals in Malta and was killed. The Canberra was not a forgiving aircraft on one engine. Of the few notable instructors at Rissy I flew often with a lovely chap, ex-helicopters, who had a splendidly irreverent attitude to the whole business and maintained an empathy with us Creamies. Sadly he was eventually killed in Oman after he returned to helicopter flying. He was shot down by a SAM in the Dhofar region during the clandestine war against the ADDU in the early '70s. In June we RAF students took great interest in the amazing victory of the Israeli Air Force in the 6-Day War. One member of our course was not so happy: a Lebanese ex-Hunter pilot, he was devastated by the total defeat of his country by the Israelis.

In very recent times CFS had been able to maintain a fleet of various aircraft which the student instructors were expected to fly for themselves with the absolute minimum of briefing. This was regarded as an essential part of instructor training – you were expected to be able to teach yourself how to fly an unfamiliar aircraft. CFS used to have Hunters, Meteors, Vampires and Canberras, but sadly this fleet was no more because of cutbacks in expenditure. The previous Commandant still kept a Mosquito in the hangar, which he would have wheeled out occasionally for him to beat up the airfield. We were still encouraged to fly with fellow student instructors in the other training aircraft as much as possible. I didn't do much of this except for a fascinating sortie with an ex-fighter pilot student in a Varsity, in which I flew quite a few circuits and bumps. Flying a largish transport aeroplane was like pulling at a gigantic rubber band, the controls were so heavy and the response so slow that you had to anticipate every manoeuvre a long way ahead.

My customary overconfidence at instrument flying was dented a bit during a hard-working 'give back' dual with our Flight Commander. The weather was pretty bad and the upper air work had been completed above 10,000 feet of solid cloud. On asking for a letdown, ATC told us to hold as there was a problem with an aircraft ahead of us. In the hold I flew a continuous 30 degree banked turn to the left for nearly thirty minutes above the clear white sheet of cloud, which I knew extended all the way down to just a couple of hundred feet above the field. This was not a good idea, I was soon to discover. As soon as I entered cloud for the instrument recovery I was immediately spatially disorientated, convinced that I was banking steeply to the right all the time, although the instruments told me the wings were level. This was because of the long left hand orbit in the clear above cloud. I had never been disorientated before and the experience was extremely unpleasant. Like all good instructors, mine refused to take control and let me off the hook. He knew that the experience of overcoming the disorientation myself, no matter how stressful, would be an invaluable experience for me, reaffirming the old lesson 'When disorientated, believe your instruments – no matter how wrong it feels'. It worked. I sweated buckets getting back on the ground and was grateful to my instructor for his good sense. A lesser instructor might have let me off the hook and taken control. That option is not available in a single-seat aircraft: you've just got to sort it out for yourself – or die.

As the CFS course progressed I felt increasingly depressed as I contemplated the awful prospect of the couple of years, teaching boring basic techniques to *ab initio* students. We Creamies spent more and more time in the bar drowning our sorrows and being teased by the ex-fighter pilots about the demeaning job of a QFI: at least they had a fund of war stories from overseas about real operational flying. There was a riotous final Dinner Night when I recall helping to throw most of the Mess anteroom furniture out of the window, a display of mindless vandalism for which we paid heavily on our final Mess bills. At my final interview with the Commandant he objected to my scruffy service dress hat and threw me out of his office. To our perverse satisfaction, we were way down the honours list of our course, although I was delighted to win an aerobatics trophy for the first time. I had asked for a posting to RAF Syerston, the most southerly of our basic flying training schools. Some hopes. As a well-deserved punishment for my churlish attitude I was posted to RAF Acklington in Northumberland, the most northerly FTS in UK. My car was now time-expired. I sold it to an air traffic controller at Rissy for £1, and took the train back to Plymouth. I went to London to visit an old school friend, now married and, after a drunken lunchtime session I bought a second-hand Sunbeam Alpine from a dealer who must have rubbed his hands in glee as I staggered into the used car lot. It was the easiest sale he ever made, and the car was a hopeless wreck. On the run back to Plymouth the oil pressure was ominously low, and the overdrive failed, never to work again. Much later I discovered that the car was a rebuilt wreck, with the whole of the right side about 2 inches further back than the left. Most of the gleaming metallic bodywork turned out to be filler. I did some posing in Plymouth with my 'new' sports car, and received a telegram from the RAF to say that I was to report to RAF Leeming instead of Acklington. (Acklington was scheduled for closure).

Notes
1. PATTER: this was talking about what you were doing while you were doing it. Not as easy as it sounds, as many pilots simply could not talk and fly accurately at the same time. Even more difficult was to fly completely accurately and say EXACTLY what you were doing: for example it was no good saying 'Here we are in the turn at 150 knots' if your airspeed was actually 160 knots.
2. Ex-fighter students would have a go straight away: they were always excellent opposition. Staff pilots would usually ignore us.

Chapter 6

Flying Instructor

After a couple of weeks' leave in Plymouth I was on my way north-wards in the Alpine with fingers crossed that I would make it to Yorkshire. No. 3 Flying Training School (FTS), RAF Leeming was the largest in the RAF, situated right alongside the A1 in the Vale of York. Until recently it had been the Javelin Operational Conversion Unit and the airfield was still littered with wrecked aircraft being used for fire practice. There were scores of Jet Provosts, plus a large Vampire T11 flight which trained Iraqi students. This was run by a charismatic, piratical West Countryman with a splendid 'Janner' accent and a loudly-professed distaste for all students . To him, all students were 'bograts', and this had become the standard QFIs' term at Leeming. He was actually a very good instructor. He had recently returned from a series of adventures as Loan Service pilot in the Falkland Isles. Sadly, the Vampires were soon to move to RAF Swinderby, before I could scrounge a trip. I was posted into No. 1 Squadron of 3 FTS, the boss at that time being a kindly old ex-bomber pilot. Straight away I was sent into Standards Flight, commanded by the lanky, acerbic squadron leader who was an ex-Hunter pilot. Here I was put through some intense warm-up training to sharpen me up (they had heard of my lousy performance at Rissy). I was impressed with the flying of the instructors. They were unbe-lievably smooth and accurate in the air, and they devoted a lot of patience and understanding to me. As my inadequacies as an instruc-tor became apparent I realized to my horror that for the first time I was about to take on a flying task for which I did not feel competent. I began to regret my idleness at CFS. Fortunately, back on 1 Squadron there were plenty of very high-class students for me to fly with and learn from. There was an old saying from CFS which I now understood:

'In your first year of instruction you learn more from your students than they do from you.'

As a Basic FTS instructor you were given a lot of freedom, combined with complete responsibility for your students. The beauty of the system was that you could stay with the same student for the whole of the 12 month BFTS course, and see them develop from stumbling *ab initio* to fully-qualified pilot, all as a direct result of your efforts. Unfortunately, my efforts were a bit of a shambles at the start, and I had to spend a lot of time apologizing to my students. The Vale of York was a splendid area to fly in, with the remote and forbidding peaks of the Pennines just to the west and the more gently curving Yorkshire moors just to the east. Our nearest large town, Darlington, was quite a cultural shock for me. We used to go there on Saturday nights for an evening in the old-time working men's clubs. The entertainment was excellent and the beer strong and cheap. Middlesbrough was something else, a dirty, sprawling heap of a town surrounded by polluting heavy industry. From the air the chimneys of the huge ICI works belched multi-coloured smoke which, trapped below an inversion layer, would often creep down the Vale of York as far as Leeming. I flew hard all the time at 3 FTS. There was a lot of it to do and quite often I was allocated four students at once. Soon I was flying up to fifty hours per month.

The better students were a pleasure to fly with. My best student was an Indian who had joined the RAF from Law School. He stayed with me for almost a year. Sadly, on the day before his Final Handling Test he came to me and said he was withdrawing himself from training and going back to practise Law in India. I was pretty shocked. Unfortunately we also had a lot students going through who were not up to the task and had to be weeded out. (The RAF was still training huge numbers of students.) These characters were hard work all the way.

It could be soul-destroying with a really bad student. It was still difficult to 'chop' anyone so we instructors had to 'build a slide' if any student was looking problematical, so that we had a clear-cut case on paper if the guy couldn't hack it. For those who pulled their socks up and turned out OK this was no problem. Up to first solo there was no big problem chopping someone, but after that landmark you had to give the guy at least another fifteen hours instruction, including the difficult introduction to instrument flying, before you could chop him.

As at Cranwell there was fierce competition amongst the better students to get posted to Valley. As instructors we were very aware of the pressures of advanced flying training on the Gnat, and we put a lot of thought into who we recommended as suitable.

We used to take the students away to other satellite airfields for circuit work all the time as there was usually no room at Leeming. We spent days away at RAF Ouston, Topcliffe, Dishforth and Elvington, watching the students pound the circuit solo while we chatted up the girls in ATC. At the end of the day there would be a race between the instructors to get back to Leeming without wasting time refuelling. From Dishforth to Leeming was only ten miles up the A1 and once I remember taking-off with just 200lb of fuel to make the run. There was a lot of night flying and we bachelors were always in demand to fly night 'cowboy' sorties when there were only solo students airborne. As 'cowboy' you were expected to lurk around the local area and keep an eye on the weather. We often flew these sorties mutual with another instructor and used to invent competitions to keep ourselves amused when we were bored with aeros. The most popular was to attempt a flapless glide landing on the numbers (the beginning of the runway) without touching the throttle, from 2,000 feet overhead the airfield. I enjoyed night flying particularly in bad weather, when there were thunderstorms about. In cloud near a storm the canopy would start to glow with a ghostly blue light as the lightning built up a static charge, ready for a strike. You could impress your students by holding up your wet glove and seeing 6 inch streams of glowing electric discharge from each finger to the canopy. I was still trying to do things as fast as possible and I had a relaxed attitude towards risks when flying solo. I think that unconsciously I was trying to build extra challenges into my flying in order to compensate for the boring routine of basic instruction – what would nowadays would be seen as the operation of the 'risk thermostat'. Fortunately I survived. Every now and then the Flight Commander would take three aircraft up for Staff Continuation Training (SCT). This would involve some enthusiastic formation aerobatics and a hard tail chase, usually degenerating into a full-blown combat. We flew close formation at very low level through the dales and peaks of the Yorkshire moors. Here you had to hang on to the leader like grim death as the trees and rocks flashed past your wingtip in your peripheral vision. You needed total and absolute trust in your leader: the slightest error by either of you and you would be wiped off in the trees.

My favourite SCT sorties were with a famous ex Swift FR5 pilot. He had flown display aerobatics in RAF Germany on the Swift 5 and was the current RAF Leeming Solo Aerobatics display pilot. My eyes were already on this slot for next year, and he was giving me a lot of unofficial coaching in display flying. Unfortunately the station 'wheels' were definitely not on my side and I was going to have to pull my socks up with my instructional flying before they would even consider me for the job. With my aerobatics mentor I flew a lot of SCT low level. My favourite valley for really low flying was Newton Dale, running north from Pickering. After a few miles there was a right-angled bend which you could just get round pulling 6g at 200 knots, if you took the correct racing line. If you screwed up you would be in the trees. My mentor showed me how to do it. He was used to flying 50 feet AGL on the Swift and Hunter, the standard operating height for recce. (in peace and war)

It wasn't always fun and games. I flew lots of SCT, (usually in the worst weather), with the old lag fighter pilots. You learned a lot just from watching how they flew. They taught me fighter-type steep turns on instruments, rolling in and out very fast. One of them was another 'black of the zero' character, who could fly a complete 360 degree steep turn without gaining or losing a foot on the altimeter, this with a snappy roll-in and roll-out. After seeing these ace instructors do this I never flew another slow 'pansy' roll-in or roll-out to an instrument steep turn.

Aside from these exciting interludes, the hard grind of basic instruction went on and on. There were many near-misses and hilarious cock-ups by students to keep away the boredom. You had to keep your wits about you near the ground when the stude was flying. A colleague's student flew him through a fence short of the runway at Topcliffe. I recall a student of mine setting up for a practice forced landing at Dishforth from 11,500 feet overhead, instead of 1,500ft. With ill-concealed sarcasm I asked him if the runway didn't look rather a long way away, but he didn't twig. I let him get on with it. This was a popular teaching technique at the time, to let the student make a mistake and carry it right through to the bitter end in order to learn the lesson properly. One of our Standards Squadron instructors, (who had been an instructor on Mosquitoes) told me that he had several times landed for refuelling at other bases miles downwind after his stude had failed to keep an eye on his position and the fuel state. This was quite a major problem for the studes during the long upper-air portion of the sorties when there could be a very strong wind drifting you away above cloud.

Sorties I enjoyed least were with the 'honkers', who suffered recurrent airsickness, particularly during the arduous spinning sorties. During these you would fly quite a few ten-turn spins from 15,000 feet down and they were the downfall of many students. Once airsickness began, the stude was sent on a deconditioning course and then rejoined the syllabus to fly all the spins again.

Although I knew my instructional technique still wasn't up to much I did my best to motivate my studes and keep them interested, especially when they were having difficulties. Although jaundiced about instructing I still loved flying with a passion and would wax lyrical about being paid to fly the Queen's aeroplanes, a job I would have willingly done for free. One of the most satisfying experiences was to take-off from Leeming – where you had been surrounded for days by low cloud, rain and generally cruddy weather – and climb up through the cloud layers to break out into the brilliant sunshine on top. An unblemished vault of blue sky, a burning sun – giving warmth even in winter – and a soft white quilt of cloud as far as the eye could see. While the poor suckers back on the ground were surrounded by gloom we had this brilliant arena as our exclusive playground until the fuel ran low. I never tired of this experience. Another favourite was looping and stunting around fluffy cumulus clouds on fine days, diving through the tops and rolling joyously down the wispy strands of white over the sun-dappled Yorkshire fields.

I was also running the squash team and the station swimming team, which took up a lot of my spare time. Social life was pretty basic as the Mess was very poorly staffed. We drank hard in the bar and at the many squadron parties, and there was a lot of horseplay with the students who shared the Mess with us. My love life continued on its usual erratic path, various girlfriends arriving and departing more or less rapidly, depending on their perceived enthusiasm for the sound of wedding bells. None of them seemed to mind too much that I was so fickle about the whole business. I just couldn't contemplate the idea of a permanent relationship until I had got away from Flying Training Command and seen a bit of the world. As time passed at 3 FTS I became progressively more obsessed with the idea of RAF Chivenor, the Devon home of the Hunter DF/GA Conversion Unit.

These were more gentlemanly and relaxed days in the RAF, where hard-up living-in bachelors formed the majority of pilots. At weekends the 'married drags' took it as a duty to invite bachelors along for a huge, boozy Sunday lunch with the family, which was very nice. I enjoyed many of these pleasant Sundays with instructor colleagues and their wives.

After some hard work on my part – and painstaking coaching by the long-suffering instructors of Standards Squadron – I was eventually awarded my B1 Instructor category. Now I could authorize myself to fly and was allowed to become the Display Aeros spare aircraft pilot and aerobatic understudy. After a series of checkouts I was cleared for solo aerobatics down to 500ft. I was heavily into negative-g manoeuvres and started and finished my display inverted. I had an ambitious 'flat show' for low cloudbase situations, which included a rolling 360 turn, (A 360 with a continous slow roll). I also had a complete low speed sequence, done entirely with the wheels down and canopy open, including loops, rolls and stall turns. The nominated display pilot generously let me take a proportion of the air displays in the summer, the biggest of which was the RAF Finningley Battle of Britain display. Low level display aerobatics was hard work, demanding the highest standard of controlled precision flying, combined with an adrenalin-fuelled 'charge' at the ten minute 'slot' you were allocated in front of a crowd. The pilot would be working his butt off in the cockpit, the horizon and display line spinning wildly about the aircraft as the g forces threatened to black him out. To the spectator the manoeuvres would look merely smooth and graceful, with not a hint of the violence going on in the cockpit. To imagine just the heat stress on the pilot, picture yourself in the heat of summer wearing heavy clothing inside a closed, poorly-ventilated plastic bubble carrying out the most violent physical exercises possible. Drenched in sweat, I loved every minute of it.

For an RAF pilot, a large part of the display flying challenge was creating a satisfying display while complying with the plethora of rules and regulations which you had to follow. There was no way round this and it was particularly difficult in recent years with high-performance aircraft like the Harrier and Tornado because of the number of things you could not do with the aeroplane. What irritated most RAF display pilots was to see foreign pilots in aircraft like the Mig29 operating with few handling restrictions[1] to produce sparkling display manoeuvres right on the edge of loss of control –

clearly aimed to impress potential customers. Sometimes they would actually lose control and crash spectacularly in front of or on top of the crowd. If any RAF pilot attempted such manoeuvres he would be taken off display flying permanently.

At Leeming we put up a 'Diamond 9' formation flypast for every student graduation parade and I tried to fly on all of them. They were great fun, always led by the laid-back and laconic Commander of Standards Squadron, and usually went ahead in just about any weather conditions. We always took passengers on the flypasts, and many of them would throw up during the sortie. The Jet Provost was not the easiest aircraft to fly in a big formation, the straight wings and tip tanks getting in the way all the time. In any turbulence we would be 'yugging' about all over the place, the less-able formation flyers overcontrolling like mad.

In the summer of '68 I wangled my way on to the Leeming contingent for a huge formation flypast for the RAF's 50th Anniversary. There were to be no less than forty-two Jet Provosts from four FTSs in the formation, spelling out the Royal Cypher EIIR. As the final rehearsals and flypast were to be operated from RAF Gaydon, this sounded like a good opportunity to have a convivial get-together with a bunch of like-minded QFIs. At Gaydon we had a ball. For rehearsals there were up to forty-five Jet Provosts on the runway for each take-off. The formation was very demanding, requiring an extra pilot in many of the cockpits to avoid collisions between the back ends of the various lines of Jet Provosts. We had a party every night and at the end Gaydon (The RAF's Advanced Navigation School) laid on a huge do for us all.

During my first year at 3 FTS I soon piled up the flying hours and gained a green instrument rating, which allowed me to fly in worse weather conditions. Soon I became an Instrument Rating Examiner, able to take students and staff for instrument tests. In September there was an epic trip to RAF Gutersloh in Germany with the Leeming display pilot, who was to give displays at two famous civilian flying clubs, Werdohl-Kuntrup and Dumpel. We had a free day and visited several local flying clubs where we drank with some of his old pals from his RAF Germany days, many of them ex-Luftwaffe aces, now instructing at flying clubs. It was pointed out that several of them had scores of kills to their credit in the Second World War. They all seemed polite and modestly dismissive about their wartime exploits, usually saying 'Ach So, but you know most of those kills were in Russia'. Barely twenty years after the end of the war these characters still showed the élan and fighting spirit of the great aces who had managed to survive the cauldron of fire that was the European air war at the end of the Second World War.

As the reserve pilot I was picked up at Gutersloh in a light aeroplane and flown to Werdohl to enjoy the display. On landing we were handed a glass and forced to consume a bottle of schnapps, as various kamikaze glider pilots beat up the field just behind us (below head height and upside down). A riotous party followed the display and we were decanted at a local German hotel at about 5 a.m. After a few hours sleep we were being flown back to Gutersloh to take the Jet Provosts back home.[2] Our commentator was with me and, as I walked out to the jet, I said 'I can't hack it. You go without me.' I finally decided to go and there followed a nightmare high level sortie at 25,000 feet (no pressurization in the JP4) on 100 per cent oxygen. The route home was via Manston in Kent, to clear customs. I started to feel better in the climb to height, and this was probably the most unpleasant experience I have ever suffered in an aircraft. For some reason this bad experience put me off flying in cloud, (much of the return flight had been in thick cloud), and I developed a bit of a phobia about it. I didn't realize it at the time but the combination of non-stop work and heavy drinking was beginning to take a toll on me. The aversion to instrument flying continued for some time; at its worst I would suffer what might now be called an anxiety attack before take-off which, of course, I had to conceal from my students. This was a bit inconvenient for my job as an Instrument Rating Examiner (IRE) – IREs were always the first to be sent airborne in bad weather, when instrument flying was the only thing you could do. Once I was airborne and actually in cloud the fear evaporated. Later on I saw a lot of this sort of thing in other pilots, particularly on the Harrier, so I was able to have some sympathy for them.

I went on my first ever package holiday, to Majorca, which was pretty disastrous, three of us having planned to go, but at the last minute the third man dropped out. This was the only bit of leave I took voluntarily during my tour at Leeming. I was so keen to fly that I just couldn't stand the thought of being without it. In retrospect this was not a good way to live and I was to regret it next year. Someone should have forced me to take some proper leave. I once took a week of leave on which I went over to RAF Valley, scrounging back-seat flying in the Gnat. I was becoming a flying junkie: although I was flying just about flat out all the time at Leeming, I still couldn't get enough to satisfy me.

In November '68 I fixed up a weekend trip to Gibraltar in a Hastings from RAF Lindholme, the Bomber Command Radar school. We took off on a bleak Friday afternoon with a dodgy weather forecast for the Gib area. I spent some time in the cockpit and was not too impressed by the intentions of the pilots, especially when I saw the latest weather reports from Gibraltar. On arrival we had the worst possible option for Gib weather – a strong south-westerly wind gusting round the rock, with a 400 feet cloudbase. The runway at Gib was like an aircraft carrier, starting and finishing in the sea. On short finals we stalled completely in a gust, (the pilot told me later that the airspeed had been going up and down by 30 knots). Sitting in a passenger seat over the wing I felt the aircraft go briefly into free fall before the power came on.[3] We overshot below the cloud, the Hastings bucking and shaking like a light aeroplane in the vicious turbulence from the Rock. As we crabbed down the runway in the fierce cross-wind the few alarmed passengers could see on the left the endless grey wall of rock, hanging like a curtain of steel from the ragged cloudbase. What we didn't know was that the crew didn't have enough fuel to take the sensible option and divert to Tangier. Things weren't looking too good.

On the next approach we were flying 30kt faster, to allow for gusts. We crossed the threshold tail-up with no sign of the Hastings wanting to land. I realized things were not going too well as we overflew the main road which crossed the runway half-way down. Options were running out fast as the pilot forced the aircraft on to the mainwheels and immediately applied full braking with the tailwheel still off the ground. I watched with a strange feeling of detached amusement as all four engines stopped, realizing that a swim was now almost inevitable. 'Hope the sea's not too cold', I thought. At last the tail came down and we finally slewed to a stop with the acrid smell of burnt rubber penetrating the cabin.

We were still on the runway. I started to breathe again as I slowly became aware of the sound of various cockpit gyros running down. After a long silence the captain walked slowly down from the cockpit, grey-faced and covered in sweat. He opened the tail door and disappeared. I got up and walked up to the cockpit. There had been not a word from the crew during the entire performance. The South African co-pilot was slumped in his seat smoking a cigarette, his hand shaking uncontrollably. The cockpit reeked of sweat. Looking out through the rain-spattered windscreen I could see only waves, uncomfortably close in front and to the side. Only by pressing my face to the windscreen could I see the last few yards of the runway and the short rocky slope leading down to the sea. There was not even enough room to turn round. We were towed back to the pan by a tractor and retired to the bar for several stiff drinks. After this stimulating start to a holiday I enjoyed a reacquaintance with the Rock, which seemed to be in the first flush of spring, all the wild flowers blooming profusely in the winter sunshine. Fortunately the return flight was uneventful.

Notes
1. I would love to read Mikoyan's Release to Service equivalent for the Mig 29.
2. We were never allowed time off in lieu of weekends away on display. The training programme at Leeming was so intense that they couldn't afford it.
3. In a propeller-driven aircraft recovery from a power-on stall was almost instantaneous with application of power as the props immediately restored the airflow over the wings.

Chapter 7

Gemini

During 1968 I had admired the punchy performances of the Leeming Gemini synchronized aeros pair. Now I was selected to make up one half of the Gemini team, flying formation on another instructor who was an ex-Hunter man and an excellent aerobatics leader. Under the professional eye of our team manager, who had been a famous member of the Red Arrows' Synchro Pair, we practised for weeks and built up a suitable display routine, involving some quite hairy-looking manoeuvres, including mirror formation, join-up loops, head-on crosses and line-abreast close formation aeros. The latter were particularly tricky in the Jet Provost, the tip tanks getting in the way all the time. From the cockpit in close line abreast, it looked as if my tiptank was almost touching my leader's 'mirror' but was easier than it sounded. My leader merely rolled inverted while I dived underneath and moved well forward to formate on his cockpit from underneath. We only had just under a minute of inverted flight , so I had to count pretty accurately to get out of the way in time, my leader couldn't roll out until I was out of the way. The main wear and tear was to my neck muscles as I had to strain my head right round and up to see him adequately. Once I had worked out the trick of offsetting my aircraft a little to one side I could afford to overlap the fins a bit and get really close. Head-on crosses were also fairly straightforward. Basically, the leader just flew a turn straight at me and, as we got closer, I aimed to hit him head on. At the last moment I would bunt just a little, to pass under his cockpit. We nearly blew it once in practice. One of the crosses required me to fly straight with my leader avoiding me. On this occasion he forgot to avoid. At the last second I managed to dodge him – it would have been an impressive collision. After this I made sure that I was doing the avoiding on all the crosses, to avoid confusion. For my leader a good close cross would be indicated by a satisfying bang from the nosewheel doors as my fin passed under his nose.

Among many things our manager taught us, was the trick of off-setting for the crowd, the aircraft closest to the crowd flying slightly lower so that they saw us pass precisely head-on, and to make it look more dangerous. A join-up loop was hard work and a bit of a lottery with the limited engine power of the Jet Provost. On these we started off head-on (with 400kt closing speed) from opposite sides of the display datum point and then both started a maximum rate turn away from the crowd with a pull-up. If I had judged the time to turn correctly I would be in close line astern on my leader before the top of a loop. This kind of thing was much more difficult in a straight-wing aircraft like the Jet Provost. Unlike swept-wing aircraft you couldn't kill speed rapidly by just pulling back on the stick.

As Gemini we went on some splendid runs overseas to display and got to know the characters of the international teams very well. Once we formed part of a flypast in Belgium with the Arrows, the Patrouille de France, the Frecce Tricolori and the Diables Rouges, the latter a wacky Belgian team of Fouga Magisters, whose speciality was inverted formation. The practice days before the actual event were by far the best for seeing uninhibited exhibitionism, especially where teams like the Arrows were concerned. The leader would give his legendary call 'Nobody below me!'[1] on the radio, and then the team would 'wire' the place right at ground level. One of the stars of the show circuit at that time did a show-stopper of a display in the Lightning. In the bar at Liege/Bierset this pilot put up with the usual jibes about Lightning pilots from the Arrows' ex-Hunter Mafia plus my leader, who also stuck his oar in. Next morning the Lighting man did a reheat rotation take-off right over our tents just off the runway, sucessfully blowing them flat and dispersing the camp furniture around the airfield. I remember looking up into two enormous flaming jetpipes for a second before the blast knocked me flat – not a good cure for a hangover. That night we had The Hollies playing live in a hangar for a cracking end-of-display party.

Our best trip by far was to Bardufoss in the far north of Norway in August of '69, for a major NATO air day. This odyssey took over a week in the short-range Jet Provost. Gemini were allocated a Dominie twin-engined jet as leader. We had no airways navigation aids and no VHF radio and, therefore, technically we could not legally fly in controlled airspace. We didn't worry too much about that kind of thing in those days so we flew in close box formation with the Dominie in cloud on airways and during letdowns into the mountains of Norway. The Dominie was also spares and duty-free booze carrier for the trip, and we set off with three Jet Provosts via Manston and Leeuwaarden in Holland to stop overnight at Aalborg in Denmark. Next day we staged through Gardermoen and Oerland and night-stopped in Bodo before flying on to Bardufoss, inside the Arctic circle. Northern Norway was like a fairyland in summertime, the magnificent fjords and mountains dwarfing our formation of tiny red and white aeroplanes as we cruised among the peaks. It was like flying through the pages of a tourist brochure. The most impressive display at Bardufoss was a thunderous routine of reheat aeros by a J35 Draken (my favourite aeroplane), and thereafter we spent most of the evening drinking in an Air Force officer's house in the village. It was strange to see the sun dip briefly below the horizon at about midnight, to rise again half an hour later. There was a rather nice unattached Swedish girl at the party, whom I attempted to chat up, seemingly without success as we packed up to go home. At about 4 a.m. to my amazement she wandered into my room on the military base at Bardufoss and climbed into my bed without saying a word!

After further adventures in Northern Norway we finally arrived back in Yorkshire after running out of money en route (I was the imprest holder and had to borrow several hundred pounds from the Norwegian Air Force).

By the end of the display season I had flown over 250 hours in six months, flying virtually non-stop with never less than three students to train during the week. I was exhausted, but I didn't know it yet. I paid a visit to RAF Leuchars, where my best friend was now flying the Mk6 Lightning on 23 Squadron. At Chivenor they had sneakily changed his posting from Hunters to Lightnings. He was making the best of it and was very much the 'married drag', living happily in married quarters. We talked about old times and commiserated with the death of our old colleague in Malta. There had been a tremendous amount of social life and boozing associated with the display circuit, and I had had my full share of it, plus the usual rounds of parties back at Leeming, where I was often acting as a disc jockey. Towards the end I had become increasingly irritable with my Gemini leader, and we would barely speak to one another socially. I believe this was an inevitable consequence of having to work so closely together in the air, sharing the same risks and trying not to make mistakes which would spoil the show. Mistakes did occur, and the natural tendency was to try to blame your partner. There had been one or two hair-raising near-misses, but we had survived. At a party at Leeming I realized just how far I had gone downhill when I decided to count how many pints of beer I needed before I could relax and enjoy myself: I counted thirteen. I was starting to have horrific nightmares – linked to the boozing – and the aversion to flying in cloud was back with a vengeance.[2] As before, once I was airborne all fear evaporated and I could relax and live again. I realized that I had to cut down on the booze and have a break.

Ironically I realized that I had finally become what I always wanted to be – a creature of the skies, more at home in the air than on the ground. Unfortunately, the old pink body was unable to take the combination of all-out flying and excessive boozing over such a long period. I didn't dare tell anyone else about the problem; the RAF medics would have grounded me straight away. Fortunately Flying Training Command had a splendid scheme whereby Creamies could be detached to RAF Transport Command for a couple of weeks, to go en route with a transport aircraft crew anywhere in the world. I put my name in for it and soon I was at the Gateway Hotel Lyneham, awaiting departure as supernumerary crew with a Britannia Far East slip crew. The slip crew would fly all the way out to Singapore and back, occasionally changing aircraft to make sure they were able to stop off regularly in all the comfortable places. I was amazed at their easier lifestyle compared with the hard day-to-day grind of Flying Training Command. First leg was a routine run to Cyprus where we spent a leisurely couple of days in a first class hotel downtown. Next leg was to Bahrain, baking in the heat, where we got the bare minimum few hours rest in an air-conditioned transit hotel before we flew on. We stopped next at Gan in the Indian Ocean, a tiny island paradise in the Maldives. The island was neatly bisected by the runway and the hutted RAF base covered most of the rest of it. The coral beaches were pure white as snow. On arrival I borrowed mask and snorkel and went straight into the sea, ignoring warnings about sharks, etc. A small group of us cavorted for hours in the amazingly clear water. At one stage, to my delight, I spotted a turtle swimming sedately along. I dived on it and hung on to its shell, hitching a ride for a while. Someone swam up in a panic and waved me away. Apparently this wasn't a very good idea; a good-sized turtle could take your fingers off if it had a mind to. I didn't mind: I was in paradise just being in the tropical heat with the beautiful turquoise sea all round. After a serious booze-up, next day I poured myself back into the Brit for a sleep en route to Singapore. The Brit in half-cargo fit was extremely comfortable for the passengers, the large rearward-facing seats reclining almost horizontal. The mighty Proteus turboprops whispered on through the tropical night and later on I watched the navigator doing astro navigation, taking star shots with his bubble sextant.

At Singapore I was met by an ex-89 colleague, now on 20 Squadron flying the Hunter FGA9, my idea of a dream posting. Before leaving RAF Changi on the Hercules line I met another ex-Cranwell colleague, who offered me a lift to Hong Kong in his Hercules. Regrettably I had to turn him down as I had made other arrangements. We went on an epic launch downtown to check out all the usual attractions; Raffles Hotel, Bugis Street, etc. The end of a splendid evening was marked by a running verbal battle with our taxi driver; apparently this was the norm for Singapore. I was overwhelmed by the magic of the place, the bright lights of the city night spots contrasting with the ever-present jungle, encroaching menacingly on the roads as you got out of town. Next morning we continued a breakneck itinerary planned by my colleague. As well as flying the Hunter he was Flight Commander of the Forward Air Control Flight at Tengah, operating the propeller-driven Single Pioneer (Single Pin) and acting as Airborne Forward Air Controller for the Hunters. The Single Pin was a splendid short take-off and landing (STOL) aircraft, capable of getting into the smallest grass strips in the mountains of the north. We were heading for Butterworth, a Royal Australian Air Force base right up in the north of Malaysia, next to the island of Penang. Flying up to Kuala Lumpur over the jungle was no fun for me in the sweaty, bouncing cabin of the Pin, recovering as I was from a gigantic hangover. KL was literally steaming in the heat and humidity when we stopped to refuel, and I wondered how anyone could bear to work there. En route to Butterworth I had sobered up somewhat and my colleague showed me some pretty hairy landings on some impossibly small strips between mountain peaks in the mist-shrouded highlands. We carried out a forward air control (FAC) exercise with the Army in the jungle and then landed at Butterworth where there were two RAAF Mirage 3 squadrons providing air defence and ground attack for the north of Malaysia. At Butterworth 20 Squadron also had a detachment of Hunters on base. The Aussies were an odd bunch, full of 'bull' in the bar which closed incredibly early, before anyone had had time to get flying speed. There followed the inevitable launch down town to Penang, an island of European civilization off the wild jungle coasts of south-east Asia. In various bars I met some stalwarts of 20 Squadron who I would encounter again later on. After a couple of nights at Butterworth I poured myself into an RAF Andover for the trip back to Singapore in the early evening. The Andover bucked and tossed like a light aircraft in the gigantic thunderstorms which boiled up from the Straits at this time every day. After a couple more days in Singapore I had to set off with my slip crew on the equally leisurely journey back to UK, this time carrying dangerous air cargo (DAC) in the form of a couple of Bloodhound missiles. No ordinary passengers were allowed so I had the cabin to myself all the way home.

Back at Leeming I was sweating on a posting. My squadron commander, who was ex-Red Arrows, offered to get me into the Arrows straight away, but I turned him down. I had seen enough of the air display world for my purposes: it was an artificial world of showmanship, showing off and non-stop public relations which I had begun to dislike.

In November we had the only fatal accident during my time at Leeming. A student was taking off in a JP3 and over-rotated to drag the aircraft off the ground at too high an angle of attack. This meant that he was going nowhere fast as there wasn't enough engine thrust to overcome the drag of the stalled wings. From the 1 Squadron ops room window we saw the aircraft waffling dangerously towards the trees north of the airfield. One of our students was squawking:

'What's he doing, what's he doing?' in a panic.

Our new American flight commander had seen it all before in his years of instructing at American flight schools. A brief, greasy ball of flame and smoke rose from beyond the trees. The student did not eject and had died in the wreck.

> But remember please, the law by which we live,
> We are not built to comprehend a lie,
> We can neither love, nor pity, nor forgive,
> If you make a slip in handling us, you die.
>
> Rudyard Kipling *Secret of the Machines*

At the New Year we were all delighted to see that my Gemini leader was awarded the Air Force Cross. My posting arrived – to the Day Fighter/Ground Attack course at RAF Chivenor. After all the waiting I was completely numb. I couldn't believe I was going to get there at last, and became ever more neurotic that something would turn up to stop me. We handed over the reins of Gemini to two new instructors who did a grand job in the following season. I flew my last ever Jet Provost sortie and left 3 FTS, having flown over 1,100 hours during my tour.

Notes
1. This was rather a superfluous call: no-one could fly the Gnat lower than this particular Arrows leader anyway.
2. Much later I discovered that part of my problem may have been 'Break-Off Phenomenon', where pilots can become anxious when flying alone and in cloud or at high level for long periods.

Chapter 8

Flying the Hunter

RAF Chivenor was a splendid old station set right on the estuary of the River Taw in north Devon. The station buildings had an unimproved wartime flavour to them: rows of small wooden accomodation huts standing in neat lines behind the single-story pre-fabricated Officers' Mess. Best of all was the mighty Hunter, whose cockpit seemed strangely familiar to me. The instrument display was reassuringly old-fashioned, many instruments being straight duplicates of those in the Jet Provost. The aeroplane itself was sleek, purposeful and powerful in its Mk 6 variety, which was the standard 'training' version. The squadrons used the heavier FGA Mk9 and 10, which had the luxury of a braking parachute and the large 230 gallon drop tanks. The 6,000 feet runway at Chivenor was barely adequate for the Mk 6, especially in a crosswind, when you were left with only half braking because of the peculiar 'bicycle' brake system. With us as students were the pre-Lightning crowd, who were being given initial training on the Hunter, omitting air-to-ground weapons, before going on to Coltishall to fly the Lightning. Ground school and simulators were handled briefly and efficiently and we were into the air with the QFIs. I got on famously with the Hunter, finding the T7 a bit under-powered with its 100-series Avon engine (7,500lb thrust). However, with a 10,000lb thrust 200-series Avon, the Mk 6 was seriously nippy and a delight to fly. At last I was in a single-seat cockpit with a gunsight in front and a trigger on the stick. Soon I had my first formation dual. I climbed into the T7 and started doing what I though was a reasonably snappy run-through of the pre-start checks. My instructor, a PAI (Pilot Attack Instructor), told me in no uncertain terms to get on with it and start the engine.

With a wry smile under my oxygen mask I hit the gangbar and pressed the button to fire the big starter cartridge. When the engine stabilized I carried on with the After Start checklist, just to see what my instructor would do. He indicated firstly, that the leader was already taxiing, secondly, that I had better get the fucking chocks away smartish. I was beginning to enjoy myself. Throwing all caution to the winds I did as requested and hammered out of dispersal after the leader, who I managed to catch up just as he released the brakes on the runway. We went straight into thick cloud after take-off, to break out on top at 10,000ft. The leader pulled straight up into a loop, without so much as a word to me. This had not been briefed on the ground. This was getting better. After an enjoyable session of formation aeros the leader settled down to take me back to base. The Hunter was a delight to fly in close formation. On my first Cine Weave sortie I was reluctantly given 100 per cent for my tracking with the gyro gunsight – the first time ever, my instructor said.

First live weapons dual was air-to-air (A/A) on the flag, a 30 feet long banner towed by a Meteor. The Meteor pilots understandably showed precious little sympathy for the students firing at them. After becoming airborne as fast as possible (my instructor still hadn't worked out that I enjoyed myself much more if I did things quickly under pressure), we arrived over the Bristol Channel on the 'perch', a waiting position abreast and above the Meteor tug. The thin streak of the banner fluttered just 1,000 feet behind the Meteor in the clear, bright sunshine above cloud. Hartland Radar gave us permission to fire HOT. From the perch it looked an awfully small target. My instructor 'demonstrated' the first pass. I was treated to the customary obscenities and blood-chilling curses as he dived viciously at the Meteor, fired a short burst, and broke violently over the flag. My feet jumped involuntarily as the gun fired, a loud pneumatic-drill hammering from just under the cockpit floor. There was a satisfying smell of cordite. Not a word of explanation was offered, and the manoeuvre he flew to end up in a firing position bore little resemblance to what we had been briefed on the ground. From the briefing (given by another PAI), I had learned that there were quite a few important points to cover: the exact time to reverse your turn, where to put the 'fixed cross' ahead of the flag and, what to do with the switches for the gun-ranging radar.[1]

My task was now clear. I would have to teach myself the technique of A/A firing. Reluctantly the instructor handed over control to me on the perch. I started my first attack. Within a couple of seconds he grabbed the stick viciously with a curse. He rolled out pointing roughly at the flag and gave me control again, without a word of explanation. Once again within seconds he grabbed the stick, dissatisfied with the way I was flying it. The same thing happened on the next pass, and the next. This was becoming tedious. If this went on there was no way I could pass this dual. However, a glance at the fuel gauge showed me that I was rapidly running out of time. I hadn't yet fired the gun, the instructor having grabbed control from me on each pass before I reached a firing position. Eventually, in total frustration I put the sight on the target from quite a long range and pulled the trigger. He blew up again.

'I just wanted to see what it was like to fire the gun,' I replied mildly. 'We've got to go home now anyway: we're on Joker fuel.'[2]

Back on the ground the debrief was predictably one-sided. I wasn't interested in anything he had to say, I was just desperate to be allowed off solo, to practise with the gun-camera for myself in a Mk 6. The Flight Commander was almost sympathetic: 'You can have another dual if you want, or go off and try it cine', he said with a grin.

He was that rare combination, a QFI who had done the PAI course. He had a pretty good idea of how some of the PAIs 'instructed' their students. I chose the solo. With no PAI hassling me I soon grasped the essentials of tracking the flag and brought back some acceptable film. 'Bit out of range, but reasonable tracking' was the verdict of the PAI who debriefed it. And then the magic words: 'Go and try it HOT!'

My first solo live shoot was uneventful, and I waited impatiently for the Meteor to drop the flag on the airfield. Each aircraft fired a different colour round (they were coated with paint), and the flag would be dumped right outside the squadron buildings on the grass. I had been the first of my course to fire live and there was a feeling of tension as a horde of sweaty, immersion-suited students crowded into the cine projection room for a debrief, the boss and one or two PAIs standing aloof at the back. There was an all-pervading smell of armpit and rubber in the darkness of the tiny, smoke-filled room. The flag was not back yet and the duty PAI ran through my gunsight film first: 'Once again, nice tracking Jerry, but you're out of range; you're ceasing fire outside 400 yards (minimum ceasefire range was 180yds). You won't get much score with that. Next film!'

I wandered out morosely, passing the boss who said: 'Get in closer, Jerry: you'll never smash it at that range'

In need of some fresh air I wandered outside into the brilliant spring sunshine. Our flag was neatly spread out on the grass, like a picnic tablecloth. I started to count the holes (I had been firing green). On my knees now I counted more and more, not daring to believe it. Twenty-six green hits out of sixty rounds fired – well into the 'exceptional' bracket. I wandered back into the smoky, sweat-laden atmosphere of the cine room. Idly I asked the boss how many hits he thought I would have got from seeing my film. 'Five or ten at the outside', he said. I told him my score and he nearly fell over.

'Jammy sod!', he said. I finished the air-to-air firing phase with an exceptional score of 45 per cent hits, having taught myself the technique without any assistance from a PAI.

Weapons duals for air-to-ground, bombing and rocketry followed. One or two guys were chopped from the pre-Lightning part of the course. One guy was suspended after a climbing accident; an ex-helicopter pilot, he had been struggling with the course.

Other duals were good value, with the one exception of my night dual. My instructor seemed to be scared stiff of night flying. He was shaking like a leaf during much of the sortie.[3] By day we practised battle formation at low level in battle four formation and at high level at 0.9 Mach at 40,000 feet in the old-fashioned 30 degree swept formation; a direct throwback to the fighter tactics of the '40s and '50s. This high altitude formation was quite tricky as the leader would turn without a radio call and the student wingman would have to try to roll out in the correct position after the turn. With the limited power available at that height, wingmen often ended up miles behind unless they flew very smoothly. Any attempt to use a notch of flap to cut the corner would lead to disaster as we cruised at 0.9 Mach. At that speed any use of flap would cause an instant, uncontrollable nose-down pitch, the Hunter diving out of control tens of thousands of feet until you re-entered thicker air.[4] Eventually we started air combat training.

My first 1-versus-1 air combat training mission was with a PAI who gave me the usual briefing that he would beat me hands-down.[5] I soon got behind him and stayed there, my old Jet Provost combat techniques working quite well in the Hunter. Later we practised some 2 versus 1 combat and, best of all, some low level 'bounced' four-ship formations where a member of staff lurked en route and attacked us. This was great sport, requiring excellent lookout by the student wingmen and lightning-fast reactions to turn the formation to counter the threat. Cruising and manoeuvring in fighting wing formation was not easy. As wingman your duty was to stick, search and report, the priority being to stay with your element leader, no matter how hard he manoeuvred. We flew well swept back at 200-400yds from the lead, always staying above him in turns – it was extremely dangerous to drop below. As well as watching the lead you had to keep your head screwed right round to watch the 6 o'clock of the other element, cruising just a mile abreast of you. The bounce would usually lurk low behind a ridge line or against the dark background of a forest. When he pitched in to attack just a wing flash or a hint of a vapour trail from his wingtip would give him away; a tiny speck on the horizon closing rapidly on the other pair:

'GOLD: HARD TURN STARBOARD GO! BOGEY RIGHT THREE O'CLOCK, RANGE 2 MILES, CLOSING.'

(A 'Bogey' was an unidentified aircraft, possibly enemy. A 'Bandit' was an identified enemy aircraft.)

This initial call from the sighting wingman had to be brief and accurate. The whole formation would now wheel to starboard and attempt to 'sandwich' the bogey between the two elements. While this was going on the leader would have to keep track of the navigation, control the formation manoeuvring and break off the engagement at the right time to continue to the target, the main priority. While the turning and weaving was going on there would be a staccato exchange of R/T between element leaders:

'GOLD 3 HAS HIM – 1 AND 2 BREAK STARBOARD, BREAK STARBOARD!'

(Gold 3 has seen the bandit closing on the lead element; he orders them to tighten their turn to avoid being shot down.)

'HE'S BREAKING OFF, 1 AND 2 REVERSE PORT, REVERSE PORT!'

(Gold 3 sees the bandit break away and orders the others to reverse back towards required track.)

'GOLD 3 IS IN YOUR LEFT EIGHT 0'CLOCK'

(This call is to help Gold Lead to pick up Gold 3 visually after rolling out)

'GOLD LEAD TALLY; ROLL OUT 340'

(Gold lead sees the other element and calls a heading for rollout which puts the formation back in line abreast.)

'HE'S RIGHT ONE 0,CLOCK RANGE 3, PARALLEL'

(Gold lead reports the position of the bandit, now departing ahead.)

'GOLD LEAD TALLY'

('Tally' means 'I can see him'.)

The way this cryptic conversation was handled was absolutely crucial to the success of the formation manoeuvring; R/T discipline was rigid and all superfluous comments were cut out. You had to pitch your voice up a bit to get a bit of urgency into the action calls; however, it was vitally important not to get carried away and start shouting in panic, in the heat of the moment – a common fault with less experienced pilots. Later on, in the Harrier, we learned to use the words 'Gold 1' rather than 'Gold Lead'. With the inferior Harrier radio 'Gold Lead' sounded too much like 'Gold 3'. Sometimes it was possible for the attacked formation to shoot down the bounce (via gun camera film). This was a feather in their caps and ignominy for the bounce, who had the initial tactical advantage of speed and surprise. His job was to prevent the formation from reaching the target by shooting them down or forcing them to manoeuvre so much that they ran short of fuel. A poorly-handled formation could be broken up by the bounce and the individual elements could then be picked off, having no rear cover.

By now I was the proud owner of a large surf board, bought secondhand from an ex-student from Leeming. The surfing was epic in the Chivenor area, with the vast expanse of Woolacombe beach just a few miles away. I spent many happy hours idling around in the surf pretending to be a real surfer. I was more interested in getting a suntan and impressing the girls. The board was really too heavy for my puny frame, and difficult to get up on. However, on the rare occasions I actually got up, it would go like a train, scattering all before it. The modern small board, more manoeuvrable and easier to mount, was just becoming popular. They didn't seem like real surf boards to me. With the board went the image, and there was a splendid laid-back surfing fraternity in the local area with some excellent bashes at various hotels and dance halls.

The combination of excellent solo flying and balmy West Country air made my time at Chivenor one of the most enjoyable periods of my RAF career. Best of all was the sure knowledge that there was only one posting available at the end of the course, to the DF/GA Wing at Bahrain in the Persian Gulf, the last operational RAF Hunter outfit. I see from my RAF log book that I finished the course with the following averages:

CINE	73 per cent
AIR TO AIR	45 per cent
AIR TO GROUND	38 per cent

Mum and Dad, 1939.

Dad, HMS *Norfolk*,
Russian Convoy
in 1943.

Mum, Dad and
Robin, 1945.

Folland Gnat T2 Advanced Trainer, 4 Flying Training School, RAF Valley.

Flying Instructor,
3 Flying Training
School, RAF Leeming.

RAF Leeming Jet
Provosts in formation
over the Pennines.

...of the Leeming Vampires. Farewell Vampire T11 formation.

Gemini. A bit more excitement! This head-on cross was not too close – they got better!

Gemini moving into Mirror formation, viewed from my cockpit.

Mirror Formation. With fins offset slightly you can get quite close together.

Flypast for Belgian Air Display. *Diables Rouges* leading, with Gemini tucked in behind; *Frecce Tricolori* on the right; *Red Arrows* on the left; *Patrouille de France* behind.

Hunters in the Gulf. FGA9 of 208 Squadron, based at RAF Muharraq.

Gemini in Norway, on the way to Bardufoss, via Holland and Denmark – the Jet Provost was a ve
short-range machine. We are in formation with an RAF Dominie, carrying spares and Duty-free!

Author in Hunter cockpit.

Hunter FGA9 at Low Level over the Trucial States.

GA9 cockpit – very traditional.

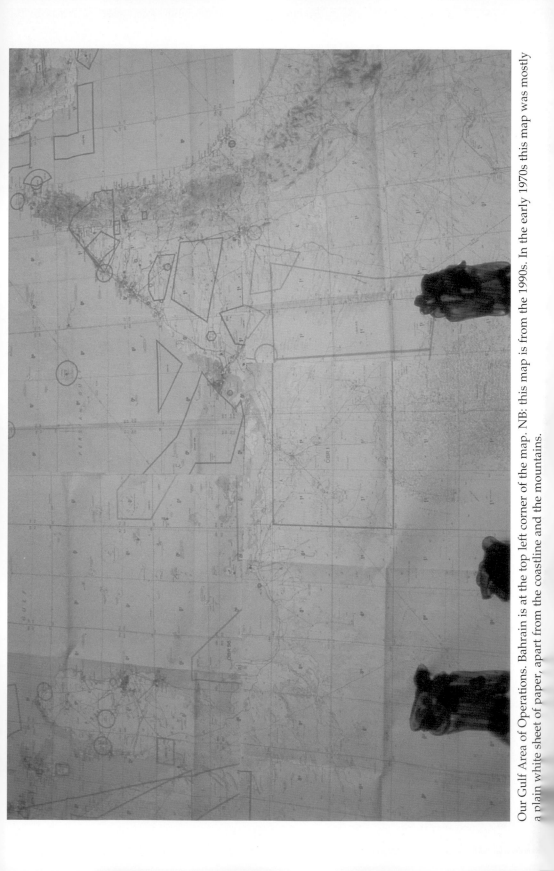

Our Gulf Area of Operations. Bahrain is at the top left corner of the map. NB: this map is from the 1990s. In the early 1970s this map was mostly a plain white sheet of paper, apart from the coastline and the mountains.

typical arab fort in the mountains of Northern Oman.

n army 'recce' of a road – the author was a nervous passenger!

SNEB anti-tank rocket impact. The rocket is doing about Mach2 as it strikes. The target is the barrel

Air Combat. The gunsight 'pipper' is almost on for the kill.

Dinghy Drill. Very nice in the Gulf, not so nice in the North Sea in winter!

The Jebel Hafit, taken from high level. This huge rock feature was visible from over 100 miles away.

Army Forward Air Controllers directing Hunters on to training targets on a tactical range. Cannon shells burst on target in the middle distance.

A typical recce target in the desert. The pilot's full report for this target would read something like this: 'Road over River Bridge, Single Span, Through-type, Parallel Chord Steel Truss, under construction, with incomplete open deck. Size: Approx 60ft by 12ft. Abutments concrete.'

SNEB(ROCKETS)   68 per cent
SKIP BOMBING   91 per cent

Notes
1. Ranging Radar: All Chivenor A/A Hunters had the nose radar well set up to give good ranging during flag firing, and they worked quite well in flight, a blue light by the gunsight indicating when you were in range. Unfortunately the kit didn't work so well on front-line squadrons.
2. JOKER fuel was the minimum fuel state to get back to base.
3. Personally I thought the Hunter was marvellous for night flying. The essential instruments were illuminated by faint ultraviolet cockpit lighting, and all other non-essential lights could be turned off to give perfect night vision outside.
4. This was a well-known handling deficiency with all marks of the Hunter; over the years many pilots had lost control because of it.
5. Air Combat Instruction. Several years later I became an Air Combat Instructor (ACI) myself. Training students to fight was not easy and meant that you had to be prepared to spend a fair bit of time manoeuvring in front of the student, allowing him to win. For the student it was far easier to grasp the rudiments of combat handling while looking forward, rather than with your head screwed round through 180 degrees to see your instructor behind you. Many instructors just weren't prepared to do this.

Chapter 9

Operational Flying in the Gulf

Shortly after leaving Chivenor I was sitting on an RAF VC10 en route to the Sheikdom of Bahrain and the famous 208 Squadron, my next posting. RAF Muharraq shared the territory of Bahrain International Airport, lying on the island of Muharraq which was linked to the main island of Bahrain by a causeway. Bahrain lies just twenty miles off the eastern coast of Saudi Arabia, a low-lying patch of dust and sand floating in the shallow, turquoise waters of the Persian Gulf. I had arrived at the hottest time of the year when daytime shade temperatures rose to 40degrees C and more, in oppressive humidity. Everything about the place reeked of the tropics; palm trees and sand everywhere, the ubiquitous bougainvillaea in permanent flower around the base, and the Bahraini Arabs, cool and mysterious in their traditional headdress and flowing white robes. Many of the women still wore the abaya, a gold-embroidered black cloak over modern dress. However Bahrain was the most progressive of Arab states and more and more women were wearing Western-style dress in public. The main town of Manama was a typical Middle Eastern hotchpotch of modern concrete and classic Byzantine architecture, the delicately-spired turrets of the mosques gleaming pink and white in the fierce glare of sunlight. The souk was a traditional Arab affair, an array of whitewashed mud cubicles overhung with hessian awnings. Dozens of small traders and artisans manufactured and sold items for the locals and the spasmodic tourist trade. There was a strong Pakistani influence everywhere .A lot of Pakistanis had built up small businesses such as barbers, tailors etc., that were much used by servicemen. One of my first tasks on arrival was to see the famous tailor Abdul Ghani, to have a decent set of tropical kit made up, the RAF issue stuff being pretty useless.

I found that the standard footwear was the desert boot, or brothel-creeper, and they were also worn for flying. This was against RAF regulations, but we had no other suitable footwear for flying in the heat. 208 Squadron was a great outfit and I had already heard of the squadron stalwarts before my arrival. The new boss was a swarthily handsome character with an engagingly eccentric approach, including a tendency to burst into operatic song at the drop of a hat. He had been on 208 Squadron in Kenya when they flew Venoms, and had a fund of hilarious war stories from those times. Only the squadron 'wheels' had an allowance from the RAF to keep their wives in Bahrain; any other married pilots had to pay for accommodation downtown out of their own resources. There were few married quarters. Life in the Mess was simple and relaxed. We lived in single-storey huts with the luxury of air-conditioning, the ancient wall-mounted units rattling away all night long to keep you awake on the rare occasions when you went to bed sober. The flight commanders were a dour and respectable Scot, and another pilot who I remembered well from Cranwell. Our two PAIs and the squadron instrument rating examiner were all flying officers who were a source of endless amusement and inspiration to the rest of us.

I received a brief rundown on the local flying regulations from the squadron QFI, who emphasized the dangers of going anywhere near Saudi Arabian airspace. The last RAF Hunter pilot to divert there had been removed from the cockpit at the point of a gun, causing a serious diplomatic incident. My squadron checkout was with a senior officer , a rather intimidating prospect. We walked out to the clapped-out squadron T7 in the searing heat of an afternoon, the engineers having worked all morning to get it serviceable. Normally we never flew after midday in summertime, it was just too hot.

'Compass is U/S', this pilot mentioned idly as we walked out. 'We've only got the standby.'

The T7 had been grounded for some time awaiting a G4 Gyro compass spare from UK. This meant that there was no accurate heading information in the cockpit.

'It'll be OK', he reassured me as we strapped into the burning hot cockpit: 'We're not going far.'

I was not so sure. The horizon looked ominously obscure in the thick, leaden haze which blanketed the island. The low line of palm trees across the runway shimmered and danced in the heat, as if chastened by a strong breeze. We took off into classic 'goldfish bowl' conditions, the tenuous horizon disappearing completely as soon as we climbed away from the runway. The intention was to fly a quick medium altitude recce to the south down the Gulf as far as the Qatar coast, some thirty miles away, and then return for some instrument flying and visual circuits. If anything the 'goldfish bowl' effect worsened the higher we went. This was outside all of my previous meteorological experience: in European flying you could always climb above a haze layer, no matter how intense. There was no air traffic control radar available to help us. Knowing the sun was in the south-west I rolled out to hold it in my 2 o'clock, checking below to see if I could pick up the east coast of the island as we headed south. The pilot disagreed with my tactic, took control and rolled out heading to the right of the sun. The tiny standby magnetic compass swung wildly with the slightest change of bank angle. Visibility everywhere was atrocious: in the thick, yellow haze at 20,000 feet it was impossible to see if we were over land or sea. I was convinced we were heading west and said as much. I could see this sortie ending up in a Saudi prison cell. By the merest chance the haze thinned somewhat, to reveal a clear yellow line which could only be the Saudi coastline, just a few miles in front of us. The pilot cursed and I breathed a sigh of relief as he turned through 180 degrees, to head back to Bahrain.

After a few days I became accustomed to the fierce heat and humidity of Bahrain, not least through trudging around the station in my new desert boots to complete the customary RAF 'arrival procedure', a tedious filling-in of forms requiring you to write out your personal details and next-of-kin addresses a score of times. My knees were becoming noticeably brown and, to my satisfaction, I felt increasingly immersed in the splendid long tradition of the RAF in the Middle East. There had been a constant RAF presence over the deserts of the region since the First World War and the fighting against the Turks. The names of the airfields embodied a permanent historical romance: Hinaidi, Habbaniyah, Shaibah, Muharraq, Sharjah, Masirah – the last three still in use by the RAF.

The primary operational task of the Muharraq Hunter Wing was to defend Kuwait against Iraqi aggression, the Iraqis having tried their hand already in the early '60s. At that time British forces had moved rapidly to forestall an invasion of the disputed territory of the Kuwaitis, with whom we had a defence pact. We had to be ready to deploy north to Kuwait at any time. The Saudis would not let us overfly their territory and so all of our peacetime training was carried out to the south and east of Bahrain. Additionally, some of the islands of the Gulf were disputed territory as far as the Iranians were concerned: they were bitter about the fact that the British government was now calling it the Arabian Gulf.

Now began my work-up training to become a pairs leader on 208 Squadron. I was under no illusion that it would be hard work, and that I would be sent home if I failed. Sadly, this had just happened to another pilot who was now on a Shackleton squadron. I soon got used to the splendid tropical work routine, starting with a Met brief at 0630, followed by first take-offs at 0700. Last take-off would be at about 1200 and we would be in the bar by 1300, to enjoy a few ice-cold beers before lunch.

Afternoons of searing heat were spent lounging around at the pool and at tea time we would wander down town for a bit of shopping as the heat of the day moderated. Trips downtown were frequent and in that age of gentler relations with the Arab world we felt free to mingle with the local crowds, shopping and browsing in the souk with no fear of violence. Although there was mutual respect (we were here as part of a defence agreement with the Bahrain government), unsurprisingly there was little social contact with the locals. The language and cultural barriers were too strong, but I for one felt completely at ease among the Arab population.

The Gulf flying was absolutely fantastic, and there was lots of it. From Muharraq we flew high-low-high sorties south-east into the United Arab Emirates territory, or across to Muscat and Oman, navigating on 1:2 million scale maps which each pilot had to illustrate for himself, there being no detail plotted inland from coastlines (in these areas the maps were just plain white paper). Fierce arguments raged amongst the old hands as to the exact location of the various features they had drawn on their jealously-guarded personal maps. A classic example of this was the famous 'lone palm tree' plotted some seventy miles inland from the southern Gulf coastline, in the middle of nowhere. Occasionally we flew low level departures from Muharraq, flying south down the Gulf of Bahrain to transit a low level corridor over the Sheikdom of Qatar. To the south and east of Qatar lay the vast open desert spaces of the United Arab Emirates, comprising Abu Dhabi, Dubai, Sharjah, Fujairah and one or two smaller countries. Along with Northern Oman this was a free-flying area for us, and almost totally unpopulated. For target navigation we had 1:100,000 scale monochrome maps, copied direct from air survey photos. They were good for topographic detail in mountainous regions, and with a lot of practice could be used for precise target navigation at low level over the desert.

On my first mission into this region I led a pair of Hunters on a familiarization exercise, one object for me being to check out the exact position of the 'lone palm tree' and one or two other features. In the crystal clear heat of the early morning we left the smooth, turquoise waters of the Gulf behind to set course inland from the rocky peak of Jebel Dhana, a favourite landmark on the southern Gulf coast. I had 'hacked' (started) the big Monte Carlo stopwatch as we crossed the coastline, to measure the ten minutes or so elapsed time to the palm tree. We soon cleared the rocky coastal terrain and settled down to a comfortable 100-150 feet height over the sand dunes; low enough to be interesting, yet not so low that you had to use all your concentration for heightkeeping, to the detriment of lookout (the squadron laid on a 'bounce' for most missions and you were liable to be attacked at any time).

'Dust devil[1] right 2 o'clock – no threat!'

'Tally'

We had no accurate measure of height, and some people's idea of 100 feet was far lower than others. The low dunes gave way occasionally to isolated patches of scrawny vegetation, consisting of gnarled trees just a few feet high. We crossed vast, featureless salt pans where depth perception was impossible, the horizon shimmering misty gold like waves on a fabulous sea. These were dangerous areas, the lack of visual clues suckering you into flying too low. Periodically we flashed over a camel trail or 'Road (Approximate Alignment)' as they were depicted on the map. Just a series of faint grooves in the sand, they were pretty useless for accurate navigation. After about eight minutes a tiny object appeared on the horizon dead ahead – the lone palm tree. It stood barely 20 feet high in the middle of nowhere, with no other distinguishable feature for miles. Having fixed the palm tree I could see why it was a favourite checkpoint and rendezvous for formations broken up after being savaged by the bounce.

On subsequent sorties we penetrated further south and east into the infamous Liwa Hollows, a moonscape of gigantic golden sand dunes interspersed with perfectly flat salt pans each 1-2 kilometres across, all virtually identical. The Liwas extended hundreds of miles south into Saudi territory, forming the north-eastern boundary of the

Rub al Khali, the forbidding Empty Quarter of legend which stretched nearly 800 miles south-west to Aden. Here and there around the edges of the hollows lay the occasional oasis, sparse patches of greenery and a few primitive dwellings. None of these places was accurately marked on our maps. Borders were pretty vague in this desolate region and we didn't bother too much about them. The interior of the Hollows was a Bermuda Triangle for low level navigation because the dunes all looked the same wherever you were. I remember my first four-ship formation attack on a tiny target in the middle of the Liwas, a stone tower barely fifteen feet high, the remains of an ancient fort now buried deep in the sand. After some ten minutes of switchback navigation the formation began the complex manoeuvring leading to a coordinated rocket attack, the aim being for each aircraft to dive on the target with minimum spacing from different points of the compass. We pointed hopefully into the salt pan, searching desperately for any feature which might be the target. No joy – missed attack. The leader had miscounted the hollows on the long run-in, an all-too-common error. As we pulled out to reform, I spotted the tower in the next hollow – too late. To the east of the Liwas lay another fascinating desert terrain consisting of immensely long and narrow salt pans separated by low sandy ridges barely 100 feet high. You could fit a whole formation into one pan and fly straight for fifty miles or more. They were 2-3 kilometres across and it was like flying down a gigantic motorway cutting. These were favourite areas for bouncing, the bounce formation 'lurking' just over the ridge in the next lane, invisible to the target formation. When a navigational turn was called the bounce would hurtle over the dividing ridge and be into the formation like a fox among chickens. A dirty trick – although splendid sport for everyone concerned.

At the extreme eastern end of the desert area lay the famous oasis of Buraimi, in those days still a smallish series of hamlets scattered amongst the lush patches of greenery. Just a few miles south of Buraimi lay the Jebel Hafit, an eight-mile long humpback rock feature rising 4,000 feet from the flat desert floor like a gigantic crashed Zeppelin. This was a favourite navigational feature and letdown point for us approaching at 35,000 feet from Bahrain, being easily visible from 100 miles away. At low level you 'hacked' the stopwatch at the Jebel and headed south-east for about five minutes, en route to the mountains of Muscat and Oman. In front and to the left you could see the gigantic impenetrable mass of the Fatah range, a sheer wall of rock rising 3,000 feet from the smooth desert floor. Closer in you could make out your turning point, the deep slash of the Al Fatah Gap, the entry point for the mountains. Your formation closed up automatically into the compact 'arrow' configuration as you turned to dive through the gap. In a flash you had left the bright, wide open spaces of the desert and were flying through an impossibly rugged terrain of deep, sandy-floored wadis and towering, razor-sharp ridgelines which extended a hundred miles north to the Strait of Hormuz. This was an excellent training area strewn with Arab dwelling forts, many of them of vast size having been extended, defended, conquered and re-occupied many times over the centuries. These majestic bleached mud constructions were favourite targets for simulated attacks and we had an extensive target library of photos of them back in the squadron.

Whilst we could operate in Oman high-low-high from Bahrain, more often than not we would land at RAF Sharjah on the Gulf coast some 250 miles to the east, often to stay the night. Sharjah was a splendid place, occupied by men only. Bits of it were straight out of *Beau Geste*. No one was allowed to bring wives or girlfriends there, not even the station commander. The only female on base was the civvy Met man's wife, who had a disturbing tendency to come into the bar wearing the shortest miniskirts. Not surprisingly, this generally all-male scenario led to some pretty wild bashes in the bar where we would sing our extensive repertoire of obscene songs. Other units on base were 210, a Mk 2 Shackleton squadron, the Andovers of 84 Squadron, plus Wessex helicopters of 78 Squadron. The men of 84 Squadron were even madder than we were. Recently they had seen the film *The Great Escape* in the camp cinema and had formed an escape committee to tunnel their way out of their accommodation hut. They had done it in fine style, just like the film, tearing up the floorboards and digging through the sandy soil towards the Officers' Mess bar. Just like the film, various squadron 'shags'[2] would wander into the bar patio area to stand around in seemingly innocent conversation while surreptitiously emptying pocketfuls of sand into the goldfish pond. Eventually, realizing that escape was impossible, they turned the excavation into an underground squadron bar for late-night drinking.

We were to spend a lot of time at Sharjah, both us and 8 Squadron, our rival Hunter outfit at Muharraq. We held regular Armament

Practice Camps there, making use of the excellent desert ranges of Rashid and Jebajib just over the border in Dubai. Additionally, there were many Army cooperation exercises and some actual operations with the British-officered Trucial Oman Scouts, some units spending a lot of time rushing about the desert with their Land Rovers painted a fetching shade of pink. Known as 'desert pink' it was a surprisingly effective camouflage colour and almost invisible from the air. Army cooperation exercises were given colourful names, often with a whimsical reference to the kind of flying we would be doing: Exercises *Jebel Bash, Arabian Nights, Bugle Call* etc., were all popular names.

My favourite fun-flying area lay in the mountains just fifty miles or so north-east from Sharjah in the Ruus al Jibal, where razor-sharp ridges alternated with deep wadis in a mathematically regular pattern for a distance of thirty miles or more. As a party trick or just for casual amusement you could fly a switchback white-knuckle route at right angles to the grain of the terrain, diving steeply into each wadi and pulling 7g to climb almost vertically up the next rock face. Well before you reached the top you rolled inverted and pulled 7g once again to zoom tight over the ridge, the rock face just a few feet above your head. When pointing straight down into the next wadi – still just a few feet clear of the rock – you rolled upright and began the next 'switchback'. Truly a sport of kings, although moderately dangerous if you overcooked it.

On my first Armament Practice Camp (APC) at Sharjah I did no range work. To my disgust the squadron T7 went U/S with a major hydraulic leak on the first day. There was a requirement for a PAI checkout on the range before new pilots were allowed to fire live in the FGA9, so I was snookered until the lads could fix the T7. I had arrived at Sharjah by Andover and been driven the thirty miles or so to Rashid range via primitive desert tracks. Our vehicle bounced viciously through the potholes as my driver, another squadron pilot, tried to equal the world land speed record for RAF Land Rovers. The range was laid out in the dunes right on the coast with a glorious coral beach between us and the sea. The only building of note was the 20 feet high range safety officers' tower from where the duty pilot controlled the range traffic, with the assistance of a sergeant. I took the squadron 'gharry'.[3] out to the skip bombing live target, a scrap Army truck. (We had hoped that the Army would have provided a larger scrap vehicle as target, but they had given up, providing anything large for us to destroy. On a recent 8 Squadron APC the huge tracked grader which they had laboriously towed into position had disappeared overnight, stolen by the enterprising 'range Arabs' who occupied the local sand dunes. The grader had disappeared completely into the desert, as if sinking into quicksand, a search by an Army helicopter finding no trace of it – not so much as a wheel track in the sand. No doubt its component parts were on sale within hours in the souks of Dubai and Sharjah.)

On the range I had my camera to take snapshots of the level bombing attacks, the squadron carrying 100 gallon tanks full of water to simulate Napalm.[4] From my position just fifty metres from the target the attacks were spectacular. At 50ft, the standard delivery height, the first FGA9 looked to be almost on the deck as it approached. The tanks tumbled immediately on release and impacted the ground with a satisfyingly powerful burst of spray. They fell about 50yds short, the ideal impact point to spray the target area with Napalm. A ton of water moving at 500 miles per hour is something you don't want to stand in the way of. The very first attack cut the truck in half and scattered the remains like matchwood. The rest of the squadron pounded the remains to bits. This was a stunningly effective demonstration of a weapons technique which I had not previously seen. Rocket firing, of 68mm calibre SNEB, was carried out on the SNEB court just next to the tower. The rockets reached Mach 2 just before impact, making a towering explosion of sand accompanied by a satisfying sonic crack. From the ground, air-to-ground strafing was less impressive. The targets were 15 feet square Hessian screens lined up to the east of the tower, and we had to go out and count the holes after each shoot. What amused me was the sight of several decrepit Arab vehicles driving around under the flight path of the attacking aircraft, their occupants leaping out to collect the valuable brass shell cases as they fell. They didn't give a damn about the danger of being brained by falling metal, and periodically we had to go out and shoo them away. The skip bombing court lay just a few yards from the tower and was used for practice bombs, simulating dive and level Napalm deliveries. The scoring court was split down the middle, the left half being for bombs hung on the left wing, and vice versa.

After a searing day out in the heat of the range it was bliss to get under the cooling fans of the Mess bar after the bumpy drive back. The 'road' between Sharjah and the range consisted merely of a strip of oiled sand of varying width which meandered all over the place around the more heavily potholed areas. However fast we drove we were always being overtaken by immaculate air-conditioned Mercedes limousines, their Arab occupants almost invisible behind heavily-tinted glass. When not on duty on the range I was allowed off on some local area sorties and spent most of my spare time working with the ground crew to fix the T7, now raised on jacks with the engine removed to reveal the damage to the hydraulic lines. On the Hunter the whole tail section had to be removed in order to get the engine out. The hangar in which we worked was a furnace during the day; although both sets of doors were wide open there was not so much as a breath of wind to cool us down. After a week of sweat we stood well clear as the engineers connected up the ground hydraulic pressure rig to see if the leak had been fixed. The control surfaces thrashed viciously for a second or two as the 3,000lb hydraulic pressure came on to the jacks. I got into the cockpit and moved the controls. Everything worked OK; there was no leak. However, the APC was nearly over and it was too late for me to get checked out this time. I would have to wait until the next APC in September.

Back at Bahrain I had settled in well and was fully acclimatized to the heat, sufficiently even to play squash, eventually winning the station tournament. The squadron 'shags' were a good bunch, a dozen or so young bachelors plus one or two married drags. There was good-natured rivalry with 8 Squadron and we tended to stick together on base and on regular launches downtown, either to the Gulf Hotel (the Hilton was not yet built) or to the Malcolm Club in downtown Manama. The usual means of transport was on the back of someone's motorbike, often three-up. Every night at about 8 p.m. a warm layer of dew would settle on the rubber-stained dusty roads, turning them into lethal skid pans on which no tyre would grip. In these conditions the sober motorcyclist negotiated each roundabout at 5 mph or less, both feet planted firmly on the ground, with all passengers assisting. The most common scars of battle at Muharraq were severe grazes and road burns resulting from skids. On arrival I had wondered why so many personnel were wandering about with net bandages on arms and knees. Cars were not popular, the heat of the day turning them into ovens after a few minutes exposure to the sun. Open sports cars were worse, the sun heating the interiors to a temperature which burned the skin. We had the same problem with the aircraft on the line, although we used specially-designed umbrellas most of the time to shade the cockpits. Despite this the ejection seat pans would have burnt the skin through our thin flying suits, had we not used real sheepskin seat covers for protection. The stick and throttles were too hot to touch without the protection of flying gloves. The dangers of heat stress were constantly emphasized by the medics. We had a strict rule that we had to get airborne within fifteen minutes of climbing into the aircraft – there was no cooling on the ground and you would be saturated with sweat after that time. Taxiing the two miles or so to the runway threshold was carried out at breakneck speed, with bared arms hanging out of the cockpit to achieve some cooling effect. Only after the gear was locked up could you feel a deliciously cool blast of air as the cockpit air conditioning switched on. This equipment was only effective at medium and high altitudes.

At low level over the desert the air temperatures could be 60 degrees C and more. Cockpits just grew steadily hotter in these conditions – the cockpit air conditioning being totally unable to cope – and you sweated buckets to compensate. After an hour of low level the luxury of cold air as you climbed for the stratosphere was indescribable. We marvelled at the fortitude of our predecessors on Vampires and Venoms who flew low level in these conditions without any air conditioning at all. On many long-range sorties to the east of Sharjah we would be 'cruise climbing' on the long high level leg back over the Gulf to Bahrain, the fuel gauges indicating uncomfortably low. A favourite trick was to get to 50,000 feet and take a picture of the altimeter. (I often carried my Minolta in the cockpit). At these heights you felt almost on the edge of space, the vault of the sky tinted deep indigo in the thin air. The usual technique was to switch the aileron control into manual (hydraulic power off), so that you could relax and fly hands-off. We didn't have the luxury of an autopilot. From 50,000 feet you could idle the engine and glide to Bahrain from over 100 miles out, using very little fuel. Our only navigation aid was an ancient radio compass (ADF) with which you could home on the Bahrain NDB (a radio beacon) and carry out an instrument letdown in poor visibility.

The flying at Muharraq, almost invariably in formation, was very competitive. Initial sorties were flown as wingman, following an experienced pilot to see how it was done and build up familiarity with the operating area. Later, the new pilot would be given an air task requiring him to lead a formation (usually four) carrying out simulated attacks on two or three smallish targets anywhere in our low flying area of operations, at the same time fighting off a bounce who could attack at any time. The bounce would have full details of the formation's route, their radio frequencies etc. The bounce would take-off before the formation and a favourite tactic was to lurk at high altitude over Muharraq, waiting to see the target formation get airborne. Then the bounce – often a pair of aircraft or more – would 'stalk' the formation from above 30,000ft, hiding in the deep blue, many miles above, before swooping down almost supersonic to attack when the formation was occupied in a turn or attacking the target. No problem 'dropping bangs' (i.e. going supersonic) over the desert. The leader would have to work out all the details of the attack and routeing to and from the target, plan and brief the mission, including tactics against the bounce, and be debriefed on his performance after landing. There would always be an experienced pilot in the formation, often one of the flight commanders.

Mission debriefs were hard-hitting and often acrimonious, the leader being told off by everyone in the formation about the mistakes he had made. The bounce would throw in his two penn'orth as well. You soon became streetwise about this and could give back as good as you got. Members of a formation would often make as many mistakes as the leader; the only problem was to notice them in flight and get someone to back you up on the ground. I enjoyed the bigger formations most of all. The in-flight action was more hectic and the debriefs were fairer as there were more witnesses to what had actually happened. Accurate debriefing of the combat engagements with the bounce was an art form in itself, not many pilots having the total recall necessary to remember accurately what had happened, who made the first call, where the bounce came from, how did we react etc. Although we had to bring back good attack film of the target, on these training missions the main aim was to avoid being shot down by the bounce, thus having 'lives' chipped off your personal score on the squadron combat ladder. This, (just like a squash ladder) showed a squadron Order of Merit in gun-camera claimed 'kills'; a good position on the ladder being prized above all other skills. All combats counted, including bounced missions.

As a new pilot I had started pretty well on the ladder after a few successful 1 versus 1 combat missions when I had got good film of the other aircraft. Air-to-air gun sighting was scored by the length of time you could hold steady tracking of the aiming 'pipper'[5] on your opponent's aircraft. Parameters were as follows:

KILL: 16 frames (1 second) STEADY tracking of
                         cockpit, thus killing pilot. 2 points.

SEVERE DAMAGE: 16 frames (1 second) STEADY tracking of
                         any part of aircraft. 1 point.

DAMAGE: 8 frames ditto above. 1/2 point.

All successful claims had to be within the range band 200-800 yards
of target, with Stadiametric ranging (set by the throttle twist-grip),
accurate to within 5 per cent.

These parameters were extremely difficult to achieve in the heat of
combat, each aircraft twisting and turning violently to avoid the
other. Additionally, the 16mm film cassettes were notoriously unreliable, often failing to turn over and record film. In that case you had
no claim. As a result, during a big combat I would change cassettes
several times (often while pulling 6g) to minimize the chance of film
failure. The nose radar, so useful for flag firing, was useless in hard
combat because it constantly broke lock at high g. I had pushed my
combat score up dramatically to reach second place on the ladder
after being bounced by another squadron pilot during a medium
altitude cine training session. He thought I looked easy meat, but I
managed to get behind him straight away and get some good killing
film. My favourite opponent in pure 1 versus 1 combat was the
squadron's acknowledged combat expert. He was almost unbeatable
in the air and his low-speed handling – known as scissoring – was
uncanny to see, his aircraft defying all the known laws of aerodynamics as he dropped behind from a seemingly hopeless position. I
learned quite a few tricks from him in my time on 208.

During my squadron work-up training I came closer to death than
on any other occasion during my whole flying career. It happened
like this:

The weather was brilliant and calm as usual, with a hazy horizon
at low level. I was flying as Number 4, i.e. as wingman to the deputy
formation leader. We were on a high-low-high bounced strike and,
for once, there was only one bounce aircraft flown by a squadron
pilot I disliked intensely. I was already starting to fancy myself at
combat and once again felt that tremendous surge of adrenalin as I
picked up the bounce – a mere speck in the deep blue vertically above
us as we descended through 20,000 feet over the sea south of Yas

Island. In spite of my early pickup and warning call on R/T, the bounce was soon in the middle of our twisting and turning formation. Determined to keep contact with my adversary, I committed the cardinal sin of losing my element leader within seconds of starting the fight. Desperate to regain some kudos, I threw myself at the bounce while shouting on the R/T that I would soon be 'claiming' him. On hearing this the rest of the formation promptly departed at Warp 9 heading for Jebel Dhana, abandoning me to my well-deserved fate. My personal duel with the bounce dragged on for several minutes and it became uncomfortably clear that I was nowhere near to getting a kill. Unbeknown to me the bounce was setting me up for a run-out[6] and, having skilfully manoeuvred me away from the last-known position of my companions, he suddenly disengaged in hot pursuit of my erstwhile formation. Incensed at the way I had been duped I dived frantically for airspeed, simultaneously 'skylining' the departing bounce as a dwindling speck just above the horizon. Throughout the engagement so far I had not checked on my height and I fondly imagined that I was still at least 10,000 feet above the sea. My whole attention was riveted on the tiny speck on the horizon as my aircraft began to hum with the famous 'blue note' at high airspeed. I couldn't afford to look in the cockpit – if I lost visual contact I knew I would never pick him up again in the haze. After a minute or two the horizon in my peripheral vision slowly began to change colour. Through the thunder of the 600 knot airflow I dimly became aware of a tiny voice in my brain repeating the same message over and over again. In a flash, and barely in time, I awoke to the awful reality – CHECK YOUR HEIGHT!

I was in a shallow dive with the altimeter slowly unwinding through 200 feet. The sea was like glass and could have been 200 or 2,000 feet away – it was impossible to judge. Just a few seconds more of doziness and I would have flown into the water at maximum speed. I pulled up violently to get away from the treacherous water that had so nearly smashed me to oblivion. Severely shaken, I flew slowly home to receive a well-deserved bawling-out for failing to stick in formation. I was too ashamed to tell of my near-disaster.

Squadron life at Muharraq was idyllic for a bunch of young bachelors on a day fighter/ground attack wing. Our squadron offices were air-conditioned and located just a few yards from the aircraft flight line. I discovered that our squadron engineering flight sergeant was an old acquaintance from Valley, where he had been an excellent ground school instructor. In the squadron there was constant good-natured rivalry and practical joking among the junior pilots. The flying was so good that it was difficult for people to unwind on the ground and so we took refuge in constant micky-taking and banter. I soon learned to avoid asking serious questions of fellow junior pilots. If you asked where a particular individual was, for example, the inevitable answer would be: 'He's on the roof with a rat in his mouth, singing 'Death to Mussolini!'

Quite where this obscure and perverse answer came from no one seemed to know – it was just a 208 Squadron tradition. I still use it to this day if someone is asking particularly stupid questions.

As well as bounced low-level strikes we flew a lot of pure combat missions, with as many as eight or ten aircraft in action. Sometimes it was four versus four, sometimes four versus six. The Persian Gulf climate, although predictable for weeks on end, was vastly different from European weather. The problem of deep haze layers has already been mentioned; such conditions made combat very difficult as it was easy to lose orientation with no horizon visible. However, the usual weather pattern was of gloriously clear conditions everywhere, with occasional layers of cumulus building up from a base above 15,000 feet, far higher than you would find at home. These clouds were ideal for hiding behind during medium altitude combat. I started to wear Polaroid sunglasses in flight, (strictly forbidden by the medics), to help to see through the murk. They were very effective in haze, although I used to get some extreme 'psychedelic' colour effects caused by the many layers of glass in the armoured windscreen. During these big combats it was absolutely vital that formations stayed together and maintained discipline. Wingmen had to stick, search and report, the primary duty being to hang on to your element leader whatever he did. Loose aeroplanes falling out of formation became a menace, the leader unable to work out who he was talking to on the radio. During combat you would often be manoeuvring several miles apart from each other, the aircraft of your supporting element mere specks in the distance. R/T discipline was rigid and there was no room at all for over-excited shouting into the mike. One of the biggest problems was keeping tabs on who was who. We had various tricks to positively identify an aircraft some distance away, one of which was to call him to roll, for example:

'GOLD 3, ROLL!'

On receiving this call Gold 3 had to carry out a 360 degree snap roll immediately in order to be visually identified by the rest of the formation. (We also used this ploy at Low Level: I would often call

'Gold Lead Rolling' and do a snap roll to identify myself to the rest of the formation. The key to survival and success during all combat engagements was early sighting of the opposition. In this, the squadron had several ace 'lookouts' with the proverbial 'eyes like a shithouse rat'. These characters were a great asset as wingmen, able to pick out the tiny speck of an enemy aircraft pitching in vertically to attack from several miles above, out of the fierce glare of the sun. Good lookout was extremely hard work, the pilot twisting and turning constantly in the cockpit, his head screwed right round to see as far behind as possible. The technique had to be learned from bitter experience. The key element was knowing exactly where to look at any one moment. No matter how much they scanned the horizon, many pilots were still unable to see other aircraft until too late. Such pilots failed to refocus their eyes at infinity at regular intervals. Without a conscious effort to do this their eyes would relax to focus just a few hundred feet away – useless for picking up a distant target. Many pilots developed a sixth sense of super-awareness, acquired via a hard-won knowledge of bounce tactics, which enabled you to be looking in the right direction at the right time, both at high and low level.

During 'Op' (Operational Work-Up) training you spent a lot of time flying as a wingman at low level, learning how to stick, search and report in a big formation. As a wingman you flew 200-400 yards well swept back on your element leader (usually an Op 2 or Op 4 pilot), and always slightly above him. Element leaders were free to manoeuvre as they wished, breaking hard into any threat and turning as required without a radio call to maintain overall formation integrity. (The better leaders would always give up just a little bit of performance to allow their wingmen to keep up.) They would fly at about 100 feet a.g.l. and you had a hard time just staying with them until you learned some tricks of the trade. A good wingman was worth his weight in gold and the squadron encouraged people to regard it as a privilege to be selected for the position on a 'difficult' mission. Many years later I was to appreciate the efforts of my wingman in the Falklands war. He literally saved my life when I was shot down.

The biggest problem facing a wingman at low level was simply staying in contact with his element leader and not flying into the ground. Imagine the situation: you are flying at about 100 feet a.g.l. at 420 knots, trying to follow another Hunter just a couple of hundred yards in front. You are expecting to be bounced at any moment (lookout was continuous – you could never relax) and your primary area of lookout is behind the opposite pair of the formation, cruising a mile away from you. To pick up a bounce you have to search deep in the six o'clock of the formation, twisting your head around almost through 180 degrees and holding this uncomfortable position for five seconds or so while you make sure your eyes focus at infinity. So, you are now travelling at 420 knots, barely 100 feet above ground and staring behind you for long periods, unable to look where you are going. When you look forward again you hope, firstly, that you are not just about to fly into the ground and secondly, that your leader is still there. To survive and become efficient at lookout in such conditions you needed the good old 'sixth sense' of situation awareness that warned you what was going to happen next. During the brief moments when you looked ahead you would check for any forthcoming obstacles which you knew the leader would be dodging around, and estimate how long it would be before he would need to turn. When any radio call was made you would immediately check your leader to see which way he was going to turn. Most difficult of all was flying in Arrow formation as a four-ship while the leader manoeuvred through narrow valleys in the mountains. In this you moved up even closer on the lead, to fifty yards or less between aircraft, slightly above him, and you also had to stick to your side of the leader's fore-and-aft axis, i.e. if you were No. 3 on the left side you had to stay that side whatever the leader did. This meant that when the leader rolled into a hard turn towards you, you had to put on an immediate bootful of bottom rudder to drop the nose and allow you to keep sight of the upper surfaces of No. 1 and No. 2 in front and below you. The great temptation was to drop below the lead and lag the turn, thus keeping him in sight more easily, but this was a lethal trap. Remember that the lead would fly as low as he wanted, and anyone dropping below his flight path would be creamed on the next piece of rising ground. After twenty minutes of hanging on in this formation, all of you were exhausted and dripping with sweat; at times I found myself thinking 'A chap could get himself killed doing this'.

We were always experimenting with tactics, trying to find out ways of attacking targets and defending ourselves more efficiently. In this we didn't limit ourselves solely to the tactical conditions of the desert. We knew our operational role in the Gulf would soon end and all of us would be back in the hard school of European theatre flying within NATO, preparing for war against the overwhelming

Communist forces of the Warsaw Pact countries. Although we couldn't simulate the weather and terrain, most of the time we were using low-level tactics which would be more appropriate in Europe. An example was low flying itself, which was seldom essential for pure desert theatre operations. If the threat was solely from air engagement by fighters on visual combat air patrol (often the situation in the desert), then we would transit to the target at about 4,000 feet, leaving no telltale shadows on the desert below and giving us maximum opportunity to pick up incoming fighters. At anywhere below this height we knew that our perfectly-camouflaged aircraft left a solid black shadow on the sand, which was easily visible to fighters lurking above.

Formation bounce tactics were highly developed on 208 Squadron. We tried to launch a minimum of a pair of aircraft as bounce, and there were various tricks used to break up an enemy formation. One of the simpler ideas was for the bounce to attack in trail, one aircraft about two miles behind the other. The target formation would react to the first aircraft, which would press the turn just enough to get them well off track. The first aircraft would then break off in the hope that the formation would reverse its turn back on to track, leaving them extremely vulnerable to the second bounce aircraft. I flew in several four-ship bounces (i.e. a formation of four bouncing a formation of eight at low level) and even led one or two myself. This kind of thing was exceptionally difficult to lead well, the main problem being to keep control of your formation during the various engagements, preventing the more hot-headed pilots from getting 'sandwiched' and shot down by the target formation. During these big fights the main hazards were flying into the ground and having a mid-air collision. In a big fight it was impossible for everyone to keep tabs on all aircraft involved, so you were often startled by the sudden appearance of an aircraft from nowhere, just a heart-stopping flash of dark green next to your canopy. If you heard the engine noise then it was really close. There were a lot of 'near misses' and some pilots used to worry a lot about them. I tried to treat the whole thing fairly philosophically: there were so many ways of getting killed flying single-seat fighter ground attack that there was no point in getting uptight about any one particular risk more than the others. In the air the key to survival was constant vigilance, achieved by pumping yourself up to a high level of arousal at all times in the air. Time to relax was on the ground. My atheism told me that there were no gods to look after me in the air and any smash for me would result in oblivion – not heavenly choirs. I just had to rely on intuition and luck. Like everyone else I had used up a lot of it already. Naturally enough, this approach to flying was not particularly good for the blood pressure. However, I loved every minute of it and could never get enough airborne time to be satisfied.

In all of this hectic action you had to remember to leave a margin for error, however small, to avoid catastrophe. I often fell back on the advice given during my flying training at Cranwell and Valley. In particular, I tried to retain some 'machine empathy' and fly smoothly during the violent combat and ground attack manoeuvres. It was all too easy to smash the aircraft around and pump the throttle indiscriminately, but I couldn't do this without a conscience. Throughout my flying career I always felt privileged to be entrusted with such beautifully-engineered machines and did my best to treat them with respect, if nothing else out of consideration for the hard-working engineers who kept them flying. I was not impressed with pilots who treated the aircraft more or less as a throwaway item – something for the engineers to sort out when the pilot had finished with it.

Hour Hogs

Most pilots on the Wing felt the same about the flying, but one or two characters were trying to hog just a bit too much for themselves. Some people had an obsession about building up the maximum number of flying hours in their log books, and would resort to any subterfuge to increase their recorded flying times. All of us had been guilty of 'sharp-pencilling' hours flown (logging a few minutes more airborne time than were actually flown), but this was because RAF rules required flying hours to be rounded to the nearest five minutes. Additionally, flying hours were taken from a pilot's report of how long he flew, not from ATC records. ATC always logged pretty accurate times of take-off and landing but, by tradition, aircrew never took much notice of what they said, especially if it was going to reduce the hours they could put in their log books. A favourite hour-hogging trick was to use up all the fuel in the aircraft right down to the minimums on every sortie flown. The worst offenders would 'lurk' idly at high altitude (where fuel consumption was lowest) overhead Bahrain, and then make a dirty dart to land at the last minute, having added an extra ten or fifteen minutes on to the sortie time. This kind of thing was objectionable for two reasons: firstly, it denied other pilots the opportunity to fly that aircraft while they were staying airborne for an unnecessary length of time; secondly – and more important – they were cheating the hard-pressed squadron engineers, who had to service all our aircraft on the basis of hours flown. A hog who used up unnecessary time airborne was literally wasting the squadron's aircraft resources for purely selfish reasons. I had been guilty of all these crimes in the past, but I was beginning to recognize the hour-hog as a menace on a hard-working ground attack squadron, where aircraft resources and flying hours were always at a premium. The majority of responsible pilots would get the job done without wasting time and then get on the ground to debrief and let the engineers turn the aircraft round for the next mission. Just exactly how many hours you had in your log book was more or less irrelevant: what was important was what you had done during your airborne time. Predictably, the hour-hogs were often the ones who bragged the most about their flying experience, being prone to wear the childish American-style 'hours flown on type' badges which were becoming increasingly popular in the RAF.

On the Hunter FGA9 we would often fly for an hour and a half or more on high-low-high missions. This had not always been the case, particularly with earlier marks of the Hunter spending most of the sortie in intense air combat manoeuvring. A couple of years later I heard a splendid tale of bouncing and low level air combat from a flight commander on my first Harrier squadron. (He had been an instructor on the RAF's famous Day Fighter Leaders' School). In the early 60s he was a keen young pilot on a Hunter F6 Squadron based at Nicosia in Cyprus. He was taxiing out, leading a six-ship formation of Hunters in short-range configuration, for some air combat against four others who were already airborne. This was a 'needle match', each formation honed to the highest pitch of combat tactics. Dirty deeds were the order of the day and a favourite bounce tactic was for the airborne formation to attack as soon as the defending formation lifted off the runway, knocking them out of the sky before they had even got their wheels up. Because of this, defensive lookout started from 'chocks away', the wingmen scanning the clear skies while taxiing, searching for the faintest hint of a contrail or sun glint off a canopy which would give away enemy fighters lurking in the deep blue far above. Without under wing tanks the F6 had barely forty minutes' endurance, and much less on full power at low altitude. While taxiing out, the Hunter formation came up behind a Hastings transport which was holding short of the runway while awaiting ATC clearance for departure to the UK.

Brusquely the Hunter formation leader asked the Hastings' captain if he would be so kind as to move aside on to a dispersal area so that the Hunters could get past and get airborne – and could he get on with it sharpish. Grudgingly, and with some bad-tempered muttering about 'Typical fighter pilot amateur dramatics', the captain agreed, moving ponderously aside as the Hunters rushed past and hurtled into the air. True to form, as the last pair of Hunters lifted off the runway four 'enemy' Hunters screamed in behind them, having carried out a perfectly-timed dive out of the sun. With the wheels still hanging, the Hunter leader called the break and ten Hunters disappeared sideways off the airfield, to begin a desperate low level dogfight in which no quarter was given. After barely twenty minutes of hectic action at full power, in which half his formation had been 'claimed' by the enemy, several of the Hunter leader's aircraft were on 'Joker' fuel. Time to go home. After a hurried reform they joined to land at Nicosia, the leader calling 'Priority Fuel' on the run-in, meaning he didn't want anyone else on the runway until his formation was safely on the ground. Meanwhile the Hastings crew – oblivious to the frantic action taking place above them – had been laboriously carrying out their pre-take-off engine runs and were only now ready for departure. The captain asked for take-off clearance just after the Hunter leader had called 'Priority Fuel', and was rendered speechless with rage when ATC told him that he was now going to have to wait for this formation to land first – this same bunch of prima donnas who had elbowed him aside to get airborne in indecent haste barely twenty minutes ago.

In September we were back at Sharjah again for an APC and I finally got my range duals. At Rashid range the only totally new events were dive skip bombing and high angle strafe, which we hadn't done at Chivenor. For dive skip you just aimed your pink body at the skip target in a shallow dive, aiming to 'pickle'[7] to release the bomb at the very last second, just as it seemed you were about to fly into the target. The technique was almost foolproof, and very accurate once you had learned the trick of getting as close as you dared before pickling. As at Chivenor, all weapon firing was recorded on 16mm film cameras attached to the gunsight. The PAIs would disallow any score where you were outside the briefed parameters for firing. There was also a major Army exercise in the mountains where we took part as friendly air assets, running a 'cab rank' system for ground attack. In this we kept a pair of aircraft orbiting at high altitude to conserve fuel, above the battle area until called down to attack under control by a forward air controller. Conditions for ground attack were deceptively easy over the low foothills to the north-east of Buraimi. On one occasion I was attacking a Land Rover in a shallow wadi very early in the morning, using a notch of flap to improve my recovery off target. I felt on top of the world as I turned in to attack. The air was as smooth as glass and I was lulled into a feeling of warm, secure relaxation in the gentle heat just after sunrise. My adrenalin level was low and there was trouble lined up for me. In the gyro gunsight the faint yellow spot of the pipper rested on top of the Land Rover's roof like a beach ball, ready for a killing burst from the guns, had I been armed. The dunes were smooth and almost featureless. I had just pressed the cine camera button when I noticed some small boulders flashing past my cockpit uncomfortably close by. I hadn't noticed a low sand dune just short of the target and I had nearly clipped the top of it while concentrating on the target.

Target fixation – one of the oldest killers in the book.

At Sharjah I flew a maritime recce sortie in one of 210 Squadron's Shackleton 2s (still armed with 20mm cannon). To my surprise the captain was the air electronics officer, the pilots merely first and second pilots. One of them was an ex- Leeming colleague.

For eight hours we cruised at low level all around the coastline of Muscat and Oman, almost as far as Salalah, looking for boats smuggling illegal immigrants. The only time we went above 250 feet was when we were back in the radar pattern at Sharjah, just to give the talkdown controllers some practice. The din from the four mighty Griffon engines was indescribable, the tips of the inboard twin propellers almost touching the cockpit canopy right next to the pilot's head. Your whole body vibrated in sympathy with the paper-thin fuselage and, by the end of the sortie, I was reduced to lying down on the rear observer's position in the glazed tail. Anything to get away from the noise.

On the Wing our standard operational readiness exercise was called HOT ROD. When HOT ROD was called at short notice, the sweating armourers would immediately arm up most aircraft with armour piercing SNEB rocket pods and 480 rounds of 30mm high explosive/ incendiary ammunition. Some aircraft were left armed with guns alone, to act as fighter defence of Bahrain. Pilots were split between attackers and defenders. As attackers we would launch off in fours down the Gulf to Jebajib range near Dubai, where the Army would lay out a line of scrap trucks for us to smash up, cans of petrol being left in them to make them burn better. We would carry out a formation attack, four at a time, under the control of our excellent forward air controller, a current Hunter pilot. All rockets were fired together in a half-second burst. On a re-attack we would fire the guns two at a time, each HE round exploding in a pinpoint of light on the ground. With a good burst you could completely destroy a truck in under a second. We weren't supposed to fire all four together because of the tremendous recoil (many of the cockpit circuit breakers would trip). I tried it once, briefly. The aircraft seemed to hit a brick wall as the guns fired. After the attacks we would head back home to act as 'bombers' and targets for the fighters defending Bahrain, attacking from all sides under the control of Romeo radar, our local air defence radar. As one of the 'fighter' pilots back at Bahrain, life was also pretty exciting. We teamed up as pairs and went out to the line to 'cock' our aircraft, i.e. prepare all switches, levers, straps, etc., for as quick a departure as possible. Then we went back to the squadron to lounge about in the coffee bar waiting for the 'scramble' order on the squawk box. It was good old Battle of Britain stuff, and great fun if there was plenty of action. This was the day fighter part of the DF/GA role. The squadron squawk box would click on: 'GOLD SCRAMBLE!, GOLD SCRAMBLE!: VECTOR 150, ANGELS 250.'

Game on! We run to the squadron gharry and hang on the back, the squadron driver breaking all speed limits on the short journey to the flight line. After a start up and take-off at maximum speed, we head 150 degrees in the climb to 25,000 feet, Romeo radar giving information on the incoming raid. Because we had no onboard search radar, we had to work out our own interceptions, Romeo just giving us bearings and distances to the raid.[8] You did this by means of a simple interception graph on your kneeboard, the aim being to roll out just half a mile behind the attackers. Occasionally we intercepted RAF Vulcans, visible from miles away as they cruised at extreme high altitude. Our only technique to shoot them down was the 'zoom climb' in which we pulled up into a vertical climb well ahead of them, hopefully to get them briefly in the gunsight at maximum range before we ran out of airspeed and stalled out. Often we were visited by Canberra PR9s from Malta, carrying out photo surveys of Oman. They were full of 'bull' about their manoeuvrability and impressive rate of climb, claiming that we wouldn't get near them in combat. One day I tried it out, intercepting a PR9 over Yas Island. After a lot of low speed milling about I managed to get some quite pretty gun-camera film of the 13 Squadron flight commander. I sent back some prints to his squadron in Malta.

At the end of my 'op' work-up training a colleague and I, the two new boys, were sent on a ranger with two experienced squadron pilots to the furthest extent of our operating area. This was a test for both of us, a final evaluation of our conversion to desert operations. We carried out simulated attacks on targets in the mountains of northern Oman and landed at Sharjah for a brief refuelling stop. Next we set off for the high-level leg down to the island of Masirah, the remotest remaining RAF outpost, lying just off the barren coast of south-east Oman.

We took off from Sharjah in the searing heat of midday. At the top of the climb we hung suspended in the brilliant blue vault of the desert sky, the green paradise of Buraimi oasis drifting by far below as we set off south-east into a landscape as forbidding and empty as the surface of the moon. We were heading for the radio beacon at Fahud, an oil well in the middle of nowhere, half way to Masirah. As we approached Fahud we saw far away to starboard the glistening white wastes of the Umm al Samim. This forbidding plain of powdery gypsum overlaid treacherous quicksand and stretched flat and unbroken for dozens of miles into the distant heat haze. From the edge of the stratosphere I felt cool and remote looking down on the harsh landscape which showed not a trace of human habitation. Not a good place to jump out, was our unspoken thought as we contrailed effortlessly in wide battle formation. Far to the west the colour of the horizon changed subtly to a warmer shade of ochre as the Umm al Samim gave way to the eastern borders of the Rub al Khali, the Empty Quarter. Seemingly close enough to touch in the crystal clear air, some eighty miles away to port, rose the forbidding dark brown peaks of the Jebel al Akhdar, a 10,000 feet mountain range in a part of Oman from which we were banned. (This was a legacy from the 1950s when RAF ground attack Vampires and Meteors had assisted the Sultan in his dispute with the warlike tribes of the mountain district.) Eventually, after what seemed like hours of cruising, the gravel and salt plains gave way to more broken terrain as we approached the coast. The desert floor was now scored in herringbone patterns by a series of deep wadis; dried-up watercourses which had not seen rain for years. Amazingly, in spite of the interminable drought, we could see tiny patches of greenery in the bends of wadis, witnesses to past rainstorms and flash floods. In this parched area, plants would continue to grow for some years after the end of a rainy period.

After a long cruise descent we flew for a time at low level, exploring the deep wadis of the coastal plain towards Salalah, which lay 250 miles along the coast to the south-west. Eventually, when the heat in the cockpit became almost unbearable, we joined in close echelon formation and ran in towards our destination. Masirah itself was a desolate place; a rocky, sun-parched island without a scrap of greenery. The runway and huts of the RAF station occupied the northern tip of the island, and the only locals inhabited an oil-drum shanty town nearby. In the Officers' Mess hut some wag had put the label 'TV ROOM' on a door leading out of the bar. Many a drunken visitor had stepped through this door, to stumble on to the soft sand outside, the brilliant stars of the desert sky gently mocking above. The only entertainment to be had was drinking and playing bar billiards. There was also a 'golf course' laid out in the rocky hills behind the Mess, with small patches of oiled sand for 'tees' and 'browns'.

In November the whole squadron flew down to Masirah again. We spent a fabulous week in this remote outpost, carrying out live FAC exercises on a mountainous live-firing range just next to the airfield. We were firing HE rockets and cannon at an array of time-expired trucks, fuel bowsers and other vehicles hidden away in odd corners of the range. It was quite a challenge to find some of them, and tremendous fun smashing them up. We recorded the firings on the excellent G90 cine cameras, mounted in the nose. Once again I came close to death on one glorious calm morning, when I was running in over the sea for a strafe attack, having set course from the mainland. The tropical sea was mirror-calm in the early morning heat and it was very difficult to judge height as we flew towards the rising sun. I was too relaxed: I should have been flying higher. My wingman saw a trail in the water behind my aircraft – the jetwash from my engine. I was almost in the sea and I hadn't realized.

'SILVER LEAD PULL UP, PULL UP!'

Thanks Pal, and Rest in Peace. (This pilot was killed in a mid-air collision in a Harrier just five years later.) I took one of the Army forward air controllers for a trip in our T7 and, in return, was given a flight in an Army Sioux helicopter. The sergeant pilot took me on an ultra-low level recce around the island and we found a huge dead whale festering in the sun on a remote beach. I asked him to land nearby so we could have a closer look but, on approaching ground level, the smell of rotting flesh was so powerful that we climbed away again. Later on the pilot revealed suicidal tendencies as he beat up a Land Rover on the way home. I have never been so low in an aircraft before, and can distinctly recall looking up at the driver of the Land Rover as we passed by at high speed. In future I declined offers of trips with Army pilots – if I was going to die in an aircraft then I wanted to be in control.

At the end of the year we enjoyed a superb Christmas and New Year at Muharraq; most of the bachelors having no UK leave. There was a traditional billet bar competition, in which all the various units of Muharraq rebuilt their accommodation as some kind of bar. 208 Squadron ground crew won the competition for the second year running, turning their hut into the stern of a magnificent galleon, HMS *Vigilant*, *Vigilant* being the squadron motto on a sphinx badge. We spent most of the week in and out of this bar, which was staffed in relays for twenty-four hours, just like all the rest of the bars. The supply of beer was unending. There was a very free and easy relationship with 'other ranks' at Muharraq, partly due to the distance from UK. The kind of officer/other rank separation – so prevalent in the UK – was minimal. We got the job done, respected each other and enjoyed ourselves, and that was that.

In the New Year we heard details of the timetable for pullout from Bahrain. Straight away our splendid Hunter Wing commander ordered that 8 and 208 Squadrons should amalgamate their flying programmes to produce more big-formation flying. He was a real gent of the old school, with the manners and charm of another age. This change of emphasis generated many improvements in an already excellent flying programme.

For the rest of our time in Bahrain we could always guarantee enough aircraft to launch eight-ship attack formations, often with a four-ship bounce, leading to the most almighty fun punch-ups in flight. Although some formations were exclusively of one squadron or another, more often we mixed personnel and learned a lot from each others' tactics. We also launched some extremely punchy dusk strike missions and even some bounced dusk strikes. In this we were merely carrying on the RAF's distinguished tradition of low level night attack, carried over from the Second World War when Spitfires and Typhoons on 'rhubarbs' (ground attack missions), would cruise over enemy territory at night, often in poor weather, looking for likely targets. Like us, pilots in those days had no night visual aids to help them out, relying solely on their own night vision to achieve success.

For a dusk strike the idea was to study the almanac to discover the precise time of sunset over the target, which could be some 300 miles east in the mountains of Oman. Take-off time would be planned to get the formation to the target at last light when, hopefully, there would be just enough light to see it but not enough for the enemy to see you. Unfortunately, things didn't often work out that well. Sometimes we would arrive in bright daylight – no problem. At other times the light would be fading fast as we ran in for the target with all our navigation lights off. On occasions there would be pandemonium during the attack:

'GOLD LEAD IN, NOT VISUAL' (Gold Lead has started his attack but can't see the target)

'GOLD 2 IN, NO TALLY ON LEAD' (It's so dark he can't even see the leader)

'GOLD 3 IN – JESUS CHRIST! – I CAN'T SEE ANYTHING!'

'GOLD 4'S LOST EVERYBODY – THIS IS BLOODY DANGEROUS!'

'GOLD LEAD'S OFF, MISS: OK, EVERYONE PUT YOUR LIGHTS ON'

'THANK CHRIST FOR THAT!'

My first bounce of a dusk attack was in a similar vein. I was leading, with a recce pilot of the other Hunter squadron as my wingman. I knew it would be impossible to pick up the formation from above. During daylight bounces you could always guarantee a nice black shadow from aircraft on the desert below. Hence we had to attack from their height, i.e. as low as we could fly in the dusk conditions. At 30,000 feet we cruised effortlessly away from the glory of the sunset over Bahrain, the powerful backlight burnishing golden highlights off our aircraft as we overflew the tapestry of Gulf offshore oil installations. In the misty grey below, they formed an endless torchlight procession, a series of gigantic braziers burning in the sea. The transition from sea to desert was marked by an abrupt cessation of the gas flares, just the faintest hint of cream showing that there was desert below us now. From ingrained habit we cruised just below contrails. We weren't expecting to be attacked but we always felt uneasy when 'trailing'; your position given away to any hostile aircraft within 100 miles. We knew the initial part of their low-level route followed the famous oil pipeline which ran for scores of miles inland from Jebel Dhana. We started the long, slow letdown into the gathering darkness below, our engines idling to conserve fuel and leave the maximum amount for the low-level fighting to come.

At 20,000 feet the glorious hues of the sunset switched off abruptly, leaving us in an uncomfortable horizon-less goldfish bowl which darkened rapidly the lower we sank. I eased the rate of descent as the altimeter passed 2,000 feet. The desert floor was indistinct and could have been 2,000 or just 200 feet below. After a couple of minutes of uncomfortable flying, half on instruments, half visually, my eyes became accustomed to the poor light and we settled into low level battle formation, to pick up the far eastern end of the pipeline as planned. Just before we set off I heard a faint radio call on UHF, indicating that the target formation was descending over Jebel Dhana, some seventy miles away to the north-west. There had been silence on the frequency for half an hour or more; once again I felt the animal surge of adrenalin and excitement in anticipation of the action to come. We then set course north-west, one on each side of the pipeline, knowing we would be bound to meet them head-on eventually. (I was hoping that they would pass between us.) Conditions were atrocious for low level, the treacherous sand dunes fading into a nebulous dark horizon, almost as if we were flying in mist. After about five minutes of mounting tension I passed two completely blacked-out Hunters, head-on and far too close for comfort. With a brief radio call to my wingman I racked it round at maximum rate to get the opposite pair. They joined the turning match in the rapidly-fading light, but as fast as it started, all the blacked-out aircraft disappeared into the gloom as if by magic, leaving me alone at low level, racing down the pipeline at maximum speed in pursuit. After a few minutes of seeing nothing I realized that it was too dark for anything else and reluctantly pulled up into a climb, turning steeply through nearly 180 degrees to head home. I had been talking to my wingman on the radio all the way: now I told him to put his lights on, in the hope that he was not too far away. By now I was passing 10,000 feet and the gas flares of the Gulf islands were beginning to reappear in the haze far to the north, like far-off bush fires. Just on my starboard side, barely a mile away, I picked up a flashing red light – Al's aircraft. By chance we had ended up in the same piece of sky.

We were back at Sharjah for yet another APC when the news arrived of a mid-air smash by the Red Arrows during one of their practice sessions. Four of their pilots had died. This made a big hole in the team and they were looking for immediate replacements. The boss called me into his office for a chat.

'The Red Arrows have lost four guys in one smash Jerry: they're in big trouble and they need people experienced at formation aerobatics straight away. You're one of the guys they're interested in. Do you want to volunteer?'

'No Sir, I'd like to stay on 208 if you don't mind'

'OK, that's it then. I'll tell them you're not interested.'

'Thanks Boss'.

One day on the gunnery range I severely embarrassed myself by doing something really stupid. In the prevailing onshore winds my windscreen had become encrusted with salt and I was having difficulty seeing the targets. With a flash of inspiration I decided I would be able to clear it off by hand. (There was no windscreen wash facility on the Hunter.) I pulled up from downwind into a stall turn and selected canopy open as the speed fell below 180 knots. With airspeed dropping below 100 knots in the manoeuvre I foolishly attempted to stick my hand out into the airflow to wipe the windscreen. Not surprisingly the powerful blast of air smacked my arm back violently against the canopy rim, nearly breaking my wrist. The stupid things some people do in the air.

Back at Bahrain I took delivery of a duty free Honda SS125 twin motorcycle; a marvellous little machine which was ideal for buzzing round the island. I booked in for a motorcycle test, waiting for hours in the stifling council offices to fill in the appropriate paperwork. The Arab civil servants gave no concessions to service personnel; if you had no favourable connections with the Sheik then you just had to wait your turn with all the other locals. Eventually I reported to the offices for my motorcycle test. I was met by an Arab policeman, resplendent in traditional white AA-style motorcycling gear, right down to the brown leather helmet, jodhpurs and puttees. He looked as cool as a cucumber in the heat. He briefed me on the route for the test and followed me closely on his immaculate Triumph 500 all over Manama, including a couple of runs through the crowded souk, presumably to see if I could get through without mowing down too many people. I passed, and could now legally take passengers on launches downtown.

In the spring I was detached on board a US Navy destroyer, the *William C. Lawe*, for a few days as an RAF observer of a major sea-air joint exercise. A pilot of our sister Hunter squadron was on the sister ship, the *McCaffery*. This was my first time on board an American ship, and we operated in company with Royal Navy ships, plus several other US destroyers. I was fascinated by the way a surface task force was organized, the American admiral controlling all operations from his gigantic 'fighting chair' on the bridge. It was hilarious to watch them manoeuvre as a formation: they used the most cumbersome and unwieldy method to pass on orders. Basically the admiral would call a manoeuvre, a 90 degree turn to port, for example; a signaller would then scrabble through a gigantic code book to find out the correct code word which would then be passed over the ship-to-ship radio link. After allowing the other ships a few seconds to decipher the code in their own code books, the signal officer would call the code word again, followed by the word 'Execute', which meant they actually had to carry out the manoeuvre. Naturally enough there were constant balls-ups as people got the codes wrong, or simply couldn't find the right page in the book. I couldn't see why they didn't just call the manoeuvre in plain language, in real time – as we did in the air. There were a host of traditional Naval-type exercises carried out. Anti-submarine patrols, boarding parties and day and night firing exercises using the 5-inch calibre guns. The concussion from these was extremely uncomfortable, but by now I had completely lost my earlier gun-shyness and – foolish bravado – stood leaning over the bridge while the forward guns banged away just a few feet away. My ears rang for months afterwards. I enjoyed the high-speed dashes most of all; there was no more impressive sight than to stand on the fantail (the back end of the boat) as we cruised at full speed, a sheer wall of water as high as a house towering up behind us as the deck pounded violently with the thrashing of the screws. In the engine room I couldn't believe the temperature in which men had to work. The duty watch stood sweating under a 'cold' air pipe which blasted air in from the deck above. Stepping out from under the pipe was like entering a furnace.

Occasionally we cruised downwind and then life became purgatory as we lost the cooling breeze of the Gulf waters, the entire ship's company sweating and listless in the stifling heat. I remembered Dad's stories of his time as an ordinary sailor on the sloop HMS *Penzance* on a two-year cruise in the Gulf in 1932-33. The ship had no air conditioning at all, and a couple of crew members died of the heat. The sloop captain was always telling the crew that he had been to the Gulf before and, in his words, 'If I can stick it, you can stick it'. The sweating crew were less than impressed to see him sleeping on his bunk each night with an overhead fan and a large block of ice below.

The main aim of my visit was to observe the coordinated attack of a large Hunter formation from Muharraq. The ship was bristling with modern radar, but they still managed to screw up their defence against the attack. I watched the radar screens as they plotted the first signs of air activity, a brief appearance of a fast-moving target far away to the north. I guessed this was only a feint attack, to concentrate their attention in the wrong direction. The air warfare officer fell for it and concentrated his attention on the northern sector as a target manoeuvred just outside missile range. (The ship was armed with up-to-date SAMs.) Very late – too late – someone in the plotting room spotted a large array of blips approaching at tremendous speed which just popped up out of nowhere to the south of us. I found out that our guys had been flying right on the water, to remain undetected for as long as possible. I scooted out on deck to watch the denouement as, by now, the ship's officers were shouting order and counter-order and rushing about like chickens with their heads cut off. Spread across the southern horizon I saw a series of tiny blips of condensation[9] approaching like enraged hornets at wave-top level. All guns and missile launchers were still pointing north, at the threat which had failed to materialize. A hapless lieutenant was supposed to be directing air defence operations from the bridge, and he hadn't a clue what was going on. Unable to contain his rage in front of the admiral, the ship's executive officer grasped the lieutenant's shoulder and forcibly swivelled him round to witness the awesome sight of eight Hunters converging on us at 600 knots, the deck shivering under the explosive crackle of their engines as they flashed overhead one after another. Too late, the exec grabbed the microphone and started shouting fire orders to the various weapon stations as a demonstration of what the lieutenant should have been doing several minutes ago. 'Gee Jerry, we sure got our ass kicked!' was all the admiral said to me as our Hunters disappeared over the horizon, to re-appear some minutes later in an immaculate close formation flypast, a piece of showmanship to demonstrate who was boss.

This pantomime showed me that surface ships without effective airborne radar cover were still vulnerable to conventional air attack, even when they were armed with the latest radars and SAMs. This was not current RAF doctrine: there was an overwhelming official belief that our kind of conventional aircraft attack would be suicidal against modern warships. Our experience was different. I took part in many air attacks on shipping and time after time we were able to achieve surprise and a successful attack, in spite of Naval claims to have shot us down with their missile systems. Unfortunately, the only real proof of the success or otherwise of a missile was to fire it against a realistic, i.e. really low and fast flying, target. Later, I discovered that most British missile firing trials (Rapier, for example) were carried out against non-manoeuvring targets flying at a comfortable height. In contrast to simulated SAM firings, we could see the immediate effect of our conventional weapons fired live against realistic targets on our many operational readiness exercises.

In July our wing commander asked me to lead a UK ferry, taking two time-expired FGA9s back to the UK. My number 2 was to be Ron Elder of 8 Squadron. UK ferries were a popular 'jolly', the main aim being to have a good time on the way home without rushing things. This was a result of the wing commander's splendid attitude towards ferrying: as an old hand he knew the pitfalls that lay in wait for pilots trying to get home in a hurry with worn-out aircraft. His standard brief to ferry pilots was: 'If you wake up with a hangover en route, don't push it! Take another day off to recover.'

There were problems involved in getting out of Bahrain and heading for UK. Because of a political dispute Iran would not accept any flight plans originating in Bahrain. As a result, our UK ferries were expected to pre-position at Sharjah before setting off. To bypass this problem we got RAF Sharjah to file the flight plan for us. After take-off we headed east for a while then turned north to enter Iranian airspace, claiming we had taken off from Sharjah. First leg was direct Muharraq-Tehran, over-flying Shiraz and Isfahan. Southern Iran was Moon country, the Zagros mountains forming gigantic razor-sharp ridgelines above 8,000 feet which extended for hundreds of miles to the north-west. Iranian airspace was Indian territory, the air traffic controllers having little idea of what was going on. Tehran International was a classic example, and we had to make our own arrangements for landing safely. We remained on the ground for the minimum time possible, just refuelling and getting out of there sharpish before the authorities had time to find something to complain about. On ferries we had an elaborate start-up ritual to follow, to get both aircraft running successfully. One pilot would take the standard start-up kit of an asbestos glove and a hammer[10] and start up the first aircraft with the other pilot in the cockpit. Then came the tricky bit. The pilot in the cockpit had to get out and start up the second aircraft, leaving his own engine running in an unmanned aircraft (strictly against RAF regulations, but the only way we could do it: we couldn't risk having untrained ground crew cock it up).

At 5,000 feet above sea level the take-off from Tehran International was distinctly sluggish in our clapped-out aircraft. The weather was crystal-clear as we climbed slowly into a brilliant vault of blue sky, the darker blue of the Caspian sea slowly materializing over the jagged peaks of the Elburz mountains in the north. We had over a thousand miles of inhospitable terrain to cover before our next destination, RAF Akrotiri in Cyprus. This was just about the limit of our range with four under-wing tanks on the aircraft. There were precious few diversion airfields in this part of the world. After the huge expanse of Lake Urmia we were over eastern Turkey, with ever-higher mountain ranges unfolding endlessly before us as I tuned in the evocatively titled radio beacons of Van, Batman, Dyarbakir and Tatvan. Fortunately there was little cloud and I was able to map read on a 1 million scale topographic map for most of the route. As expected, towards the end of the route we were running short of fuel and had to take a few short cuts despite protests from ATC.

The next day we flew on up the Med to RAF Luqa in Malta, to spend a pleasant couple of days looking around while some minor snags were fixed on our aircraft. We finished the ferry uneventfully, completing the last leg to Kemble after a refuelling stop at Istres in southern France. I had been expecting more problems en route and was mildly surprised that we had made it so easily. Most of our returned aircraft were found to have some sand-related engine damage after deep strip examination: however, the engines usually kept running, sometimes with many of the compressor blades missing or damaged. The Avon 201 was a good engine. Some previous ferries had taken over a month to reach UK, with engine changes and God knows what U/S en route. After a couple of days off at home, I got back to Bahrain as quickly as possible, in order not to miss out on the splendid flying that was going on.

The integration of the Wing was going well: we had been refreshing the 8 Squadron recce pilots on formation ground attack and combat tactics, while a selected few of us were given some fighter recce training. It sounded interesting to me so I volunteered for it. At the end of August I was lucky to be selected for the mini fighter recce course during which I was authorized to fly at an eye-watering fifty feet above ground. The old hands told me, 'Fifty feet flying is dead easy – you just try to fly as low as you possibly can and after a couple of days you'll be down around the right height!'

They were right, but it never felt easy. Flying that low at seven miles per minute (700 feet per second) puts a lot of pressure on the pilot. Time available for map reading was minimal, and all cockpit tasks had to be done instinctively, with the absolute minimum of time spent looking in. Every second with your head in the office was another moment closer to eternity, you and your machine smeared across the landscape in an obscene orange streak of burning fuel and disintegrating wreckage. The proximity of sudden death concentrated the mind wonderfully: even so there was no opportunity to look around and cover other members of a formation, (most FR flying was as a singleton anyway) – the phenomenon of 'tunnel vision' was well-known while under pressure. Like a computer close to overload, the brain was unable to take on the simplest extra task: calculating how long your fuel was going to last became almost impossible. I felt really at home in the Hunter FR10. The gunsight was offset to one side, leaving an almost unobstructed forward view through the optically-perfect flat of the armoured windscreen. The extremely accurate G4 compass was mounted high in the cockpit, just below the pilot's sightline, enabling precision course-keeping at all times. The ergonomics of the Hunter FR10 were perfect for ultra-low level flying. (This was in stark contrast to more modern British ground attack aircraft where the pilot's forward view was interrupted by a head up display (HUD), After a few days practice I was doing OK at the low flying bit. My 'chase' pilot asked me casually during one debrief:

'Uh, Jerry; how low do you think you were over those rocks in the mountains today?' (He had been following close behind to check up on me.)

'Uh, about twenty feet or so – is that OK?' (I didn't want him to think I was trying to push it.)

'Yeah, that's fine – just as long as you know how low you are.'

The recce part was hard work. First of all your low level navigation had to be right on the ball. The best recce pilots had a genuine photographic memory, able to record and remember the details of the target during the few seconds you flashed past it. We had good cameras and I soon got the hang of getting satisfactory target pictures, but that was the relatively easy bit – most ground attack pilots could do that with a bit of practice. The real recce honours went to the aces who could remember accurately the details of every target. That aspect had nothing to do with flying ability – it was a mental trick, like those people who could remember the sequence of an entire deck of cards. You either had it or you hadn't.

As the training went on I got better and the 'chase' pilots immediately stepped up the pressure, giving in-flight targets which you had to plot on your map during the sortie, while still flying and navigating at fifty feet. When things looked too relaxed the chase would tell you, 'Push it up to 480', i.e. push up your speed to 480 knots. This immediately increased the pressure, tempting you to fly higher – which was not allowed. The course was tremendous fun and I enjoyed the tactical freedom and independence of singleton operation, although I still preferred the cut-and-thrust of big formation operations.

By the end of September '71 my all-too-brief tour in Bahrain was over. Although I had left it a bit late I was determined to get my Honda back to the UK. I fixed up with a colleague, who was now a Hercules captain, to load it aboard a Herc when he came through Bahrain next time round. By then I would already be in the UK and I promised to meet him at Lyneham to collect it off the aircraft and avoid any embarrassment with customs. We put away the squadron standard at an emotional disbandment ceremony at which I was the standard bearer. I had already heard that I was to get my first choice of posting again, to the new Harrier OCU at RAF Wittering. I was nominated for the last UK ferry of 208 Squadron, to be led by the new boss. The third pilot was a fiercely keen and talented young New Zealander who had recently joined the squadron.[11]

We set off from Bahrain with the last three 208 Squadron Hunters. With us we had our clapped-out T7, and as passenger we carried a sergeant technician , hopefully to fix any en route snags. Ferrying with the T7 could be a bit tricky at the best of times. Its range was considerably less than that of the single-seaters, requiring a lot of extra stops en route. We made it to Teheran OK, and I was nominated to fly the T7 on the next leg to Dyarbakir in Turkey. The take-off from Teheran was very sluggish and distinctly unpleasant. At one stage I was convinced we weren't going to get airborne before the end of the runway. (The T7 was considerably underpowered compared with the FGA9). Diyarbakir was a remote and primitive Turkish Air Force base in the mountains of eastern Turkey. After the long trek from Bahrain we were already tired as we refuelled ready for departure to Cyprus: we had no intention of getting stuck there overnight. There were no snags and, with some relief, we got away, with me flying the T7 again on the boss's orders. The boss didn't offer any explanation at the time; later on I found out why he wouldn't let me fly his aircraft – he had got a flickering fuel low pressure light, a serious technical 'snag' which could mean that the engine was about to fail. Naturally, he wanted to take the risk himself and not pass it on to anyone else.

We made it to Akrotiri and abandoned the aircraft to the technicians to sort out while we motored north to Kyrenia in a hired car, to spend an idyllic few days in a holiday cottage borrowed from an acquaintance of the boss. This was before the tiresome invasion by the Turks, and Kyrenia harbour was a visitor's paradise with few tourists, awash with Turkish and Greek character.

On return to Akrotiri for some light entertainment we arranged a low level air combat sortie with some 5 Squadron Lightnings whose boss we had met in the bar. This was my first true dissimilar combat mission and I was impressed to see the big fighters running in supersonic behind us, the back of the aircraft enveloped in a cloud of condensation marking out the position of the base shock.[12] This made them rather easy to pick up at low level over the sea. As expected, they made initial kill claims with their Red Top missiles, which we took with a pinch of salt in the debrief. We reckoned we had sorted them out with guns when they foolishly slowed down to mix it with us in close air combat. The next day we flew on to Souda Bay in Crete where we were sent on our way by surly, uncooperative Greek Air Force technicians. This was the Greece of the infamous 'Colonels' Regime', and we got out of there pretty smartly. The next desirable stop was at Capodicino, Naples. We were hosted in fine style by a US Navy communications pilot we knew well from his regular trips to Bahrain, ferrying admirals to and from NATO HQ.

Nursing severe Valpolicella hangovers we pressed on to Istres after a night in Naples, landing in France in a torrential rainstorm on minimum fuel. I carried out my first-ever true formation landing on the wing of the ever-reliable boss, who was in the T7, (equipped with windscreen wipers). Being unable to see anything forward from the single-seaters, as wingmen we just hung on in close formation until we hit the runway. After our weary arrival at Kemble I spent a few days in Dawlish (Mum and Dad had moved back there the previous year), and then headed for Wittering in the green MG Midget I had bought from my brother. In just over eighteen months I had flown

420 hours on the Hunter, and it had been action-packed stuff. There had been no accidents on the Desert Hunter Wing in that time. From what I had heard of the Harrier, the flying was going to be even more interesting. Since I had seen my first RAF GR1 Harrier at Leeming a couple of years previously there had been a lot of accidents, several of them fatal. The VSTOL handling aspect of the aircraft was causing a lot of problems – even for the high calibre of pilots recruited to fly the beast. Up to now all of them had been experienced ex-Hunter men, with just one or two ex-helicopter pilots, as an experiment. Only now were they starting to take the cream of the first tourists from Valley. After an exciting eighteen months or so of operational Hunter flying, I felt well up to the challenge and this promised to be an interesting flying tour.

Notes
1. Dust Devils, or mini dust tornados were a common sight, a ghostly spiral of sand moving through the desert. We called them on the radio for lookout practice.
2. A Shag was an ordinary squadron pilot, not a 'wheel'.
3. A Gharry was a squadron vehicle for use by pilots.
4. Ersatz Napalm could be made up quite easily by any competent armourer, to be delivered in spare fuel tanks. However, we did not practise live drops. This was unfortunate, as Napalm was an extremely useful weapon against troops and armour, being cheap and easy to drop accurately.
5. The Pipper was a spot of light used as the aiming point for the guns and rockets. Its position in the gunsight was gyroscopically controlled to allow for gravity drop and crossing speed of your target. There was also a 'fixed cross' index, harmonized to the exact point where the guns pointed on the ground. In manoeuvring combat the pipper and fixed cross rarely coincided. At the same time as aiming with the pipper, the pilot had to use the throttle-mounted twist grip to match the ranging reticles to the exact wingspan of the target. Without radar ranging this was essential for accurate shooting.
6. There was a lot of skill in judging when to escape from an opponent you didn't want to fight with. If you screwed it up he would be hard behind you and would shoot you down as you ran. The trick was to disengage when your oppo was committed nose-high and you were head on and accelerating nose-down. You could then make plenty of distance on him before he could get round

behind you. This tactic was even more risky against a missile-armed fighter.

7. Pickling meant pressing the bomb release button on the stick top. This had to be done very precisely: an error of half a second would throw the bomb hundreds of feet away from the target.

8. Broadcast Control was a Cold War air defence radar procedure for use in heavy voice jamming. In this way many fighters could receive instructions at once.

9. At high airspeed (550-600 knots) in humid conditions, a jet generates a ball of steam around it as the local air pressure drops suddenly and precipitates water vapour.

10. The Avon 200 series was started by an Avpin-fuelled starter turbine, Avpin being an explosive fluid rather like rocket fuel. There was only enough Avpin for three starts, and only RAF stations kept the wretched stuff, so you had to get it right first time. The glove was used to extinguish any residual fuselage fire after the starter had operated; the hammer was available to beat some sense into the starter relay box in the event of an all-too-common misfire. It was not unheard of for the whole aircraft to blow up during an unsuccessful start attempt, because of Avpin leakage into the fuselage.

11. Sadly, this pilot did not survive for long. After his time on 208 he went on loan service, flying Hunters with the Sultan of Oman's Air Force. He died in a silly accident, running off the runway with brake failure.

12. When a jet goes supersonic various shockwaves form around it. The base shock is the biggest and is usually located around the wing root.

Chapter 10

Harrier Student

RAF Wittering, the home of the Harrier, lay just a couple of miles south of the beautiful and ancient stone-built town of Stamford. The Harrier – which was still suffering serious teething troubles – was by far the RAF's most exciting and demanding new single-seat aircraft for decades, and I felt honoured to be selected for the course.

On arrival at 233 OCU I introduced myself to the flight commander, a hunched, thin-faced flight lieutenant. With his steel-framed specs he had more the look of a world-weary schoolmaster than a fighter pilot instructing on the RAF's most demanding new aircraft. He appeared permanently grumpy and deployed a biting sarcasm which cut like a knife. Soon I discovered that he was immensely popular, an absolute ace pilot and instructor, who was an old Hunter fighter recce hand. During the course he would keep us in fits with his endless fund of lewd jokes and hilarious flying anecdotes. The flight commander told me straight away that my course didn't start until mid-December, that there was an acute shortage of two-seaters, and the prospect of gash flying was non-existent. If I really wanted a job then I could hang around and he would find me one. If I didn't – then I knew my course starting date. I took the hint. Without filling in a leave pass or even carrying out station arrival procedure I departed hot foot for the West Country for a couple of months of 'gardening leave'. I took golf lessons from the old Scottish professional at the Teignmouth golf club and joined the Exeter Golf & Country Club, then situated near the Countess Wear roundabout. Here I played for their squash team and enjoyed golf on their 9-hole course. I lived the life of Reilly for a couple of months, having made a bit of money in Bahrain. After a couple of weeks at home there was sad news. An RAF Hercules had flown into the sea off of Italy on a night paratroop training mission, killing all on board. A few days later I read the name of the captain – it was my old Cranwell colleague

Feeling refreshed after my two months' gash leave, I reported to RAF Ternhill for the pre-Harrier helicopter course, to be flown on the Whirlwind 10, the RAF's standard advanced helicopter trainer. Some thoughtful genius had realized that fighter pilots needed some experience of hovering to prepare them for the totally unnatural experience of hovering the Harrier. The course was brilliant. After no more than forty-five minutes of briefing on how a helicopter 'helicoptered' (omitting all the boring technical bits), I was issued with a rather jaundiced-looking helicopter QFI and sent out to the flight line. The QFI did all the tedious bits and cranked up the machine. After moving a discreet distance away from the parking area, he demonstrated hovering for a brief period and then handed over control to me. Hovering was great sport, and not too difficult once you had learned to coordinate rudder with changes in collective pitch control. The Whirlwind seemed super-sensitive on the controls, and you had to be really relaxed to get good results. All of us progressed rapidly through take-offs, landings, transitions to forward flight and autorotation (engine-off landings). The final sortie included low flying, sloping ground landings and, most difficult of all, landings and take-offs in small clearings. The clearings were in woodland surrounded by tall trees, with barely enough space to take the rotor disc. After my helicopter flying practice with an old friend at Valley I got on reasonably well, but none of us had any particular problems. After barely six hours of helicopter flying we were doing what the helicopter students on the formal course did after almost fifty hours' flying instruction. This was because we could concentrate entirely on the techniques of helicoptering without having our brains cluttered with all the extraneous dross of aircraft technical knowledge, hovering aerodynamics and emergency procedures. The course worked so well and the Ternhill staff were so impressed with the speed at which we picked up the techniques that they soon started an experiment whereby their own students learned to fly in the same manner, with no formal technical ground school. This was also a great success.

Back at Wittering, No. 5 Harrier course got on famously together and played a lot of golf. We were all more or less fanatical golfers at this stage. As the 'new boys' we were immediately regaled with tales of Harrier derring-do by the senior course. The Harrier ground school lasted just one week, all lectures being given by the excellent bunch of QFIs of B Squadron. I flew my first Harrier duals at the end of December. First impressions of the cockpit were that it was very cramped and extremely noisy. The big Pegasus turbofan rotated just a couple of feet behind the pilot's head, always sounding to me as if the bearings were about to break up, sending a permanent, low-frequency vibration through the back of the ejection seat. The fan itself gave out a piercing, rusty-bacon slicer whine, which you could use to judge engine revolutions fairly accurately. Straight away I missed the smooth, civilized hiss of the Avon, unobtrusive yet powerful. But this engine was in another class, pushing out an astonishing ten tons of thrust – double the power of the Avon – in a lighter airframe. More significantly, the engine acceleration time from fast idle to maximum power was just three seconds; an explosive performance which literally hurled you into the air before you could take a breath. This scorching engine performance made for unbelievably snappy acceleration on the runway, even in the heavyweight two-seater. On a lightweight short strip take-off you would slam from zero to 150 knots in about five seconds, with over one g longitudinal acceleration. This was outside all of our experience, and we soon learned to treat the engine and nozzle controls with the utmost respect. We listened to the briefings on VSTOL techniques, with wholehearted attention: failure to get the message first time would usually lead to disaster – the evidence available for all to see in the severely-bent Harriers being repaired in the hangar downstairs. Engine and nozzle handling drills for the various VSTOL exercises were hammered into us like parade-ground drills, with the constant reminder that: 'Thrust is where you point it!'.

By means of the nozzles the ten tons of jet thrust could be swivelled from fully aft to forward of the hover position (the braking stop) in just over one second. This dramatic change of force vector would have a violent effect on the aircraft, and you had to know exactly what you were going to do once you put your hand on the nozzle lever.

Bad weather interrupted training for over a week at the beginning of January and we were given an extra dual before our first solos, which consisted solely of hovering. The two-seater was very new to the RAF and, not long previously, courses had trained without dual sorties. There had been a lot of accidents. Just a couple of months previously, a United States Marine Corps student had suffered a technical failure of the nozzle drive system, allowing the nozzles to run away to the hover position after take-off. Sadly, he did not survive.

All solo exercises were filmed with a 16mm cine camera, in case of crashes and handling screw-ups, of which there were many. Things happened so fast in the beast that the only way to find out exactly what had gone wrong was to run the film in slow motion. A typical example was the infamous 'roll on vertical take-off' which was still catching out pilots during a vertical take-off. Basically these early Harriers were totally unstable in roll just after lift-off. If the wing dropped then you had less than a second to take violent corrective action. Failing this you would crash on one wing, severely damaging the aircraft. If you persisted with the take-off you would crash upside down.

After our initial hovering solos we were shown how to do conventional landings, with a touchdown speed of over 160 knots. This, if anything, was more difficult than the VSTOL work. The Harrier was definitely short of wing area and its turning performance was mediocre in comparison with the Hunter. It was also uncomfortable and unstable to fly at low level. It yugged about and whistled and whined as if it was about to fall apart when pulling g. Most ex-Hunter pilots thought that it felt a bit like a fairground machine to fly. However, we got used to it.

During the twenty-one sorties of the convex phase we learned every aspect of handling the Harrier: Vertical landings and take-offs in small clearings and on tiny Mexe pads, short strip take-offs and rolling vertical landings, accelerating and decelerating transitions, mini-circuits, grass operations etc. All solos were supervised by the duty Harrier instructor, call-sign Pegasus, who sat close by in a Land Rover in direct communication with the pilot by radio. The calm, measured voice of Pegasus was always there to give us confidence, debrief errors in technique and give advice on handling in the air.

A smooth touch on the controls was absolutely essential in all Harrier VSTOL flying, as any stick-stirring bled off too much reaction control air, thus reducing the lifting capacity of the engine. I have never before or since felt so 'stretched' by a new aircraft type and the constant impression was that you were just barely in control of the jet, and that if you relaxed for just a moment then it was going to bite you – hard. This was more or less correct, and those who couldn't keep up the concentration soon bit the dust, either literally crashing and damaging the aircraft or voluntarily withdrawing from training because of the constant pressure. Sadly, this happened to one

member of our course, who confided that he was having the most
appalling nightmares and couldn't sleep because of the constant
tension. His helicopter experience hadn't prepared him for the
pressures of single-seat FGA flying, for that was all the Harrier was
– a vertical take-off Hunter. As soon as we had cracked the convex
phase then we were into all the normal ground attack training: Air
combat, low-level navigation and attack, air combat and weapons
firing. The Harrier's head up display (HUD) at this time was
appalling. The green symbols danced and jiggled constantly with
every change of attitude and engine rpm. This was a first-generation
HUD, and it was barely useable for instrument flying. It was constantly giving erroneous information and often failed completely in
flight. Worse still, the large HUD reflector glass almost completely
obscured forward view, particularly in bad weather. Problems with
the INAS meant that quite a few single-seaters had no INAS (Inertial
Navigation and Attack System) at all. In these aircraft (designated
GR1 Mod 9s), the HUD showed only airspeed and height, with an
adjustable weapon-aiming reticule in the middle. The latter was
adjusted by means of a setting wheel in the cockpit. The only navigation aid was a basic C2G compass, which swung wildly with every
change of bank angle. In an obscure corner of the cockpit was a
TACAN indicator, not heading-resolved. The moving map display
was replaced by a 1940s-vintage turn and slip indicator. Basically,
the Harrier was not particularly easy to fly on instruments, seeming
unstable and over-sensitive on the controls. There were many other
technical problems with the aircraft, which seemed to us to be an
over-complicated box of tricks. There was considerable tension
between pilots and engineers at this time, with the pilots frustrated
at constant technical problems and the engineers at their wits' end
trying to sort things out.

During the convex phase we had been constantly warned about the
dangers of intake momentum drag, a unique characteristic of the
Harrier which made the aircraft dangerously unstable in the speed
range 30-90 knots. Whenever the pilot accelerated or decelerated
through this speed range he had to use rudder to make sure the
aircraft was pointing directly into the airflow, taking care to
eliminate any sideslip as soon as it started. To help him there was a
sideslip indicator in the HUD and, more useful, a tiny weather vane
mounted on the nose, right in front of the windscreen. Intake
momentum drag was caused by the tremendous 'suck' of the huge
engine intakes, which drew in a ton of air per second at maximum

power (a hangar full of air per second). As soon as the aircraft developed any sideslip, a lateral component of the intake 'suck' would tend to pull the nose of the aircraft further away from the relative airflow. This exaggerated sideslip would cause a powerful rolling force which would be out of control in less than a second, the power of the roll reaction controls being insufficient to counter the roll. The result of lack of attention to sideslip control would be that the aircraft would roll over in a flash, the pilot unable to use the ejection seat because the powerful rocket motor would merely drive him and the seat into the ground. At the end of the convex phase all students watched the Harrier 'horror film', a compilation of film clips showing the more disastrous VSTOL accidents. The last clip, in lurid Technicolor, showed an American student suffering an out-of-control roll after a too-punchy accelerating transition from a vertical take-off. Just before impact the pilot ejects – too late to save himself. The film was entirely successful in eliminating the over-confidence we felt on completing the convex phase.

Range work was carried out on the excellent Holbeach range in the Wash. Unfortunately we had a very poor system for weapon aiming. By now it was supposed to give us wind and speed-resolved aiming solutions for bombs, rockets and guns. At this time the system could not do any of these things properly, the big floppy aiming bug positioning itself at random in the sight glass, to deliver weapons anywhere but on the target. Because of this we had to use suitable bits of the various HUD test pictures to achieve any worthwhile results on the range. For bombing we used the bottom of the Test 2 picture, for SNEB we aimed roughly with the target between the legs of the break cross in the Test 2 picture, and for strafe we had to use a bit of the Test 1 picture. These test displays, (intended only for a pre-flight checkout of the HUD on the ground), could only be selected ON by holding your finger on a tiny button on the left coaming. The Harrier GR1 also had a tiresome design fault with the throttle, meaning that the engine would go to idle when you pulled out of the attack – just when you needed full power. This meant that – apart from the difficulties of aiming – you had to juggle between the HUD test buttons and the throttle during an attack. There was some disillusionment with progress with the aircraft and we students were amazed to be briefed on the unofficial 'Gibbs SR Modification'. In order to avoid having to hold the HUD test buttons during range work, some pilots had discovered that the cap on the smallest Gibbs SR toothpaste tube exactly fitted the screw threads around the test buttons. The pilot would screw on the cap at the start of a range detail, leaving the test picture displayed permanently throughout the weapon firing exercise. Naturally, this meant that the HUD – inadequate though it was – was unavailable for use as an instrument flying reference in the rest of the range pattern.

The Harrier's development test flying, particularly of the weapon system, had so far produced less than optimum results. An example was the development of the Harrier's air-to-air gunsight. Initially it had been recommended to the manufacturers that the ranging aspect of the sight must be a duplication of the six-diamond stadiametric ranging ring of the old Mk 8 gyro gunsight found on the Hunter. The only reason the Hunter had this inconvenient arrangement of six separate diamonds in a circle was because of the limitations of the 1940's technology mechanical-optical construction. The HUD was an entirely electronically-generated image, and by far the simplest option would have been to have a ranging ring of an unbroken circle, which was also by far the easiest display for the pilot to use. It took ages for the firm to make the HUD mimic the old Mk 8 Gyro gunsight, and we ended up with a sight that was difficult to use in air combat. Yet another example was the SNEB full pod firing trial. After many months of work by the manufacturer on the sighting arrangements the squadrons were cleared to fire full pods also. Immediately, squadron pilots complained about the huge nose-down pitch which occurred on firing, which cause the rockets to impact well short. The test pilots (who had approved the system) were asked whether they had noticed this and, if so, why hadn't they reported it? The rather inadequate answer came back: 'We didn't think it would effect your firing.'

As a direct result the newly-developed INAS rocket aiming pictures were found to be more or less useless for full-pod, i.e. operational firing, and yet more expensive modifications were necessary.

This saga was just one of many examples of the difficulties experienced during development flying on the Harrier GR1, which led to many problems for its operators in its early years.

With these disappointments going on in the background, we students adopted an attitude of: 'Who cares – let's just enjoy what we've got and get on with some golf if there's no flying available'. With aircraft constantly unserviceable this was often the case, and No. 5 course spent a lot of time on the various golf courses around Stamford. Apart from the inadequacies of the weapon system, the weapon phases were very enjoyable under the aegis of a good crew of QWIs (Qualified Weapon Instructors – the new name for PAIs). They were excellent value both on the ground and in the air.

Part of the advanced phase of the course was formal recce training for all students, making use of the inbuilt F95 recce camera in the nose. The Harrier GR1 was to be used for attack and recce, in theory giving equal prominence to both roles. Straight away the RAF came up against the inbuilt anti-recce prejudice of the 'Mud Moving' fraternity. Many of these guys – ex-Hunters like me – regarded recce as a job fit only for wimps, whereas 'real men' fired weapons and dropped bombs. They were reluctant to learn the techniques of recce and constantly derided recce pilots as the 'killum with fillum' brigade. I was still interested in recce but I had to admit I much preferred the more intense action of ground attack and air combat. At Wittering I enjoyed refreshing the techniques of flying pinpoints, area searches and line searches. On a line search task you were given a stretch of road, say 20-30 kilometres long, which you had to fly along and report and film all targets seen. The position of the targets had to be plotted in flight and reported by radio – not an easy task. There were a lot of techniques involved in planning and flying a line search if you wanted to be sure of staying on the line and finding all the targets. First of all, the approach to the start point was treated like any normal initial point run, making use of an easily-identified feature to start your run-in about one minute away. You then had to carry out careful map study to identify possible target areas and major checkpoints on the line, i.e. points where you would cross over to fly round a bend. Having marked your 1:50,000 map with all this information, you were ready to get airborne. On the line itself you had to work very hard, firstly to keep the line in view and secondly to see, film and plot any targets found. Planning where to make turns was critical to success: at 500 mph you don't get round bends as easily as a car. Constant anticipation was the key to success, the slightest loss of concentration meant that you would 'fall off the line' and miss out large chunks of it.

In flight we used mid flap for line searches and all exercises where we needed a tight turn, including air combat. We were cleared to use it up to 475 knots, pulling quite a lot of g. Soon we were to discover that there were problems with the ruggedness of the flap design. Apparently one of the test specifications for the Harrier GR1 could not be met during the initial flight test programme at Boscombe. This 'spec' involved turning performance at medium altitude and, to improve this, the manufacturer merely introduced a mid flap setting so that the flaps could be used in an intermediate position. Unknown to us pilots, in its initial design the Harrier's flaps had been built for use purely as a low speed device, with only an 'up' and fully 'down' selection available (like the Lightning). Using it for high-g manoeuvring at high airspeeds put a much greater strain on the mechanism. The consequences of this were to become apparent later on when the flaps' mechanism started to break up in flight. The early Harrier's structural weakness was a direct consequence of the desperate attempts to save weight, which had been undertaken when it was discovered that initial versions of the Pegasus couldn't produce enough thrust to give satisfactory VTOL performance. This problem was exacerbated by the financial constraints on equipping the aircraft. The most blatant example was the overweight UHF radio installation which never worked properly in service. The USMC, realizing that they needed to save weight on their version of the Harrier (the AV8A) installed a state-of-the-art lightweight radio which was entirely contained in the cockpit. The GR1 made use of the RAF's old PTR175 radio, an obsolete, heavy radio set which required a lot of space in the rear fuselage, plus a control box and antenna switching unit in the cockpit. Apart from the excess weight, this installation meant a lot of extra cable looms to take the signal from the cockpit to the radio and then back to the cockpit again. These long cable runs – in an aircraft with an extremely noisy electromagnetic background – led to lousy radio transmission and reception at all times, on both main and standby radio. I couldn't believe how bad radio communications were when I first flew the aircraft; some of the problem was also due to excess cockpit noise picked up in the mike. In my view the aircraft was disadvantaged operationally with such a poor radio.

Towards the end of the course there was sad news. One of my greatest friends from Cranwell, one of the last true gentlemen in this world, had been killed. It was a night mid-air collision in a Lightning. His wingman survived but his body was never found.

I was tired of living in the Mess. After nearly ten years in the RAF in bachelor accommodation I decided to live out for a while. With two other students I shared a flat in St George's Street in Stamford and had a ball. There were some epic parties and, on one occasion, a collapsed ceiling due to a tap left running. The landlord and the tenants downstairs were not impressed.

The high-level pressure to show off the new aeroplane was intense at this period. Essential training was regularly interrupted by orders from Group HQ to send an aircraft to this or that location and give a VSTOL display.

On one occasion a Harrier unit had been tasked to provide a VSTOL demonstration on a Mexe pad for a senior officer at RAF White Waltham, a small grass airfield to the west of London which was surrounded by built-up area. This was not the easiest airfield to get into for a display, and a suitably-qualified pilot had been carefully briefed about the task, which involved a short hover, vertical landing and then a vertical take-off to fly straight to Farnborough to refuel, no fuel being available at White Waltham. Everything was tight about the task, as the pilot would have barely enough fuel to carry it out. The squadron prepared two immaculately-clean aircraft for the task. On the day of the display the primary aircraft went U/S on the ground, and the pilot jumped into the clean spare, which also went U/S after take-off. There were no other aircraft available on the ground at Wittering. The only remaining aircraft was already airborne en route to Wales for a recce training mission. The squadronduty authorizer contacted the pilot via the squadron radio and instructed him to divert immediately to White Waltham (for which the pilot had no map) and carry out the display. The pilot would have been fully justified in refusing the task but, true to the prevailing spirit of 'can-do', he carried out the display exactly as briefed in a professional and efficient manner. Afterwards, Group HQ responded with a reprimand because the unit had sent a dirty aeroplane for a display in front of a senior officer.

For some time I had toyed with the idea of buying a light aeroplane for commuting between UK and RAF Wildenrath in Germany, my next posting. Devon was a tiresome journey from RAF Wildenrath by surface transport. In late spring I renewed my PPL and bought a second-hand Jodel DR1050 Ambassadeur, a lovely little wood-and-fabric 4-seater powered by a RR Continental flat four engine. She was a tail-dragger by choice. I enjoyed the challenge of a tail wheel aircraft as it took a bit of effort to make a nice landing. With a coarse-pitch prop she was good for long range cruising although not much good at short-field operations. However, I fully intended to make use of long RAF runways as much as possible.

Before the end of the course we had another crash on base. A pilot on 1(F) Squadron, had an extremely lucky escape after losing control during a deceleration to the hover – the good old intake momentum drag problem. He had pulled the handle just in time to earn his free Martin-Baker tie.

At RAF Wildenrath, (the only other Harrier base), there had just been a similar ejection at a high angle of bank. As well as this accident there had also been two recent fatal crashes and two wheels-up landings. One of those killed had been another delightful ex-Cranwell character. He had been flying a low level air display and had lost control after inadvertently entering cloud.

We were building up to a peak of accidents in the Harrier force, after the period of the aircraft's initial introduction into service. The latest technical problem was the tendency of the Pegasus to 'lock in' to a surge condition after a bird strike. In this case you had just a few seconds to shut down the engine, clear the surge and relight before you would have to eject; engine-off, the Harrier glided like a piano. This had just happened to a pilot on 4 Squadron, who had hit a bird while low flying in north Germany. The engine surge locked in and he ejected successfully fairly low down. As he floated earthward he was disgusted to see his erstwhile mount fly off into the distance – apparently fully serviceable. The blast of the seat rocket had cleared the surge, allowing the aircraft to fly pilot-less for another thirty minutes or so, carrying out various death-defying stunts until it ran out of fuel. The German Air Force had already scrambled a couple of Starfighters with orders to shoot it down. The locked-in surge was soon to claim another Harrier when a squadron commander had to eject in Germany. Straight away at Wittering one of the flight commanders also had a locked-in surge following a bird strike. Barely able to complete the surge recovery drill in time, he just managed to achieve a successful relight and recover the jet before it hit the ground, coming within an ace of losing his life.

The result of this ongoing saga was for the RAF to order the immediate introduction of a back-up manual fuel control system for the engine, to allow quick recovery from a surge.

Chapter 11

RAF Germany – Fighting the Cold War

At the end of the Harrier course I loaded up my kit in the Jodel at Exeter Airport and set course for RAF Wildenrath on the German/Dutch border. My navigation in the Jodel was straight-line stuff, using the same technique as I used in the Hunter and Harrier. I flew at whatever height was most convenient for wind and turbulence and cloud base. In strong winds it was uncomfortable to fly too low; however, you had no choice but to get right down into the tree tops to get under frontal weather systems, the forward visibility reduced to just a few hundred yards. There was supposed to be a light aircraft corridor across the Channel, but I just drew a straight line between Ashford in Kent (where I refuelled) and Wildenrath, with only the minimum deviations to avoid the more important airfields. I was a bit nervous of flying over sea, even in summer, and kept my radio permanently tuned to the emergency frequency in case of engine trouble. Over land I usually switched the radio off. If I ended up in the sea my RAF sea survival training told me that I would not survive long in the water, even in summer. Hence I flew quite high over the Channel and wore an RAF immersion suit and lifejacket in winter. Even so, I suffered the usual uncertainties about the engine's reliability as soon as I coasted out, imagining all kinds of engine problems developing as I listened carefully for the slightest change of note which might signal an impending failure. Fortunately for me my Jodel and its engine were to prove an extremely reliable combination.

I arrived at RAF Wildenrath one stifling summer's afternoon in late June, to find a scene of intense Harrier activity as three separate squadrons were working up to a peak of operational efficiency. No. 4(AC) Squadron had been the first to reform at Wildenrath, followed closely by No. 20(AC) Squadron. 3(F) Squadron had formed most recently, and was still not declared combat ready, the NATO criterion for operational readiness. The Cold War was still very much a hot war as far as our commanders were concerned and RAF Germany at this time was still at a peak of readiness to counter the obvious threat of the huge Warsaw Pact (WP) communist forces just over the inner German border, barely 100 miles away. This threat, both in conventional weapons and also nuclear, biological and chemical (NBC) weapon capability, was almost overwhelming, and we were under no illusions that we would survive for long in the event of a determined invasion by WP forces. Because of the reduction of British armed forces under successive governments our strength was sadly depleted since I had last seen RAFG in 1965. However, despite being totally outnumbered by the enemy, there was a job to be done to the best of our ability, and our training centred on immediate readiness to meet a surprise attack. Equally important was last-ditch survival in the event of nuclear, biological or chemical (NBC) attack. On the ground we could only hope to delay the onrush of Soviet-built armour, which was capable of advancing 100 kilometres per day. In the event of war the whole Wildenrath Harrier Wing planned to deploy forward into the field and operate from the fields and roads of rural Germany, our aircraft, tents and weapons concealed under camouflage nets. This plan suited the extremely short operational radius of action of the aircraft – barely eighty miles with a full weapon load – and was practised regularly in our peacetime training. I was delighted to discover that our Commander-in-Chief of RAFG was one of the legendary Second World War Dambuster pilots. I was soon to meet him; he was a splendid old buffer, still totally enthusiastic about the low level attack role which he had helped to pioneer in the Second World War.

I had been posted to 3 Squadron, but on arrival I was told that my posting had been changed and I was to report immediately to OC 20 Squadron. This squadron had suffered the brunt of the accidents that summer and no less than three separate boards of inquiry were still in progress. I found OC 20 Squadron's office on the flight line in a Portakabin right in front of the aircraft line. I introduced myself to the boss, a softly-spoken bear of a man who had already been a squadron commander on Hunters in Aden. He told me that he had been OC 3 Squadron the day before, but was now OC 20 Squadron. He welcomed me aboard, having originally picked me personally for 3 Squadron. He warned me that things were going to be tough as the squadron was well and truly on the spot and any misdemeanour would be hammered. The other major problem, obvious to see, was that the squadron's new hangar accommodation was not ready, and all of our briefing rooms, planning rooms etc. were located in Portakabins and time-expired British Army ops caravans, parked at random around the aircraft flight line. This meant the constant, brain-numbing shriek of Pegasus engines disrupting conversation and briefings, and an extremely sweaty existence for us pilots, virtually permanently dressed in g-suits and the uncomfortable torso harness for flying. There was no air conditioning of any sort, not so much as a fan to cool the interiors of the cabins, made unbearable by daytime temperatures of over 90 degrees F. With windows open the noise of engines destroyed all conversation. These difficult operating conditions – and the extremely tight supervision generated by the recent accidents – put a lot of pressure on the pilots and flight commanders.

One flight commander was an ex-staff member of the RAF's famous day fighter combat school, while another was a tall, imposing character of patrician tones who seemed to have stepped out of a pre-war RAF training film. Sporting an ultra-traditional RAF handlebar moustache he was a character from a different era. He looked as if he would have made an excellent commander of a Wapiti squadron on the north-west frontier of India. He had been one of the original RAF aces selected to fly on the famous Kestrel Tripartite Evaluation squadron, formed in the mid '60s to evaluate the operational possibilities of VSTOL attack aircraft. Overwhelmed by total enthusiasm for the VSTOL concept, he envisioned a large RAF Harrier force of small, independent flights training and operating virtually full-time under field conditions. Although the aircraft had been brought into service, hardly anything had been done yet to equip the force with the essential off-base ground equipment for rough-field operations. For example, until the boss latched on to the excellent German-manufactured 4-wheel drive Unimog, the RAF expected us to tow and manoeuvre aircraft in and out of 'hides' using standard RAF airfield towing tractors, which were virtually useless on soft ground. Because of this the Wildenrath Wing was forced to use unwieldy 4-ton trucks as tow vehicles, the only ones available which would not bog down in soft ground. The standard RAF refuelling vehicle was supplied for our off-base operations with a suspension designed for operation from smooth concrete surfaces. On rough ground the chassis frames immediately started to crack up. As the expected off-base equipment failed to materialize, there was disappointment at the delay in realizing the potential of VSTOL operations. Like all of the squadron command- ers, our boss had a big job on his hands in these tough times. The rest of 20 Squadron were an interesting crowd, mostly experienced ex-Hunter people with just one first tourist. Across the Wing at Wildenrath there was a host of excellent characters – ex-Bahrain Hunters.

As in Bahrain, Mess life was idyllic for young bachelors. The station provided accommodation for dozens of young female schoolteachers who taught in local BFES schools, and they were all members of the Officers' Mess. In the bar the men were often outnumbered by women, which we didn't complain about too much. Social life was frantic, with the exchange rate at ten Deutschmarks to the pound and an extremely generous local overseas pay allowance. Booze, fags and petrol were ridiculously cheap. All bachelors lived on base, on orders of HQ RAF Germany, who were afraid we might be corrupted and compromised by lurking Soviet agents if we were allowed to live off base. Apart from a constant round of squadron parties, Mess guest nights and married quarter "dos" there were two regular nights of the week written off for regular discos. Every Wednesday night people turned up from as far away as RAF Gutersloh for the disco night at Wildenrath. On Saturday night virtually the whole of RAFG decamped to RAF Bruggen for their weekend disco and steak night.

On the ground the pace was punishing, while the flying was mar- vellous, in spite of a tedious couple of months when no one was allowed to fly below 1,000 feet because of the engine problem. Western Germany was still an armed camp in the early '70s, being virtually under occupation by NATO forces. This meant that every time you got airborne you would come across Army units either camped out or mobile on the vast sandy training areas spread across the country. You couldn't fly for more than a couple of minutes without encountering some military activity on the ground. This plethora of targets made for extremely realistic training, particularly in the all-important armed recce role (seek and destroy), which we knew would be the most likely task in wartime. A typical training mission would route via a series of training areas, looking for columns of tanks, troops, guns, missile launchers etc., either on the move or camouflaged in woodland. We soon learned to recognize and follow the tracks of heavy armoured vehicles in soft ground and could home in on the huge dust clouds raised by tanks on the move in hot weather. Even well-camouflaged tanks in woodland could be pinpointed by the puff of black smoke pushed up when they started engines. During a good mission you could spend most of your airborne time carrying out various simulated attacks on these targets, to return to base sweaty and exhausted from all the g you had pulled. There would then follow a critical debrief of your HUD camera film, to confirm whether or not your attacks had been accurate. And then off again for the next mission. In the low level airspace over West Germany conditions were blissful for anyone enthusiastic about air combat. The sky was stiff with Air Defence fighters – Phantoms, Lightnings, Starfighters, Mirages, Drakens – all spoiling for a fight with anyone they found. We were not prepared just to sit back and be intercepted; if we were not actually engaged in an attack on ground targets then we would attack any other military aircraft we saw, engaging in the most hectic low level fights until we ran low on fuel. This was legal under the RAFG rules of the time. Lightnings from Gutersloh (Mk 2As) were the most worthy opponents, being prepared to fight anyone at any time. However, because of their ludicrously short range they could only mount realistic combat air patrols (CAPs) within a few miles of Gutersloh airfield. Wherever possible we would try to route outbound and inbound via these CAPs, to pounce on any Lightning we could find.

Attack/recce training was interspersed with regular live firing on the ranges of Nordhorn, Helchteren and Hohne, the latter an Army training area where we fired high explosive ammunition under FAC control on tanks and soft targets. Additionally, at regular intervals, there were arduous no-notice alerts to test the reaction of the whole base to a surprise attack from communist Warsaw Pact forces. The chilling alert klaxon would sound in the early hours of the morning and you had to get up fast and sprint to work, drunk or sober, to be briefed on what was going on. We never knew if it was a practise or a 'real' alert until we got into work. This was the whole aim of the exercise, to ensure everyone reacted instantly regardless of the threat. Specifically, there was no time allowed to make arrangements for families and loved ones if it was a real war – they just had to fend for themselves. Delaying at home to shave, have breakfast or even so much as a cup of coffee was totally forbidden. There was always an Armageddon scenario at the end, the exercise finishing up with simulated nuclear attack, everyone stifling in gas masks and full NBC suits for hours on end, praying for 'Endex' to be called. This got you used to the idea of fighting a war where you were all probably going to die anyway: 'At least we'll take some of the bastards with us', we thought. Not much different from Bomber Command in the Second World War: the aircrews' life expectancy in action then was about the same as ours would have been – measured in weeks, not months. On many of these exercises the whole of NATO would be on alert, from the northern tip of Norway in an arc through central Europe and the Med to the eastern borders of Turkey; hundreds of thousands of troops and several thousand aircraft on immediate standby, fully-armed and ready to move to meet any threat. Our enemy were the forces of the Warsaw Pact nations: The Soviet Union, East Germany, Hungary, Czechoslovakia, Poland and Bulgaria. – all the nations of the Communist bloc. A formidable and determined group. The only reason the communists didn't take over the whole of western Europe was because of this enormous, highly-tuned and aggressive NATO defensive effort. We stood absolutely in the front line: this was the reality of the Cold War in the early 1970s

On exercise, first take-offs would be just before dawn – a grisly experience with a hangover and no breakfast – and there would sometimes be several days of exercises, including launching attacks on field targets, local air defence of Wildenrath airfield, arming and re-arming aircraft with live weapons, intruder alerts, simulated NBC warfare etc., the whole tedious business going on twenty-four hours a day.

When the alert klaxon sounded, our first task after arriving at work would be to disperse the aircraft around the airfield to frustrate any surprise air attack. In the freezing cold and dark of the early hours we would be taxiing, still half asleep, to the old Canberra dispersal revetments on the south side. The RAF had not yet started to invest in proper hardened aircraft shelters (HASs) and hardened bunkers, so our dispersal policy was a pretty ramshackle arrangement. The aircraft were parked two to a pan – I was amazed we didn't have more collisions in the dark – and then all pilots had to hole up in the various broom cupboard sized cubby holes in the sides of the concrete revetments. These were only big enough for half a dozen pilots at most, and we were widely spread out among the many revetments. One cubby hole would serve as squadron ops, and we would lay out old-fashioned army field telephone lines to link the various locations together. Because of the phone lines we couldn't shut the doors, which let in the freezing night air and there were no heaters. There we would sit shivering for hour after hour, waiting for the first air tasks to come in via Wing operations. A favourite trick of our tasking agencies would be to send us a four-ship attack task with an 'as soon as possible' (ASAP) time-on-target (TOT). This was the joker in the pack; any four-ship needed extra care and expertise and the 'attack ASAP' designation meant that we had to complete planning and briefing within thirty minutes of arrival of the task on station. Because there was inevitably a ten minute delay while Wing ops got the task to us, this left under twenty minutes to plan and brief – truly panic stations all round. The only way we could hack this was for the formation to carry out an extensive pre-brief on likely mission options and then get dressed in full flying clothing and sign out, ready to run for the jets. Then, when the actual air task came in we just needed to throw the target position on the map, scribble an initial point run and go for it. Experienced pilots would lead, making planning easier. Any competent Harrier pilot could navigate a hundred miles or so to the general target area without a map, using local knowledge of our likely areas of operation towards the Communist border. Detailed planning and map study was only required for target runs.

We would always be required to practise a survival scramble, in which the whole Wing would have to get airborne as fast as possible from a no-notice standing start. The launch was carefully planned so that all three squadrons took-off from different areas of the airfield without conflicting with one another; one from the main runway and one each from the northern and southern taxiways, regardless of the wind. This evolution was often practised in fog, when we were not supposed to get airborne, but just taxi round to the take-off point, roll down the runway and then return to our squadron dispersal. Naturally enough this led to some hilarious cock-ups as the 'launch' or 'taxi only' order was passed on by air traffic control. On several occasions a pilot would arrive at the take-off point convinced that it was taxi only, not strapped-in to save time. On seeing the aircraft in front actually take-off there would follow an uncomfortable delay while the pilot frantically strapped in for take-off. Similarly, on several taxi only occasions a pilot would find himself airborne above a solid layer of fog, wondering why he was the only RAF aircraft airborne in Germany.

We took our squadron training very seriously in the difficult armed recce role. We experimented constantly in two-ship and four-ship formations, trying to find the most effective ways to attack opportunity targets found in the field, allowing for the likely defences we would have to face. In my opinion we were hindered more than helped by some of our more unimaginative QWIs, (qualified weapon instructors), some of whom seemed concerned only with peacetime range firing procedures. As a result, our squadron standard attack procedures, produced by QWIs, were unnecessarily vulnerable to ground defences because the QWIs insisted on using the unrealistic peacetime attack parameters for our simulated attacks. An example was our cluster bomb which, for peacetime training, had to be dropped from a minimum of 200 feet pass distance (we were never given any to practise with anyway-they were far too expensive). This limitation was imposed to avoid the slight risk of self-damage from the explosion of the bomblets. Erroneously, in my view, it was not accepted that in wartime we could use lower pass distances to ensure more accuracy and a more tactical approach to the target. In war the resulting increased risk of self-damage would be a drop in the ocean compared with the very real risk of damage from all the guns and SAMs firing at us (this proved to be very much the case in the Falklands war ten years later). I made myself pretty unpopular with flight commanders and the QWIs by arguing forcibly that we should change our attack standard operating procedures to reflect the acceptance of much greater self-damage risks in wartime operations. I felt that practising using peacetime safety parameters was wasted effort. As we weren't firing real weapons there was no extra hazard. Another example concerned the war loads of our Aden cannon. I found out from the squadron armourers that all of our war-ready belts of 30mm ammo were belted up with twenty high explosive rounds followed by ten armour piercing, simply because it was easier for the armourers to do it that way – that was how the ammo arrived from the bomb dump. Our QWIs hadn't even considered how this would work out in practice – firing on a real target in wartime, when you wanted a good mix of the two types going down the barrels. We were constantly suffering gun failures on the Harrier and were extremely likely to be strafing with only one gun in wartime. At twenty rounds per second a whole burst could consist of just HE only. The obvious solution was to mix the rounds up much more.

My Jodel was now parked in the 20 Squadron hangar and I had bought a second-hand Beetle as a runabout. There was so much social life going on that I hardly had time to get airborne in the Jodel. One memorable trip in late summer was with a couple of colleagues down to the Mosel valley, where we had contacts with a vineyard owner at Urzig. On a beautiful Saturday morning we cruised through the soft, rolling hills of the Eifel to the Mosel. My aim was to land at a small German flying club field spectacularly perched on a high plateau above a hairpin bend of the river. I was suffering radio problems and was a bit concerned to see a German 'Oompah' band marching down the middle of the grass landing strip. I flew a couple of orbits and then managed to land when they cleared the strip, dodging various glider towlines on the approach. After taxiing to the parking area I was met by a beaming flying club official who welcomed us with a tray of foaming Steins of beer, apologizing for our having to overshoot a couple of times. 'Today is our Air Day', he said with pride, 'Everybody is going to enjoy themselves!'

This was pretty obvious from the state of the other civilian pilots, who were getting stuck into the beer at a tremendous rate, before getting airborne again. He waved away my apologies for having no radio and called up his refuelling team who proceeded to refuel the Jodel from galvanized buckets of 100 octane aviation fuel, filtered through a large chamois leather in a funnel. We stepped back discreetly as we realized that several onlookers were smoking right next to the open buckets of high-octane fuel. Noticing our concern, our host raised his Stein in salute. He pointed to his refuelling crew and said with pride, 'This is to show that flying is fun!'

Inevitably we were soon overwhelmed by the juggernaut of traditional German flying club hospitality and abandoned ourselves to the spirit of the day. They were a wacky crew, and about as mad a bunch of flyers as you could wish to meet. I made a mental note never to risk getting airborne with any of them. Much later in the afternoon we managed to escape to the vineyard and finish the day sampling various Mosel vintage wines. The Sunday was spent in glorious sunshine in the *Bier Stuben* of the Mosel valley. Somehow at the end of the day I convinced myself that I was sober enough to fly back to Wildenrath.

There were more trips like that when I could raise the money to buy fuel (I was pretty broke), plus some interesting runs back to Devon with a stop off at the pretty little airfield at Ashford to clear customs. On one occasion I routed back via Wattisham to visit my best friend, who was now OC Target Facilities Flight and also the Lightning solo display pilot. He did a tremendous show and was a worthy successor to previous Lightning aeros exponents. As we stood in the evening sunshine at the visiting aircraft pan, my friend

introduced me to the Wattisham station commander, a legendary
South African. My friend amused me by relating the story of a recent
similar occasion when he stood outside TFF talking to the station
commander while a Lightning took off in the background. He
watched in horror as the pilot did the usual 'wheels-up take-off' and
piled into the barrier in a gigantic ball of flame at 150 knots, being
last seen leaping from the burning wreck and sprinting off towards
the horizon. Amazingly he was uninjured. The pilot had whipped the
wheels up too early and sunk back on to the runway. Fifteen tons of
Lightning then slid along the runway on the belly tank, whose
leaking fuel immediately ignited in a sheet of flame hundreds of
yards long.

Soon there was news of another fatal accident at Wittering. A
student had speared in on one of his last Harrier training flights. He
had been leading a 233 OCU instructor at low level in Scotland and
had entered a dead-end valley which was blocked by poor weather.
This was quite a normal event for OCU training sorties, and the
student was expected to cope with it. He had pulled up into the clag
with the instructor following at a distance, when over the radio came
the chilling call:

'I think I've lost control!'

To his eternal credit, a very quick-witted instructor shouted back
immediately:

'Don't be afraid to eject!'

To no avail. Within a few seconds the student had crashed.

In late August, 20 Squadron deployed to Sardinia for our five-week
annual armament practice camp at the NATO air base of
Decimomannu. Southern Sardinia was blissfully hot and dry and we
soon settled into the routine of six or seven waves per day of four
aircraft to the huge Capo Frasca bombing range. The local town of
Cagliari was an excellent place to eat and drink, and we spent many
pleasant evenings lounging at pavement cafes and eyeing up the
extremely attractive local girls. We were dissuaded from chatting
them up by the language barrier and the thought that their
boyfriends were certain to be unfriendly. We spent a lot of time on
the beaches, sunbathing and waterskiing, having worked our butts
off back at Wildenrath during the summer. I started to play guitar in
the 20 Squadron Trad Jazz 'Band'. Various other amateurs would
join in at times. Rehearsing in the 'Pig and Tapeworm' pilots' rest
room, we made hideous noises late at night on paper and comb, to

the fury of those trying to get some sleep upstairs. Only two players had any real talent, but we had a lot of fun.

Frasca was hard work as an air-to-ground range, the excitable range safety officers (RSOs) restricting range missions if we didn't obey all the rules meticulously. I dropped my first 1,000lb bomb, a concrete-filled parachute retard version which seemed to fly for miles before it hit the ground. We only had one each to drop, (their cost must have been peanuts) and I discovered that opportunities to drop live 1,000lb bombs were almost non-existent. At this time the RAF were just about to stop live drops at Otterburn, leaving only Garvie Island in the extreme north of Scotland as a live bombing range. All our normal range bombing practice was carried out with the 4lb practice bomb, a small smoke-and-flash device whose ballistic characteristics were unrepresentative of either the 1,000lb retard or the cluster bomb. This meant that all of the practice bombing techniques we had learned had to be readjusted when it came to operational weapon delivery. This was fairly typical of the RAF's lack of preparedness for war, almost an exact parallel of the pre-Second World War situation where very few of the RAF's bombs had been properly evaluated in live drops. (See *Bombs Gone* by John A MacBean and Arthur S Hogben). In an attempt to improve the ballistics of the 4lb practice bomb, some enterprising souls at one RAF base had experimented by drilling some extra holes in the base plate. This produced a bomb which simulated the 1,000lb retard bomb much better but they were unable to get the modification officially adopted.

Many of our weapons were made less effective operationally because of the RAF's insistence on, in my view, unrealistically high safety standards. A classic example was the new BL755 cluster bomb. It had no less than seven different safety devices to stop it going bang at the wrong time. We were convinced that it would never work reliably under operational conditions. However, none of us was allowed to drop one and see – they were far too expensive to practise with, in spite of the fact that they were the number one weapon in our inventory for use against WP armoured forces. Later on in the Falklands War – in defiance of staff instructions – we disabled two of the safety devices on the cluster bomb, to make them more reliable when dropped from much lower heights.

At the end of the armament practice camp the QWIs organized a weapons competition combined with the 'operational' phase of our firing practice. During the 'op' phase we would try to make all of our attacks as operationally realistic as possible, including staying at low level all the way round the pattern until turning in for the attack. Op range patterns were extremely demanding and great fun to fly. There were no practice shots to assess the wind – we were in hot first time for every weapon, and we fired a different weapon on each successive pass: one bomb, one rocket, one 30mm strafe pass, then repeat four times. The four aircraft would join the range aiming to get rid of four practice bombs, four SNEB rockets and fire four gun passes. Although operationally unrealistic (for real you could leave most weapon switches at live throughout), the constant change of weapon selection and firing technique with each pass offered unlimited scope for the notorious 'switch pigs'.

The whole thing was, as usual, an extremely demanding flying exercise at the same time as a keenly-fought competition for the best overall score. We would fly the tightest range pattern possible, just barely giving time to reset the weapon control panel and the HUD between attacks. To the fury of the range safety officers, less competent pilots would fire rockets at the bombs' target or drop bombs on the rockets' target. (Both were fired by the same button on the stick.) You needed hyperactive tendencies just to keep up with the pattern directions, which changed depending on which weapon you were firing next. All too often a switched-off pilot would get lost by turning the wrong way off-target and be unable to join the pattern again. In that case his score was forfeit – hard rules.

Chapter 12

Harrier Wing Field Operations

Back at Wildenrath in October the whole Wing deployed to the huge Sennelager training area to practise our off-base operational role. The three squadrons occupied six different Harrier sites hidden in the woods and fields of the tank training area. A first look at an operational Harrier site was extremely impressive. I flew into our primary sites and was given a detailed briefing on exactly how to find the Mexe landing pad, hidden in a clearing in the woods. (I had not flown to any deployed site before.) Armed with a 1:50,000 map showing the run-in, I set off from the initial point to the east of Paderborn in a steadily lowering cloud base, the visibility decreasing ominously the closer I got to the site. At various planned checkpoints on the map I progressively slowed down from 420 knots, putting down flaps, then gear and finally selecting the braking nozzles to reduce the speed to zero, all the while continuing to map read on the 1:50,000 map. I hoped that I had got the right piece of woodland – it all looked the same in the sandy terrain. There was only one chance to make a pad landing – after that I would have to divert immediately to Gutersloh on the minimum fuel of 1,200lbs – barely seven minutes running time at full power. The Harrier GR1s could only hover with less than about 1,500lb of fuel, so everything was right on the limit.

Out of the corner of my eye I picked up one of the small Dayglo pad markers, then the pad itself – just a nondescript grey sheet of metal 50 feet square in the corner of a greyish-looking field. Checking that the airspeed was below 30 knots I shuffled sideways to pick up the markers, then the corner of the pad below and just to the side of me. I used the 'pad corner' technique exclusively to achieve a vertical landing – it never failed, even in the most difficult circumstances. The 'pad corner' landing technique was taught (entirely unofficially) by one very well-respected instructor at the Harrier OCU. It involved keeping one corner of the pad in view throughout the vertical descent; at the same time the usual pad markers could be safely ignored. Inevitably, this involved a slight sideways movement during the descent, which had to be arrested just before touchdown in order to achieve a smooth landing. This was not at all difficult, and the tremendous advantage of the technique was your independence from the usual pad markers, which were sometimes misplaced or difficult to see in certain light conditions. I had the greatest respect for this instructor, both as a VSTOL flyer and as a lateral thinker, and I used his technique exclusively from then on. I used to pride myself on the speed with which I could get from the hover on to the ground. This was not due to any unusual skill on my part – the technique itself was almost foolproof and, in my view, should have been adopted throughout the Harrier force.

After landing you were entirely under the control of the marshallers, who quickly got you off the pad and rolling fast towards the hide area under the canopy of trees. On the soft grass you had to have the flaps and nozzles up (to avoid burning the grass), and had to keep moving fairly swiftly to avoid the dreaded bogging-in. Driven by 3,000lb of hydraulic pressure, the steerable nose wheel of the Harrier acted as a very efficient plough. Once you had cut through the turf into the softer ground beneath, it was all over until they came to dig you out. No amount of engine power would blast you out of the hole you had made. Moving at seemingly reckless speeds you ended up being marshalled into the impossibly tight space of a camouflage-netted hide under the trees, the leafy canopy closing over your cockpit as you chopped the engine on a signal from the ground crew. With the engine still winding down you were surrounded by ground crew who swarmed on to the aircraft to refuel and, if necessary, rearm it. On these exercises we kept no live ordnance in the field, but the hide area was surrounded by dummy bombs, CBUs and rocket pods so that the armourers could get some exercise. After climbing out you were led through woodland paths to the 'ops' complex, a couple of well-camouflaged Army ops trucks equipped with all the communications necessary for wartime operations. Each site was in contact with the Field Wing Operations Centre (FWOC), which received air tasks direct from Army HQ. We had our own permanent Army ground liaison officer (GLO) and intelligence officer (IO), who operated next to the ops caravan. Their task was to interpret incoming air tasks and brief pilots on specific aspects of the current ground situation. The GLO kept a large situation map of the whole battle area, showing all our own troops and known 'enemy' dispositions. For each exercise our staff would produce a hypothetical tactical and intelligence situation, always related to the routes likely to be used in a Communist armoured thrust over the border into West Germany. Our exercise targets would operate on these routes and we could find them easily without maps.

The flying on these field exercises was first-class, and there was lots of it. There was invariably a large Army exercise going on at the same time and we would join in, in support of one side or the other. Our normal operating unit was as a pair, although we occasionally flew four-ships for special tasks. We were often cleared to operate right up to the inner German border itself, to get experience of navigating in our wartime area of operations. In peacetime there was a strictly-enforced 'buffer zone', the air defence identification zone, or ADIZ, designed to keep NATO aircraft away from East German airspace. Over the years there had been a number of cock-ups where NATO aircraft had penetrated deep into Soviet-controlled territory by mistake. Some of them had been shot down by the Communists. An air vice-marshal once told me that he had led his entire squadron of Vampires through Soviet-controlled East Germany in the early '50s after a navigation error. Ironically, my first 'border run' was in a Mod 9, (we still had one on 20), with no navigational kit whatsoever. I was leading a flight commander who was supposed to be checking on my navigation. I was unimpressed that he – supposedly an experienced Harrier operator – had given me the poorly equipped Mod 9 to fly, while he flew a Harrier with all the serviceable navigation kit and HUD. In my view any flight commander worth his salt would take the more difficult aeroplane for themselves, leaving a non-combat ready pilot with the fully-serviceable machine. That was the attitude I adopted later when I became a flight commander, on the principle that you should never ask any of your subordinates to do anything you were not fully confident of doing yourself.

Strip take-offs from Harrier field sites were never dull. Because of the need to preserve the grass surface, an absolute minimum of time was allowed between leaving the hide and getting airborne. No stopping was permitted on the grass. Take-off checks were completed in the hide and then you were off for the start point, marked by a small wooden marker on the grass. The take-off line was varied during the day as the surface became progressively more cut up. As you made the final turn to line up with the strip direction, you juggled the throttle to carry out some semblance of an acceleration check on the engine, screwing the throttle friction down to make sure the lever would stay where it was put. Flaps went to the take-off position as you turned on to the strip; if you forgot this you were doomed to crash on take-off. You had to make sure you were pretty accurately lined up with the strip before slamming to full power. Once you accelerated any major attempt to correct direction would carve up the strip in a bad way. As you hit full power the full 10 tons of thrust hit you and you were committed, rather like a ship deck take-off. The Harrier's puny brakes could not stop you even if you could avoid skidding on the grass. It was essential to have the short take-off nozzle stop (STO stop) correctly set for the lift-off nozzle angle as it was impossible to judge this accurately on the tiny cockpit gauge. You couldn't afford to look in the cockpit anyway because once your speed increased above about 40 knots (this took just a couple of seconds) cockpit vibration was so great on grass that you couldn't read any of the instruments any more and there was the possibility of your hand being shaken right off the throttle lever. Because of this vibration you also had to get your hand off the throttle and firmly grasping the nozzle lever as soon as you had slammed to full power. As you approached the lift-off marker (a small Dayglo board) you smashed the nozzle lever to the STO stop and the aircraft leapt into the air, a slight pull on the stick setting you up in the correct nose-high attitude to clear the obstacles in a climbing transition. There were usually trees or high tension pylons at the end of the strip, and your eyes would be riveted on the obstacle as you pulled sufficiently to clear the tops. This was entirely an eyeball exercise: you did it on feel – and the state of your underpants. Pitch control was extremely sensitive at this stage. Once clear of the obstacle, and not before, you slowly moved the nozzle lever forward to transition away as the gear came up. With the aircraft cleaned up you stayed low over the trees as you accelerated away to the RV point, to wait for the rest of the formation to join up.

There were to be many more of these three-week deployments at Wildenrath, three per year for my time there. Most of the time we operated from grass; however, the infamous aluminium strips were already coming into use with other squadrons. These strips, consisting of about 500 feet of pierced aluminium planking (PAP), would allow pilots to carry out take-offs and creeping vertical landings (CVLs), thus reducing the dependency on fickle grass surfaces in wet weather. On 20 Squadron we scorned the use of PAP, preferring the fun of skidding around and bogging-in on grass. On several occasions we used the Paderborn flying club grass field, making rolling vertical landings (RVLs) on the grass strip which was once used to launch Me 109s and FW 190s in the Second World War. On our next deployment, in the wet spring of '73, we had a lot of trouble with bogged-down jets because of the mud. The boss, resourceful as ever, saw a local farmer driving serenely through the mud in a Unimog 4WD and persuaded the man to lend it to us for a trial. The machine proved ideal for towing Harriers and eventually RAFG agreed to order them for the whole Harrier force. At last we could stop using the cumbersome 4-ton trucks to tow aircraft off-base.

At Wildenrath the social life continued at a hectic pace, with regular joint parties with the occupants of the 'schoolies' block and weekend runs out across the Dutch and Belgian borders to various discos and night clubs.

Back at work the latest technical problem was making itself felt in our daily training. The aileron hinge brackets were starting to crack up under the stresses of flight. Basically, the Harrier wing tip was in pre-stall buffet all the time at low speed or during manoeuvre, and there was grave danger that an aileron would fall off, with disastrous results. The RAF forbade us from carrying out any manoeuvre which involved buffet until the problem could be solved.

By now I had completed the splendid RAF winter 'survival' course at Bad Kohlgrub in Bavaria, during which we learnt to ski and drink vast quantities of Hacker Bräu, not both at the same time. For the final three-day escape and evasion exercise, we were dropped at one end of a large exercise area in the Bavarian Alps to build a para-teepee and survive overnight in sub-zero temperatures. Late the following night we were to be sent off in pairs to penetrate to the western end of the area through deep snow, avoiding the defending forces of German Alpine troops on skis. We knew that our chances of evading that lot were slim and their prisoner interrogation techniques were not too comfortable. At the same time the staff had briefed us that in wartime the absolute priority was to avoid capture – by any means possible. I decided to take their advice at face value, having done my share of practice bleeding at Cranwell. Remembering some ploys from winter survival in the Cairngorms, a colleague and I secretly made white camouflage snow suits from parachute material, which we put on as soon as we were dropped from the truck. We had to spend an uncomfortable period lying flat in snowdrifts to avoid the mobile patrols, but eventually the coast was clear. We then trekked east out of the exercise area, in the opposite direction from the final RV. When safely clear of the area we discarded the snow suits and flagged down a taxi which took us by a roundabout route as near the final RV as we dared. We bedded down for the night in a comfortable barn under enormous piles of hay and, in the early morning, walked serenely into the RV without being caught.

I was also playing regularly in the RAFG squash team, and we had some enjoyable engagements all round the region, from Brussels to Copenhagen. They were a good sociable crowd in the team and we had a lot of good times. On one occasion we played against a BAOR team which included my brother Robin, then based at Osnabruck. Soon Robin was posted on secondment to the Duke of Edinburgh's Royal Regiment in Berlin, to take charge of their recce element who were charged with the difficult and hazardous task of 'snooping' around the Communist military installations of East Berlin. Apparently this was great sport, although you had to keep your wits about you to avoid being nobbled by one or other of the many East German security forces. Robin would travel with a team of observers in an unmarked car, and they would pick up a Communist 'tail' as soon as they crossed the border into East Berlin. The next job was to lose the 'tail' as soon as possible, by some speedy driving, Bond-like, through the lesser-known back streets so that they could carry out their recce mission more or less unhindered. This was part of the cat-and-mouse game. A favourite dirty trick of the East Germans was to set up an ambush for the recce car, positioning a heavy BTR152 armoured car up a side alley which would race out into the street on a radio call from the 'tail', hopefully to squash the recce car flat. This had been tried out a few times already and the Army had been lucky to avoid casualties.

Robin invited me and a couple of other Harrier pilots on a trip to Berlin to see the East German May Day parade. This was a great opportunity to be shown the sights of the city and also to see our potential enemy at close range. Because of the Four-Power Agreement the British military had rights of access across into East Berlin at any time, as long as you wore uniform. We were met by Robin's Army friend at Braunschweig railway station to join the British military train to Berlin. On the train, guarded by a British Army detachment, the three of us were glued to the windows for our first sight of Communist territory. East Germany was a sombre sight, seemingly barely recovered from the devastation of the Second World War, the landscape drab and oppressive with primitive roads and crumbling, unpainted buildings everywhere. There was hardly a private car to be seen. The whole atmosphere was that of a John Le Carré spy novel. At every railway siding there was military equipment on view: tanks, guns, SAM launchers etc., and radar sites on hilltops in the distance. All of this equipment was thoroughly familiar to us from our daily training sessions with slide shows of enemy materiel and it was fascinating to see it close up. The trip across into East Berlin via Checkpoint Charlie was even better. We strolled among squads of East German troops, warming up for the parade with their sinister goose-step. We had our photos taken posing next to all the latest Soviet hardware, T62 tanks, ZSU 23/4 guns, SAM 6 launchers BTR 60s etc. Most striking to me were the fiercely aggressive paramilitary police, of which there were at least half a dozen different organizations, all spying on each other. The porcine East German communist police scowled fiercely at our RAF uniforms, their loathsome Dobermann and Alsatian dogs snarling and straining at the leash to give a clear impression of what they would like to do to us. I shuddered at the thought of the cruel tyranny these forces represented, and pitied the ordinary East German citizens who had been terrorized and subjugated for so many years.

The parade itself, an unashamed demonstration of military muscle, gave a clear indication of what we would be up against in any future war. After the parade we stayed on in Berlin for a few days, to enjoy the full range of tourist attractions. Robin was an excellent host, and we were privileged to be able to spend some time in his regimental Mess. We were pleasantly surprised at the easy-going relationship between different ranks in the Mess, with officers addressing each other by their first name, regardless of rank. Before leaving Berlin I flew on a fascinating Army helicopter trip along the Berlin Wall, including a recce of all the WP military installations within visual range of the border. Before landing I took a photo of the infamous Spandau jail, where Rudolf Hess was passing his last few years of captivity.

In the spring we started to run into the next major technical problem with the Harrier. Our new Mk 103 Pegasus engines started to come apart in the air. First of all in the spring our USMC exchange officer had to eject after engine failure. Then, in July we had three accidents at Wildenrath on three successive Fridays. A pilot had to eject over the runway after an engine problem on take-off. A week later I was leading a formation when the No. 4 had to eject after take-off. Finally, a USMC pilot lost control on landing and ran off the runway. In each case the aircraft came to rest conveniently in front of the crash rescue vehicles' shed. After the third event the crash crew chief formally asked for a metal strip to be laid out on the grass in front of the crash vehicles so that they could get there more quickly – as it was clear that this was now the favoured spot for Harrier crashes at Wildenrath.

The second of these accidents was unrelated to the engine problem, and turned out to be a timely setback to my customary overconfidence in the air. I was leading an armed four-ship to go to Nordhorn range and we lined up on the runway in the usual two-up and two-back formation, the front pair some 500 yards in front of the back pair. Standard drill for take-off was for the leader to call 'Gold, 55 per cent GO', wait a few seconds for everyone to stabilize at this power setting, and then call 'Rolling, rolling, GO!' On this call all four aircraft would slam to full power and we would leap airborne together. After a 90 degree turn you would be in defensive battle formation. That was the theory, and I had done it many times. On this occasion I ballsed it up, forgetting to call '55 per cent, GO!' I called 'Rolling, rolling, GO!' and slammed the throttle, to leap ahead of my mildly surprised wingman, who was still at idle power. Feeling miffed that I had so rudely cleared off without him, he used his initiative and carried out a conventional take-off, just about catching me up at lift-off. Also staying cool at the back, the back pair leader hand-signalled a wind-up to his wingman (No. 4) and nodded for a standard no-radio pairs take-off, which worked fine until lift-off. I knew nothing of this until later.

Meanwhile, back in my cockpit, having left my wingman behind I knew that something had gone wrong with the take-off procedure. As I called the frequency change to departures I could hear the familiar 'pip, pip, pip' autotone given out when a pilot ejects from a Harrier. This was ominous.

On departure frequency I made the classic radio call:
'Gold, Check in.'
'Gold 2.'
'Gold 3.'
Silence.

'Gold 4, Check in!'

More silence.

'He crashed on take-off WIN – I think he hit slipstream!'

(This was Gold 3 being helpful.)

My mind in turmoil I racked it round in a turn back towards the field. In the hot sunlight a sickening, oily black cloud was rising above the runway. 'God! What have I done?' I thought: the ballsed-up take-off must have caused the crash. My heart sinking, I led the three remaining aircraft of Gold formation back over the field. The sight that greeted us was as grim as it could have been. Close to the still-smoking wreck – too close – lay a pathetic little pile of multi-coloured material, obviously an un-deployed parachute. 'God,' I thought, 'Gold 4's under that – I've killed him!'. The crash vehicles were already hosing down the wreck and I didn't dare make another pass to see what they found under the parachute: clearly he had ejected too late to save himself. I couldn't ask ATC what was going on; as expected they were in panic and there was pandemonium on the frequency as other Harriers returned short of fuel and were diverted to other airfields . We orbited for twenty minutes or so before being given clearance to land. I taxied in devastated, to shut down on the 20 Squadron line and ask frantically what had happened.

'They've taken him to the medical centre,' was all I got before I rushed for the nearest Land Rover and drove off in a panic.

In the medical centre Gold 4 was sitting on a bed looking pleased with himself. A pretty nurse was taking his blood pressure as I dashed in and did the classic double take. I didn't know what to say – for a few seconds I was absolutely speechless. He was unharmed, except for the usual MDC 'splatter' of facial cuts.

'Err – what happened?' I spluttered eventually, still unable to believe my eyes.

'Oh, I just clobbered a load of birds on lift-off; they went down the engine and it surged straight away. I pitched up out of control and pulled the handle.'

Fortunately, Gold 4 had flown Buccaneers with the Navy: he wasn't at all shy about leaving an aeroplane that didn't want to fly any more.

'So you didn't hit my slipstream then?' I sighed with relief.

'No that wasn't it – relax WIN, it wasn't your fault!'

Jesus wept. That balls-up cost me some beer – a price I was willing to pay.

Squadron Exchange

In midsummer we carried out a brilliant squadron exchange visit to
RDAF Karup in Denmark, to see how the Danes operated and
sample some draft Carlsberg. The Danes flew the magnificent Saab
J35 Draken, my favourite design, and I was lucky enough to be
given a flight in their 2-seater. The Draken was a remarkably
smooth and zippy machine, like a supersonic Hunter and very nice
to fly. The main drawback was having to keep the canopy fully
closed all the time on the ground. With the air temperature above
30 degrees C things were very sweaty until we got airborne. There
was also a squadron of vintage F100 Super Sabres at Karup, for
ground attack. The Danish pilots of these were a very hairy bunch,
the RDAF having an extremely liberal attitude towards its servicemen. Some young pilots had such splendid bouffant curls that we
couldn't understand how they got a bone dome on. Also the
Mudmovers flew like savages, as demonstrated in an impromptu
airfield attack they carried out when one F100 almost lost control
while pointing directly at us (he overcooked the pullout and
stalled). Some of us were already running when the pilot – one of
the hairiest we had met in the bar – just recovered control in time. I
made a mental note to turn down any offers of trips with this
bunch. The Danes were an aggressive mob in the air and we had
some good fights with them over the sea. We also encountered
some of their air defence fighters, the famous F104G Starfighter.
Over the sea they would bounce us supersonic, the tiny, slim dart
almost invisible as they rushed in to make slashing missile attacks
before departing at Warp Snot over the horizon. But they were wise
enough not to slow down and try to mix it with us at low speed.

Within a few weeks there was yet another 20 Squadron accident. I
was No. 2 on a four-ship to Helchteren range in Belgium. We were
on our second attempt to complete a TACEVAL shoot. We had
aborted again because of atrocious weather over the targets. While
flying back over the River Maas in Arrow formation at about 1,500
feet I saw a large puff of black smoke from engine.

'Silver Lead has engine failure!' was all we heard then a brief
period of heavy breathing, interspersed with a terse description of
the symptoms, (in case he didn't survive).

'RPM 15 per cent, JPT 700deg: Trying a relight', his voice was
urgent but still cool as he struggled to restart the engine.

I took over the lead and called Silver out into loose formation. At
the same time I put out a brief 'mayday' call to Wildenrath. Now

there was nothing more we could do to help him. The aircraft was decelerating rapidly. I was already using deflected nozzles and flaps trying to stay alongside him. We were only at 1,500 feet so there wasn't much time. Too late I realized that I was on the wrong side to film the inevitable ejection with my port-facing F95. I thought about moving to the other side but held off when I sensed that he was about to eject. We were already diving steeply at an uncomfortably low speed. There was a flash of the rocket as the seat whistled close by to leave the pilot hanging safely on his parachute well above me. Quickly I accelerated and told No. 3 to monitor the parachute landing. I continued to weave above the doomed aircraft until it piled into a field with remarkably little commotion, just a cloud of dust as the disintegrating wreckage ploughed a long furrow in the soft ground. I had made a point of keeping enough speed to recover from the dive – the USMC had just lost yet another wingman in exactly similar circumstances when his leader had engine failure. The wingman had slowed down too much and followed his leader's aircraft into the same hole in the ground.

So, we had lost yet another Harrier with a suspicious engine failure. Soon we heard the electrifying news that witness marks on the fan blades were caused by damage from bolts originating within the engine itself. In other words the engines were destroying themselves from the inside. Because of this the RAF had lost three Harriers, and now we had to replace all the bolts on all the engines in the fleet. Each engine change took a minimum of three days to complete, followed by several air tests on the reassembled aircraft once the engine was back in. The wing had to come off to get the engine out. All told the engine bolts saga cost the RAF tens of thousands of hours of work and severely limited our operational capability for months.

In the summer and autumn there were the usual field deployments which were becoming more extensive in scope and better-equipped for us in the field. To make things as realistic as possible we would start out with a major TACEVAL exercise on base at Wildenrath and spend a few days practising our on-base operations. When everything was ready we would set off in pukka Army-style convoys to take all the ground equipment forward to the sites, the aircraft following up as soon as the sites were manned. Slowly, more effective equipment had been brought into use. Now we had the splendid German Unimog 4WD aircraft tow vehicle, better communications and hydrant fuel supplies on site, among many other improvements. We were also provided with a portable TACAN beacon, located 'somewhere near' the sites. Its operators, RAF signals people, had been told that the Harrier force was very tactical and obsessed with concealment; their interpretation of this was to keep their beacon moving around without telling us where it was, bless them. They didn't understand that the beacon was useless if we didn't know its exact location. On site we were heavily into cockpit tasking, to save time on changing over pilots in the cockpit. This was only made possible by our likely wartime tasking options whereby we would be going back to the same target area again and again to attack a particular armoured thrust. The concept of 'surge flying' was coming in and each site was aiming to fly up to fifty sorties a day with only six aircraft. With six sites that meant 300 attack sorties per day – quite a useful effort for the Northern Army Group area.

Interspersed with intensive flying, more experienced pilots had to do stints of duty in the ops caravan as duty authorizer, where you were responsible for the whole flying programme. This was hard work, especially under TACEVAL conditions when you would be working for long hours in stifling heat wearing full gas kit. Although I was wholly in favour of the surge flying concept I took a jaundiced view of the childish 'sortie race' game. Each site was now vying to achieve the first fifty-sortie day with just six aircraft. To achieve this, people were taking unnecessary risks to fly unproductive sorties just to get near to the magic fifty. This was the same kind of thing as hour-hogging in my view and, although keen to launch as many productive sorties as was reasonably possible, I refused to take part in the game. On one occasion as duty authorizer I deliberately cancelled our fiftieth sortie of the day because there was no useful air task for the pilot. Fifty was just another number as far as I was concerned, no more significant than forty-nine or fifty-one.

Cockpit tasking was great fun and you could get in a lot of flying in a short time. The daily routine on site would be as follows: After breakfast in the Mess tent at an impossibly early hour you would report to the GLO and IO for a briefing on the latest exercise (or war) situation. After a Met brief you would update your navigational maps with any information given. Then the duty authorizer, (who controlled flying operations) would divide you up into formations and issue a 'batting order' for the day's flying. You then got together with your wingman and carried out an extensive pre-brief of how you were going to fly any mission given. By now sweltering in full flying clothing you sat around waiting for the first air tasks to come in. When this happened the GLO briefed you on the target, updated your intelligence information and you signed out after a short authorizer brief. You then literally ran to the jets and the game was on. Everything was done as fast as possible, the only way to make sure we could achieve some impossibly difficult TOTs (time-on-target), and get in the maximum number of effective sorties per day. After duffing up the target and a brief punch-up with any fighters we could find, we would land back on as quickly as possible. Hanging around airborne to claim extra flying time was stamped on in 20 Squadron. Hour hogs need not apply. Back in the hide a telebrief line would be plugged in as the ground crew refuelled and re-armed. Sitting in the cockpit under a cam net was pretty relaxing compared with the hassle of climbing out and trekking back to ops with all your heavy gear. (Your steel helmet, sleeping bag, 9mm pistol, gas mask and gas kit were all lugged around in a large plastic sack.) On telebrief you debriefed with the GLO and duty authorizer and received details of your next task. We could then switch to a quiet channel to re-brief within our formation. After the minimum time on the ground we would launch again for the next target and repeat the cycle for a maximum of six sorties per pilot per day. After the fourth sortie of the day the peacetime rules said you had to get out of the cockpit for a stroll, just to ease your muscles and break the routine.

Cockpit tasking meant long hours sitting on an ejection seat and was very tiring day after day. On one occasion I flew twenty-three sorties in four consecutive flying days, all under TACEVAL conditions. By the end of that time I was so fatigued that I barely had the strength to pull enough g to recover off target. Air combat was a lost cause when you were so tired. In spite of our fatigue we usually found enough energy to launch most nights to the nearest 'schoolies' Mess or a suitable *Stube* for some beers. The drive back was usually pretty fraught in the dark, our ultra-keen junior GLO insisting on exercising his driver in lights-off driving over the sandy wastes of the tank range. This was done in order to conceal the location of our sites, which were often under attack by 'enemy' saboteurs and ground forces during the night. (Sometimes the pilots had to do a stint of 'stag', or site guarding at night.) We all became completely at ease living under canvas, bringing various aids to help make life more comfortable. I always used an air bed on top of a camp bed, to sleep like a log most nights. Those unwise enough to rely solely on the air bed were often left floating around in the not-uncommon floods we experienced. Grub was always at a high standard under canvas from the RAF's mobile caterers. For me the main black spot of any deployment was the enforced reliance on Elsans for essential functions. After a few days many of these were full to overflowing: not a pretty sight.

A lot of our airborne tasking on field deployments (and from Wildenrath) was on forward air controller (FAC) missions. After my experiences with the excellent ex-Hunter FACs in the Middle East the standard of NATO FACs was a big disappointment. Few of them were capable of giving adequate control, even the British ones. In 1973 RAF FAC techniques were little changed from those used successfully in the Second World War. The FAC observed likely targets from a front-line position and gave attack details to ground attack aircraft orbiting in a safe area within radio range. Having spotted a likely target, the FAC would plot it as a six-figure grid reference and then work out a suitable run-in track and time from a known initial point some 10-20 kilometres back from the target. The waiting attack pilots would have a large-scale map (usually 1:250,000 scale) on which were drawn up a large number of initial points which had been agreed with the FAC. Having passed all of these details to the pilot, the latter would be cleared to run in from the initial point to carry out the attack, usually under the direct control of the FAC. As the FAC observed the aircraft pull up for the attack, he would then begin a rapid commentary, designed to get the pilot's eyes on to the target as soon as possible. Bear in mind that there would be a maximum of about fifteen seconds available for the FAC to talk, from first seeing the attacking aircraft to completion of the attack. FACs had to choose their words extremely carefully.

Problems with FAC at this time can be summed up as follows:

Quality of Current FACs: Traditionally, primary FACs had been selected from the ranks of ex-ground attack pilots. As these became scarcer, other aircrew and many non-aircrew types were brought into the trade, with predictable results on the quality of control.

Radio Communications: The Harrier radio, as already stated, was of a scandalously poor quality and it was usually impossible to hear what the FAC was saying unless the pilot got so close to him that he was within range of enemy defences. During peacetime exercises in Germany some of us would refuse to fly any closer to the FAC than we thought was 'realistic' (i.e. staying out of range of the enemy's weapons and radars until cleared to attack). This meant that communication with the FAC was almost impossible and therefore we would fail to carry out the required attacks. This would be reported on the mission report after the sortie, invariably without follow-up action from higher echelons. We were trying to make the point that FAC would be virtually impossible in wartime, but they just weren't interested.

Choice of Initial Points: The choice of initial points was entirely out of the control of the attacking pilots, and was often inept. Because of the average FAC's lack of fast jet low level navigation experience, they had only the vaguest idea of what kind of feature could easily be found from the air. Initial points such as minor road junctions hidden in woodland, farmhouses amongst a profusion of the same, tiny, thin masts visible from only half a mile: – all of these and many more appeared with depressing regularity on our FAC initial point maps. In many cases it was easier to find the target than the initial point. The most common error by FACs was failure to take account of terrain in hilly areas. Many attacks would fail simply because the initial point or the target was hidden behind a hill until the last moment.

Target Acquisition: At the end of the initial point run – assuming that the pilot had flown 100 per cent accurate track and distance, allowing for wind effect – he would pull up and look for the main reference point indicated by the FAC. Like the initial points, these reference points were often poorly chosen. The pilot had, at most, only a few seconds to correctly identify the reference point and then look from there to the target, with the assistance of a commentary from the FAC.

Target Marking: Often the FAC would offer to 'mark' the target or reference point with coloured smoke. In the confusion of battle, this was often difficult to pick up. Yellow smoke in a yellow cornfield was a fairly normal FAC trick.

Our FAC Techniques: In order to achieve at least some measure of success in our peacetime FAC exercises we adopted the following measures:

Rear Briefing: If at all possible we would insist that target details were passed to us as we overflew ground forces HQ in a safe rear area. From then on the FAC acted merely as a veto, cancelling the attack if it was not required.

In-Flight Target Study: After rear briefing the better pilots would be able to plot the target position on their own 1:50, 000 scale map in the cockpit – at the same time flying and navigating at low level in battle formation at 420 knots and also looking out for hostile aircraft. A little bit of 'target study' carried out before the attack could make the difference between a successful first pass attack and a miss. Often this 'target study' would reveal a useful reference point that the FAC had not noticed, which would also help during the attack – in effect the pilot doing most of the FAC's job for him.

Straight-In Attacks: By the end of my Harrier tour in Germany we had abandoned the old-fashioned 'turning' tip-in and adopted the straight-in run at the target, nicknamed 'Iron Spike'. The turning attack was always a source of errors. With a straight run at the target it was possible for the better pilots to draw a line on their cockpit maps, in flight, and fly along this line to the target. This proved to be a much more reliable method than listening to the FAC's commentary.

All of these ongoing problems with FAC were repeated with tedious monotony on each and every FAC exercise. In spite of constant bitter protests from front-line pilots, little if anything was done by our staffs to improve the situation and – inevitably – we were to lose aircraft shot down while carrying out FAC attacks in the Falklands War some ten years later, when the chickens came home to roost.

In midsummer I had an accident with a Harrier engine which dented my selfconfidence somewhat. We were on field deployment and on MAXEVAL at Geseke site, some ten miles east of Bad Lippspringe. I was sitting in a cockpit in a hide, awaiting start-up time as various other formations taxied out through the dust right in front of me. Normally our big engine intake covers were removed when the aircraft was ready for start, but each time another Harrier taxied past I told the ground crew to put them back in to avoid getting stones down the engine. When the coast was clear the ground crew removed them again. This happened several times and, sure enough, when the order to start engines came they were still in the intakes, unknown to me. I should have double-checked. During engine start the covers were sucked in, causing some expensive damage to the engine. The boss played a blinder. In shame I explained what had happened, expecting some pretty severe disciplinary action. After hearing my account of the incident he said straight away: 'Forget about it Jerry: it wasn't your fault.'

What a player. With the current spate of accidents, with Harriers falling out of the sky left, right and centre, our senior commanders were of a mind to 'kick' any pilot ruthlessly for the most minor incident. Shortly before this incident the boss had astonished me by telling me that the Chief of the Air Staff was interested in getting me as an ADC. I told him that I was not the least bit interested in the job and that I was desperate to remain on 20 Squadron. He sympathized but told me I would have to go through the motions and be 'interviewed' in London. I duly turned up at the Ministry of Defence wearing my scruffiest sports jacket. I hadn't bothered to shave or comb my rather long hair – I didn't want the job anyway. I was interviewed by a squadron leader who sniffed at my scruffy appearance and told me what a privilege it would be to be selected for this 'demanding staff appointment'. I told him no thanks, and can I go back to my squadron now? That was the end of that.

A job I really did want to be selected for was the QWI course at Wittering. There were two slots available for 20 Squadron on the course that year, and to my delight, the boss said I could have one of them. Close to the course starting date I was disappointed to hear that one of the slots was cancelled, and I had lost out. I determined to get on the first course next year, but meanwhile an event was taking place in the Middle East which was to have far-reaching consequences for all of us. The Arab-Israeli Yom Kippur war was an epic struggle as far as we were concerned in the RAF. We followed the reports of the air combat engagements and ground attacks avidly, keen to learn as much as we could from the experiences of both sides. For a long time all of our operational training in RAFG had been carried out in a vacuum – we had little idea of how things would pan out in a real shooting war in the central region. Apart from the rather specialized experience of Vietnam (we had some American Vietnam 'vets' flying on the Wildenrath Wing), no modern Air Force had been put to the test at low level against up-to-date SAMs and radar-laid gun systems. We studied the reports of the Yom Kippur war with great interest, keen to find out which tactics would work in realistic defence conditions. By now I had been appointed as squadron tactics officer, responsible for keeping everyone up-to-date

with the latest enemy weapon systems and tactics. This was a fascinating job and, when not flying, I spent many hours in the station
bunker studying reports of the capabilities and tactics of the WP
forces.

One day in late summer a friend and I, and a couple of girls, piled
into the Jodel for a trip across to France for lunch. The trip turned
out to be a little more adventurous than we had bargained for. I
refuelled at Saarbrucken and we flew across the border to land at a
small French club flying field. While taxiing in to the empty parking
area we saw a small turbine-powered helicopter appear around the
side of the hangars, hover-taxiing towards us. As it passed the corner
of the hangar the rotor blades clipped a metal support and we
watched in horror as the machine rolled over in a flash, the rotor
blades beating the machine to death barely 100 yards away. Without
thinking I was out of the cockpit and running, the prop of the Jodel
still spinning after I had cut the ignition. With my friend pounding
close behind I ran straight for the smoking tangle of wreckage. The
engine was still winding down and spewing out a jet of vaporized
fuel from the red-hot, mangled turbine. 'Just give us a few seconds,'
I prayed. 'Don't burn yet, please.'

A bloodstained, dishevelled figure was staggering away from the
wreck: somehow he had been able to drag himself clear. I could see
a leg sticking out of the wreck of the cockpit. The body didn't look
too badly damaged, although the face was badly cut up by broken
perspex. There was no choice; we couldn't leave him in the wreck,
which might burn at any moment. My friend and I pounced on the
unconscious body and dragged him clear upwind. There was no one
else in the wreck and we seemed to be alone on the airfield which
was still paralysed with inactivity after the drama of the accident.
After a brief checkout we established that he was still breathing and
not bleeding to death. We cleared his airways and left him in the
recovery position, awaiting professional medical help.

No chance. The whole action was over in less than two minutes,
from seeing the crash to dragging the body away, and now the
airfield erupted with action. A bunch of hysterical French civilians
appeared from nowhere and rushed at us, pushing us aside pulling
him about and trying to give him mouth-to-mouth, all the while
screaming at each other in unintelligible French. Realizing that there
was nothing more we could do in the face of this uncomprehending
mob, my friend and I walked slowly back to the Jodel, our clothes
still stained with the blood of the casualty. After a brief cleaning-up

session away from the scene of the accident we strolled into town for a well-earned drink. I never found out what happened to the casualty in the end. We didn't identify ourselves to the local authorities – I had no intention of being stuck in France to be interrogated about the accident.

I managed to get some leave later in the summer, having had a promising trip to Vienna cancelled by the squadron. I invited a couple of passengers along for a trip in the Jodel to the south of France. First leg was to Lyon, where hangarage and landing fees came to the princely sum of ten francs at the International Airport. After looking round the city we stayed overnight in a sweaty, noisy old hotel in the centre of town. Next day we set off through the Alps to Nice. I remembered a bit about mountain flying from my helicopter trips back at Valley. I took very careful note of the wind forecast – I had no intention of flying over mountainous terrain in a strong wind. Even though the wind was relatively light I was still a bit caught out as I approached a sheer, razor-sharp ridge line just south of Grenoble. The headwind spilling over the ridge put us in a strong downdraught and I needed full power for a long time to clear the ridge safely. After the long, easy glide downhill to the coast we landed at Nice and put the Jodel away in a hangar for a week at ten francs a night. We had an idyllic week of lounging around Nice, staying in a splendid old hotel close to the sea front. We took a taxi around the headland to Monaco to marvel at the sights and the fleets of luxury yachts in the harbour.

All too soon we had to set off back, on the 'John Wayne' scenic route right through the middle of the Alps. I checked the weather very carefully and we loaded up with enough fuel to make southern Germany. With three up the Jodel was distinctly short on power and I wasn't sure that I could get high enough to get over the Alps. If we couldn't hack it on the route I had planned then we would have to retrace our steps all the way back to Nice and fly back to Lyons via lower ground. I hadn't told the girls of my doubts, and we took off in rather hazy conditions to head east along the coast for Genoa. After some distance I struck north into the Alpes Maritimes to get into the northern Italian plain. The weather in the mountains was a bit tricky and the girls got a bit agitated about the amount of cloud I was dodging around between the mountain peaks. However, all went well until I broke out of the mountainous region to discover that I was completely lost. Back to basics. I had taught lost procedure enough times on the Jet Provost, so I found a line feature and flew

along it. After a while I had found out where I was, the technique
working perfectly the first time I had to use it in anger. I headed
straight for Lake Maggiore and we started the long, slow climb up
to 8,000 feet. By now the weather had cleared and in the crystal-clear
air we could see the magnificent sight of the entire Alpine range
spread out in front, just a few cumulus clouds decorating some
distant, snow-capped peaks. All very pretty, but could we make it
over the highest point of the route?

By now we had been climbing in the High Alps for over an hour
and were in Swiss airspace. We had left the beautiful blue waters of
the lake behind, following the valley which led to the Simplon Pass,
the lowest passage through the peaks. As far as I could tell from the
half million scale map, ground level in the pass was between 7,500
and 8,000 feet. Could we get that high? We were still only at 6,000
feet and the rate of climb was pitifully slow. Meanwhile the ground
in the valley below was rising ominously to our level, with large
areas of snow between the rocks on either side. The valley was
getting noticeably narrower and I knew that I would have to judge it
pretty carefully if we had to abort and turn round. With limited
engine performance I couldn't afford to make any strenuous
manoeuvres or we would stall straight into the rocks below. At last
we made 7,000 feet, the rate of climb less than 100 feet per minute
as we approached the final bend in the valley, after which I knew I
should be able to see the pass just a few miles ahead. For over an
hour now I had been hanging on to our exact climbing speed with
the lightest possible touch on the stick. With our limited power we
would need all of the distance up to the pass to gain sufficient height.
Happily, the engine was droning on perfectly: any sign of a problem
would mean an immediate 180 degree turn to retrace our steps back
down the valley. We drifted slowly round the final bend and I could
see the level floor of the pass and the dead ground of the valley
beyond. Not daring to move the stick in case I lost another knot of
airspeed, I focussed intently on the ground ahead, trying to see if our
flight path was going to clear the ridge. There was silence in the
cockpit, as by now the passengers had realized how tight things were
going to be. For a moment I regretted taking this route: what could
I say if we had to turn back now?

Imperceptibly – painfully slowly – I saw that progressively more of
the valley wall beyond was rising above the ridge line ahead. Like a
sailor using transits to see if he was being 'headed' from his destination by the tide, a pilot could see if his flight path was going to clear

any given obstacle ahead. We were going to make it and I was sure of it just before we lost the turn-back option. We flew through the narrow pass at a comfortable 300 feet above the rocks, the engine at maximum power and the speed a comfortable 10 knots above the stall. The altimeter read 7,800 feet, the highest I ever saw in the Jodel. As the ground started to recede below us I knew it was downhill all the way into northern Europe. I started to breathe again.

From here on I could relax all the way to Germany and I pulled the throttle back almost to idle to begin the long glide down past Trun in the Vorderrhein valley. Turning left at Chur we passed the borders of Liechtenstein and saw the silver sparkling line of Lake Constance far away to the north. I had not spoken to anyone on the radio since leaving Nice. The only embarrassment would have been an interception by air defence fighters. However, we were flying too low for that to be much of a risk. The waters of Lake Constance looked calm and peaceful in the late afternoon sunlight as I glided in to land at Friedrichshaven airfield. We had a snack and a coffee and flew on to Wildenrath in the early evening.

At the end of that year we went on APC again to Decimommannu in Sardinia, not the nicest time of year to be there. The weather was cool and cloudy, and we shivered at nights in the inadequately heated blocks. A new squadron arrival joined us on the APC, having just started his squadron work-up training. This pilot was an original character and a self-confident maverick who was not prepared to be overawed by the RAF's way of doing things. I latched on to him as a kindred spirit straight away. An ex-Phantom pilot, he was pretty sharp at air combat and soon learned the tricks of the Harrier. Our new boss turned up on a visit to Deci.. He appeared to us as impossibly young-looking for a wing commander with a squadron commander's tour already behind him. He had been OC of a Hunter squadron in the late '60s and was to be an excellent boss too.

At Christmas I drove home to find Britain in the grip of the so-called oil crisis. There had been no sign of this in Germany and I was horrified to find empty petrol stations and morons on the roads driving everywhere at 40 mph in third gear. These fools thought they were saving fuel, but by forcing everyone behind them to drive in a lower gear in fact they were pushing up everyone's fuel consumption. You couldn't tell them: they automatically associated speed with high fuel consumption. They didn't understand that if you drove in anything other than top gear you were wasting fuel.

My final year in Germany seemed to race past, the pace of our flying programme becoming steadily more hectic with each day. Exercise followed exercise with bewildering rapidity, and there seemed to be no end to the complexity of our wartime task. In my capacity as tactics officer, nowadays named Warlord, I had to continually update the squadron on changes to our war plans and procedures, as well as passing on tactical advice gained from studying intelligence reports. It was a sobering experience to be reminded regularly of the vast superiority of forces the WP had over us and our puny ability to strike back in the event of an invasion. We had to plan for it, and aim to get the best possible value from our limited force size. Among many other wartime procedures, the 2 ATAF routeing and recovery plan was fiendishly complex through the maze of NATO SAM sites between us and the enemy.

We surmised that the procedures would be difficult to follow accurately in the heat of battle and if so, might expose us to the risk of being shot down by our own defences. At the same time our poor radios would scupper any effective control of air attacks from the ground. Consequently we regularly practised NO COMM target-of-opportunity attacks on vehicles and armour, simulating no radio contact with each other or with ground agencies. Finally, we knew that in war there was little chance of our surviving many missions in the face of the expected overwhelming enemy flak and SAM barrages.

Many of us practised the difficult technique of free navigation back to an opportunity target, which was to come in useful for me later on in the Falklands War. In this a likely target, found on a line or area search, was mentally plotted and a return track worked out after completing the line. At the end of the line, having assessed all the likely targets seen, we would turn back (usually flying in pairs) to attack the most juicy targets. Bear in mind that we would now be maybe 30 kilometres away from the target and would have to 'free nav' all the way back, making use of all terrain cover possible to make a tactical attack. In this demanding exercise you had to make your brain work in reverse, remembering all the geographical features of the line in reverse order. There was little time to consult a hand-held map. The technique was difficult but essential, and we refined it to a bit of an art. This kind of thing was commonly done in the latter days of the Second World War, but Typhoon, Tempest and Spitfire pilots usually had the luxury of searching for targets from medium altitude (5,000-10,000 feet), while we had to do everything as low as we could possibly fly to avoid SAMs. This, combined with our higher speeds, made the navigation problem extremely challenging. We were used to dealing with this problem. Since the advent of jet low flying speeds the success of any ground attack or recce pilot, depended mostly on his ability to navigate at low level, and our squadron training recognized this. Upgrading to combat ready status depended mostly on how well the new pilot could find his way around with confidence, leading a formation. Some older hands would cheat at the game and show off their navigational skills only in familiar areas, where they knew the terrain well. An old training tactic from the fighter reconnaissance instructor course was that you always tried to train in unfamiliar areas, as you could never be sure where you would be tasked to fly in wartime. This was the true test of low level navigation: to set off in totally unfamiliar terrain and still be able to follow the route and find the targets.

We flew in almost any weather conditions, few excuses being accepted for not getting airborne. If the weather forecast was bad for a particular area where you wanted to go, then you just went anyway, to have a look and see if the Met man was right. Practising our SOP formation attacks could be slightly hazardous in the prevailing summertime conditions of Germany, when an impenetrable Ruhr haze drifted about the whole of the central region. In such conditions flight visibility would be as bad as 2-3 kilometres at best, and almost impossible directly into sun. To add to the problem the windscreen would be covered in squashed insects soon after you got airborne. In summertime I grew to hate the unhelpful green writing and general mechanical clutter of the HUD, which formed a permanent obstacle to my forward vision. I just wanted to tear it out of the way, remembering the clear, uncluttered forward view from the Hunter FR10. One of our more punchy low-level manoeuvres was the rotate attack, used in battle four formation when the lead or No. 3 spotted a ground target passing down the middle of the formation. We would all fly on for about ten seconds and then the lead would turn hard inwards back towards the target, to pull up and make an attack with his wingman. Meanwhile the No. 3 would delay slightly then carry out a similar manoeuvre towards the lead so that we ended up with four aircraft attacking with a 90 degree separation with the minimum time separation over the target. With practice we got pretty good at it and wingmen became used to making close pairs attacks with their element leader, an essential requirement to minimize time spent over the target. We could also fly the rotate attack NO COMM. Timing was everything and the element leads had to be careful to identify both aircraft of the opposite element before committing to an attack. At low level a constant worry was the proliferation of tall, thin TV masts which were springing up everywhere, usually in the middle of our favourite low-level routes. These masts, often 1,000 feet high, were supported by a cat's cradle of steel wires which extended many hundreds of metres from the base. Many NATO pilots had flown into them with fatal results over the years – they were very difficult to see in the customary poor low level visibility. One particular obstacle, which literally gave me nightmares, lay in the middle of the north German plain, close to the Mittelland canal. This was a large 'antenna farm' of dozens of 1,200 feet masts interlinked with multiple steel cables, the whole thing over a kilometre across. In poor weather you were never exactly certain of their position over the featureless north German plain and we had a lot of near misses with this low level flytrap when people got just a bit too close. Once you were in it there was no point in trying to pull up, you would be bound to hit one of the cables anyway. Some of my worst nightmares ended up with me discovering that I had flown into the middle of the flytrap and had no choice but to fly on, cringing and hoping I wasn't about to be cut in half by one of the cables.

A certain senior officer was finally leaving Wildenrath after an exhausting round of farewells. His last flight on 20 Squadron was to be a memorable occasion for me. As duty pilot, I was dozing in the tower when he taxied out for his last trip. At the end of his sortie I heard him call up to ask if he was clear for a 'flypast', the usual euphemism for the customary 'knee trembler'. Idly I watched from my position slumped in the duty pilot's chair as he appeared over the top of the Bloodhound SAM site at the eastern end of the field. This pilot was a good aviator and I had no qualms about the flypast as he flashed past down the northern taxiway at a good head height. Within a few seconds the 'squawk box' from Met buzzed:

'Who was that idiot?'

I passed on the pilot's name and rank.

'Well you can tell him if he does that again we're all walking out of here!'

'Typical Met Office: – no sense of humour,' I thought.

OC operations' box buzzed angrily next. His office was next to Met.

I explained who it was, forestalling the obvious question. Silence.

The box switched off. Five Seconds later it buzzed again.

'Doesn't he KNOW who's on the station down at the visiting aircraft flight?'

'Er, no sir. What do you mean?' (With a sinking heart I realized that I should have checked earlier.)

'Well, there's the Chief of the Air Staff, the Commander in Chief and the Station Commander for a start – who else does he want in the audience?' This with heavy sarcasm.

By sheer bad luck the aforementioned VIPs had just landed in an Andover and were standing in the sunshine right next to the taxiway as the Harrier flashed past. Apparently nobody said a word at the time, just a raised eyebrow from CAS to the Station Commander. The senior officer was furious with me after he landed:

'You dull shit WIN, why didn't you TELL me?'

'I'm sorry, sir, I didn't know they were there – honest,' I apologized, genuinely mortified.

After a series of accidents we were becoming snowed under with flying orders and instructions, all of which were supposed to be obeyed without question. These orders continually filtered down from on high, in order to prevent that particular accident from ever happening again. In my view this was an erroneous philosophy as, by their nature, accidents were a classic chaotic event, subject only to the laws of chance. What really mattered was the quality of our aircrew, their flying accuracy, self-discipline and standard of training – especially their poor-weather flying capability.

In poor weather the RAF, Dutch and Belgian Air Forces had Germany to themselves. The Americans and the GAF weren't even allowed to plan to fly in any area where the met man forecast weather below low flying limits (5 kilometres visibility and cloud base 500 feet above cruising height). We never took instructions from the met man: his forecasts were merely advisory, to be checked out by a pilot on the spot if necessary. In really appalling weather we would meet the occasional Dutch or Belgian recce aircraft, but no one else. (Never one of our so-called all-weather fighters.)

The low flying regulations were about to be altered for ever as a result of an accident involving an RAF Jaguar pilot. The pilot accidentally flew under a set of power lines and clipped the fin off, leading to an inevitable ejection. Our commanders immediately introduced new low level rules so that we now had to fly a minimum height of 250 feet minimum separation distance (MSD). With the old

250 feet a.g.l. rules you could always claim that you were 250 feet above ground if you clobbered an obstacle. The new rules, when introduced in the mid '70s, increased our low flying training heights at a stroke, in my view degrading our training at the same time.

Medium altitude air combat training was the standard default exercise when really bad weather prevented low level training. There was one overriding reason for this:- ACT was fun. It was the most challenging and exhilarating of all forms of fighter flying by a long way, and we were drunk with the thrill of it. Air combat was the ultimate demonstration of the pilot's art: it required him to handle his aircraft instinctively to the far limits of its performance while under severe physical and mental pressure, while at the same time maintaining a cool chess-like appreciation of three-dimensional positioning, involving large numbers of competing aircraft. On most squadrons, skill at air combat was the most envied and sought-after quality for a pilot. The ACT 'kill' ladder, (showing which pilots had achieved the highest number of simulated 'kills') was the most important barometer of a squadron's morale and motivation. Jokingly we called it 'the sport of kings' and this was no exaggeration.

Within the RAF this overriding preference for ACT had a strong influence on the training of all squadrons, both air defence and ground attack. From the early 1970s there were just two basic types of fast jet squadron in the RAF (ignoring the few specialist recce units). Air defence squadrons practised all-weather air interception and carried out ACT. Fighter bomber squadrons practised ground attack and also carried out a lot of ACT, much of it at low level. I once asked an old colleague (an ex-Creamy with me at Leeming, now flying Lightnings at Gutersloh), how many ACT missions he had flown recently. I found out that I had flown more ACT missions in the previous week than he had flown in the previous three months.

My customary overconfidence in the air was given another jolt on my annual standardization trip with our standards officer in the T4 in late July. Each pilot on the Wing had to fly a check ride once a year to demonstrate that his VSTOL handling was up to scratch. In the circuit at Wildenrath he asked me to do a braking stop slow landing on the southern taxiway. This manoeuvre, involving selection of braking stop just before touchdown, had led to several accidents in the past when pilots got the timing wrong. At Wittering they had banned the manoeuvre but the standards officer was still holding out for us practising it at Wildenrath. The problem was that if you selected braking stop a fraction of a second too early the aircraft would pitch nose up, out of control, whereas if you were too late then it would pitch down, out of control. You had only one chance to get it right. I was too early and I smashed the stick into the instrument panel in a hopeless attempt to stop the nose pitching up. The standards officer was on the controls in a flash and recovered immediately with a deft movement of the nozzle lever: that was the secret, as only by reducing the nozzle angle could you regain pitch control. In the heat of the moment I hadn't moved fast enough and without him in the aircraft I would have been a smoking wreck. As we walked in he was in a subdued mood. He confided in me that he was probably going to recommend that we should also ban the manoeuvre in RAFG, and that is what happened. Thus, by default, I became the last RAF Harrier pilot to attempt a braking stop slow landing. Actually in my view the manoeuvre always was a bit overrated, demanding far too much skill and concentration from the pilot. We were better off without it. Ironically, the RAF's Tornado pilots were to go through a similar painful experience in the '80s with the pre-selected thrust reverse landing, also designed to minimize the landing roll. This manoeuvre was also re-evaluated and severely restricted by various regulations.

In September we completed our final Wing deployment of the year, to the Mandalay site in Sennelager, 20 primary site once again on grass. This was my last deployment and I was uncomfortably aware that I would, once again, be 'peddling trash' as a QFI at Wittering within a few months. The exercise flying was glorious and action-packed as usual, and our new boss was on top form, having settled in well.

During the TACEVAL phase of the deployment we went all-out to support a major Army exercise as usual, in this case a river-crossing evolution on the River Weser, in one of the prettiest parts of the Sauerland. This generated a large number of interesting air tasks for us to attack troops, armour and bridging equipment as the Army played with their toys in the water. It was always a source of wonderment to me that we were being paid for this. After each day's flying the pilots would sit down in a tent with the TACEVAL team and 16mm cine projector to debrief the day's missions. As usual this involved correlating the claims of targets destroyed or damaged on the mission reports with the actual HUD film obtained. If the team considered that your HUD aiming accuracy was poor then they would disallow the claim and this would affect our operational assessment at the end of the TACEVAL. This was all good clean fun and generated a lot of ribald comments as some over-ambitious claims were exposed to close technical scrutiny. Bull-shitters and Walter Mittys need not apply. I remember one particular piece of a certain pilot's film which had us all on the edge of our seats. Clearly he had made a last-second split-arse turn on to the target. The very first frame of film showed a close-up plan view of part of a German Army barracks from a horrific dive angle. There was a sharp intake of breath from the assembled mob – this was going to be interesting. After no more than a fraction of a second of extremely unsteady tracking, the weapon release pulse appeared at the corner of the frame, followed by an extremely rapid pullout with extensive wing rock, the pilot pulling deep into the stall to avoid hitting the ground. After a death-defying close shave on the roofs of the barrack buildings – individual slates of which were clearly visible on film – everything went blank as the camera switched off, to the sound of ribald cheers from the onlooking cynics. No undue disrespect was intended: most of us held this particular pilot in great esteem as a fully paid-up member of the human race; we were merely demonstrating our relief that he had survived a close shave and spared us yet another tiresome Board of Inquiry. The cheers subsided. In the stunned silence the evaluator spoke, his voice earnest and deferential with the polite sarcasm reserved particularly for senior officers who had screwed up badly:

'Er, I see from your MISREP you claimed a damage on this target, Sir?'

'I think we'd better write this one off to experience', said the pilot, sheepishly.

We had all seen too many examples of this kind of target film before, some of them resulting in the death of the pilot concerned. Fortunately for boards of inquiry, gunsight films often survive the resulting collision with the ground or the hill behind the target which you hadn't noticed – the final, embarrassingly public testament to the foolhardiness or sheer bad luck of the pilot concerned.

The 20 Squadron band had gone from strength to strength over the years and we all took our instruments to every field deployment. On several occasions we had a full squadron dining-in night in the field, after which we would play for a while, with steadily increasing derision from the other squadrons – who clearly had no musical taste. Many of our songs were corrupt versions of Trad Jazz standards, with obscene comments on the other squadrons added to the lyrics. To our delight the boss would bring a mangy old violin on all deployments and insist on scraping along with some band numbers, even playing the occasional solo. This inevitably brought the house down with people rolling about in fits at the awful noise he was making, tongue firmly in cheek and a seraphic smile on his face as if he was playing like Paganini.

At the end of this deployment I was last airborne to return to base, and turned back for an impromptu low pass over Mandalay site before chasing off after the rest of the formation. In my usual hurry I killed an almighty overtake with a handful of braking nozzle and piled into the 'box' slot behind the boss, who was doing about 350 knots. A hangover from the Gemini days, I always took pride in getting into a formation position as fast as possible, leaving the braking to the very last moment. Looking to my left I could see there was something wrong with Gold 3's jet alongside me.

'Uh, Gold 3 – your wheels are still down.' No one else had noticed.

'Shit!' Gold 3 explained. 'Back in a sec.'

With that he pulled up out of formation into a high speed yo-yo above us, putting the gear up as he went over the top. Within a few seconds he dropped back into immaculate formation.

There were more deployments for the Wing that autumn. No. 3 Squadron went to Solingen on an exchange visit with the extremely sociable pilots of the RCAF, and a bunch of Canadian Starfighters arrived at Wildenrath. During their deployment I was asked to deliver a 3 Squadron jet to Solingen and was invited to stay overnight for a massive party, with the promise of a Starfighter trip in the morning. Feeling very much the worse for wear after an epic booze-up, I was shovelled into the back seat of a TF 104G in rather unfriendly-looking weather conditions. Solingen sits below a heavily-wooded ridgeline on the plain of the Rhine, and the hilltops all round were covered in low stratus as we took off. I was amazed at the smoothness and power of the Starfighter after the constant vibration and noise of the Harrier. When the pilot cancelled afterburner I thought the engine had stopped, it was so quiet. We cruised around in and out of the cloud tops far too low for comfort, the pilot demonstrating how the radar could pick out the hill tops and keep you from spearing in. We climbed above a virginal white layer of solid stratocumulus for some gentle aeros. The stick seemed heavy after the Harrier, but the power of the afterburner gave scintillating

acceleration in and out of manoeuvres. After about half an hour I
was quite used to the stick forces and was beginning to enjoy myself.
The pilot took over for a dirty dart down through the clouds, once
again using the radar picture to fix his position. This was the first
time I had used an air-to-ground radar and I was much impressed.
Unlike our unreliable INAS system, the radar never lied. It always
showed exactly what was there below the cloud, the only problem
being in interpretation of the picture. In contrast, our INAS-driven
projected map was child's play to interpret (it was the same low level
map that we used for normal LL navigation). However, Sod's Law
had given the INAS a sixth sense of when the pilot was uncertain of
position, especially above cloud. In that case it would invariably drift
off miles away from the correct position, leading the pilot completely astray. Old Harrier hands had learned from bitter experience never
to rely on INAS when it would have been really useful, i.e. when you
were lost. Ironically, in good weather when you didn't need it the
INAS would stay accurate for hour after hour, showing exactly
where you were. Back at Solingen we flew a couple of patterns, at a
good Harrier looping speed around finals. I found the machine unbe-
lievably smooth and very nice to fly, more of a re-entry vehicle than
an aircraft.

Straight away 20 Squadron was off on the final exercise of the
year, this time to the German Air Force base of Diepholz in the north
German plain. This was our annual 'Red Rat' exercise, in support of
4 Armoured Brigade in their annual exercises. We had an epic week
of flying with the longest and most liberal entries in the flight author-
ization sheets that I had ever seen. On each mission we were
authorized first of all, to provide local airfield defence, then to
proceed to the target area and savage any enemy tanks we could find
(there were hundreds of them). In the target area we were allowed to
bounce any 'enemy' fighters we encountered and on return to base
we had to carry out an airfield attack to exercise the Diepholz
defences. After a week of this we were whacked and grateful to
return to base.

At Wildenrath the social life continued non-stop and we had some
epic Mess guest nights with the usual fun and games. One of the
pilots owned a Honda monkey bike and would always wheel that
out for us to give the girls a ride round the ante room, often three up.
On one occasion we managed to get someone's Mini through the
front door of the Mess and drive it up and down the corridor. The
20 Squadron dining-out was an uncomfortable occasion for me as I

had no wish to leave Germany. However, in the end you went where you were posted: there was no room for sentiment in the RAF's personnel department at this time – there were too few QFIs willing and able to take on the difficult and demanding job on the Harrier OCU, which was no easy option as I was soon to discover. There were also a lot more accidents to come before the end of my time on the Harrier.

So far I had learned that the whole ethos of the Harrier force was not conducive to a careful, measured approach to aviation – which was unfortunate for those few individuals who couldn't keep up the pace. The essential timing requirements of our air tasking system and the constraints of field operations meant that things usually had to be done at the run, or we wouldn't have been able to do the job in wartime. Risks were being taken every day in order to get the job done and make sure we were ready for war. There was an old saying within the RAF Harrier force: 'If it isn't done quickly then it's not worth doing!'

That just about summed up our approach to flying. It suited me down to the ground and I had become a total speed-freak, keen to do everything as fast as possible. After the hectic action of field deployments you became progressively more reluctant to slow down to a more civilized pace on return to base; after all, the faster you got on with it the more flying you could get in and the sooner you could stack to the bar. At the same time I was becoming steadily more cavalier in my attitude towards risks in the air. I remember one particular incident towards the end of my tour when I was leading a four which got tangled up with some Lightnings on combat air patrol near Gutersloh. This was a fairly typical engagement, no more or less hazardous than any others we were getting into on a daily basis. This time my reaction to it gave me cause to stop and think for a while.

Dogshit low level Air Combat weather. A bruised, dark layer of nimbostratus hung ominously low over the Teutoburgerwald. The ridge was a long, wooded feature lying just north of Gutersloh and was a favourite place for the bad guys to lurk in wait for passing formations, their dark green camouflage almost invisible against the dark forest background. It was raining intermittently over the ridge, with sheets of grey/black mist interspersed with occasional clearer patches. My deputy lead was a droll, laid-back ex-creamy who had been sent to us recently from another squadron. The sinister dark green shapes of the big fighters appeared as if by magic in the middle of our formation, materializing out of one of the mist patches like sharks in a tuna school.

'Gold, break starboard, break starboard! Two bandits down the middle!'

Now began a frantic turning match in and out of the showers, each pilot trying desperately to keep the Lightnings off. Within a few seconds our formation was falling apart, the wingmen dragging arse and the element leads losing touch. Angry at our failure to stick together, I was determined to claim both of the Lightnings before they could get any one of my formation. The first one was easy, just drifting along ahead of me in the ragged cloud base, for a few seconds fatally unsure of whether to stay in the fight or abort and pull up through cloud. Get the sight on and get some film fast. I 'claimed' him just before he disappeared into the murk. Turning hard back and down towards the ridge I spotted the lead Lightning chasing hard behind two Harriers who were, in turn, pulling as hard as they could to avoid him. All aircraft were trailing thick wing tip vortices, which snaked back and down into the dark treetops just a few feet below.

We were all getting far too low for comfort: the stratus, the rain and the adrenalin flow driving us lower and lower on to the ridge line. A third Harrier was pursuing the Lightning, too far back to get a guns kill. I pointed straight at the middle of the fight, calling No. 3 to break out of the way as I closed in. As I had hoped, the Lightning had been watching No. 3 over his shoulder and now judged it prudent to break out of the unequal fight to make good his escape. He had lost track of me and was going to 'die', on film, as a result. Although only a few hundred yards in front of me, his all-over dark green camouflage made him almost invisible in the rain and against the forest background; I was relying on his tip trails to stay visual. Suddenly the trails crossed over as he reversed for the run-out – he had lost speed in the turn and I was on him like a ton of bricks, pressing the camera button for a burst of film which ended with just a glowing pair of reheat nozzles filling the whole frame. I had pressed in just a fraction of a second too long: with a lot of overtake I had to bunt violently down towards the trees to avoid colliding with my target. During the debrief I bollocked the rest for failing to maintain formation integrity and, after a few moment's reflection, had the grace to apologize for continuing the fight so long in such lousy weather conditions. Two of the formation members were pretty green, and No. 3 made it clear that he didn't appreciate the way I had summarily turfed him out of the way to get a kill. Thinking about it later on I realized that I was getting a bit too 'gung-ho', and could do with calming down a bit. On the Red Rat deployment the boss had had to interview me about the same sort of thing, and had passed on a gentlemanly warning about sticking my neck out too far in peacetime flying. This was probably as good a time as any for a change of scenery.

My time in Germany was nearly over. I went to Bavaria with some RAF and Army types for a skiing 'expedition'. Arriving back at Wildenrath in time for New Year's Eve and nursing a king-sized hangover, I set off for UK and Wittering at the beginning of January.

Chapter 13

Harrier Instructor

In the summer of 1975 I got married to Trisha. We had met in Germany and had now bought a house in Stamford. Life on the Harrier OCU was enjoyable and extremely busy, with few dull moments. On 'B' squadron we kept ourselves to ourselves and had a happy ship. The first thing I had to do was the IRE (instrument rating examiner) course which lasted a month and involved some hard work in the air. The Harrier was a bit of a pig on instruments and you were working pretty hard to keep everything under control and yet still fly smoothly. In particular, with the HUD switched off, the standby flight instruments were the usual cheap and nasty rubbish which were hard work to fly on. After twenty hours of solid instrument flying on the IRE course I was checked out on the various instructional sorties in the T4, and soon became more at home in the back seat than in the front. One major disadvantage of the T4 was the fact that the student in the front had control of the intercom volume, invariably setting it to maximum to compensate for the well-known phenomenon of student deafness under pressure. (Harrier students were under pressure all the time, especially on an instructional ride in the T4 when every minute had to count.) Because of the high intercom volume cockpit noise in the back of the T4 was even worse than that in the GR3, and I was rapidly going deaf because of it. I saw a report from the aviation medics on a cockpit noise survey in 1975: the GR3 came out as the second worst cockpit in the RAF. They hadn't tested the T4.

I enjoyed the challenge of instruction on the Harrier all the time, and quickly developed the usual survival techniques to enable me to last through a tour without a student 'bending' an aeroplane I had signed for. Some examples were: keep your left hand hard up behind the throttle whenever the 'stude' was flying VSTOL; keep the thumb of your left hand touching the nozzle lever all the time, so you would know the instant the stude started to move it; keep your right hand very close to the stick during any touchdown and lift off; monitor the footbrake pressure during slow and conventional landings, to check if they were resting their feet too hard on the rudder pedals etc. By far the most tense sorties were the initial hovers and short strip landing duals. On initial vertical take-offs we briefed the student that we wanted a bruised thigh from full roll stick in the event of a roll on vertical take-off. If you didn't get this the instructor had to take control within less than a second to prevent a crash. Similarly, on short strip landings, when the view from the rear seat was restricted anyway, throttle control was absolutely critical during the touchdown and you had to smash on power in an instant to prevent a hard landing.

In summertime temperatures all VSTOL practice in the T4 was strictly limited, and you only had one chance to get an instructional demo right. You were also working right on the limits of VSTOL performance most of the time during your demos, to give the stude the maximum opportunity to practise it himself before he was sent solo. Solo supervision was a bit tedious, and I soon grew bored with sitting out on the airfield in a Land Rover watching the students screw up various VSTOL manoeuvres. If they made a major error then you had to choose your words extremely carefully and talk fast to prevent an accident. It was absolutely crucial not to say the wrong thing, as you could easily make the situation worse. A typical example – which I had to deal with once – was the infamous '40 nozzles vertical take-off', which had been done by quite a few Harrier pilots already. The engine checks before lift-off involved a check of duct pressure with the nozzles set at 40 degrees, after which you moved them to the hover stop and immediately slammed to full power. Several students got in such a panic that they slammed to full power with the nozzles still at 40 degrees, causing the aircraft to lurch forward violently before lifting off. From bitter experience we QFIs had learned that any student in that situation instantly pulled the stick fully back in a classic Pavlovian reaction, to drag the aircraft off the ground in a horrific nose-up attitude. There was not enough brain capacity left to do the sensible thing and pull the throttle back to idle before you lifted off. Your student – who you had briefed and authorized, and for whom you were entirely respon-sible – was now lurching up into the air virtually out of control, with the controls gripped in a frenzy of panic because he couldn't work out why the aircraft was pointing up at the sky. Fortunately, once airborne the instinctive reaction in a panic was to bend the throttle into the fully-open position, so the aircraft was at least climbing away from the ground. The big danger was that forward speed would build up along with sideslip, leading to instant doom. On the radio you had to shout: 'Select hover stop, select hover stop!' several times before there would be any response.

Other VSTOL errors were equally traumatic and often it was clear that a stude had become so 'bunched' after a mistake that he just couldn't carry on safely. In that case you would give the red card on the radio and tell him to taxi back in for a thorough debrief. After this we would invariably send the stude out to try the manoeuvre again straight away. Like falling off a horse you had to get them in the air again quickly before they lost too much confidence.

In the summer I headed back to Germany and rejoined 20 Squadron primary site once again for its summer deployment exercise; this was a common arrangement for OCU instructors. Based once again on grass at Hovelhof and Moosdorf we had a great time and I felt right back in the swing of things, flying twenty-seven sorties in nine days. There were the usual fun and games to be had during the exercise and, on one occasion, I fixed up with another pilot for a bit of illicit combat after we took off from separate sites (he was flying out of 20 sub-site). Taking off from Hovelhof in the early evening I spotted my opponent far away to the east, just lifting off from the sub-site. We turned hard towards each other in the dusk at low level and zoomed up into the first high-speed yo-yo. As we crossed over at the top, in bright evening sunshine, I noticed that my opponent still had his wheels down. There was a slight problem as we were on different radio channels. There followed a frantic few seconds of flashing through the radio channels until I could find a common one where I could tell my opponent to slow down and get his wheels up.

In September there was an accident to an OCU pilot. He had been to RNAS Yeovilton for an air display and the ejection seat activated as he climbed out of the cockpit. I had taken over responsibility for air combat training on the OCU. I introduced some formal Vectoring in Forward Flight training for the studes, to try and up the standard of air combat on the machine. 'Viffing' – much hyped by the media at the time – involved using the nozzles to make sudden changes to the aircraft's flight path in combat manoeuvring. Used properly it could give an edge over a pilot not used to countering it. However, there were numerous tedious limitations involved, concerned with the strength of the nozzle system and few pilots were able to make use of it to any great effect; more likely they would 'viff' in the wrong place and make things worse for themselves. Additionally, there were a lot of major handling problems associated with VIFF, not least of which was an almighty pitch-up effect when the nozzles were deflected. The pilot had to compensate for this automatically, or he would lose control – the infamous 'departure' where the aircraft would yaw and roll out of control until the nozzles were put aft again. I had taught myself to use VIFF during my time in Germany (there was precious little air combat instruction available), and it was common to see Harriers gyrating out of control in an undignified fashion in the middle of a fight.

As a result of the steadily increasing interest in VIFF, there had already been a formal VIFF trial part 1, in which our pilots had flown a specially-modified Harrier in combat against some other types. The trial was heavy stuff, jointly organized by Hawker Siddeley, McDonnell Douglas, the USMC, NASA and the RAF. The whole thing was organized formally by test pilots and scientists of the Royal Aeronautical Establishment at Bedford. There had been limited results from the part 1 trial, partly because the aircraft involved had not had the nozzle system strengthened to the proposed level. Now we heard that there was to be a much more extensive VIFF trial part 2, using an experimental souped-up Harrier GR3 with the full strengthening mods to the engine and nozzle system. In this ultimate Harrier hot rod (XV277 – now at the Scottish Aviation Museum, East Fortune) the lucky pilot could use full power and full nozzle deflection at any airspeed. XV277 was to be armed with Sidewinder acquisition rounds and – joy of joys – a good old Mk 8 gyro gunsight and recorder camera instead of the existing HUD/Telford camera. All this had been going on in the background while I was settling in at the OCU and I was delighted to hear that I had been selected as the RAF operational pilot for the trial, due to start in September.

I had an extensive lead-in work-up for the trial, involving dissimilar air combat (DACT) against Hunters and Lightnings. For the purposes of the trial, XV277 was to be flown alternately by the three Harrier pilots in various set-ups against a Lightning, and also a very much souped-up lightweight Mk 6 Hunter.

I soon met the other trial pilots. All Lightning flying, initially in the Mk 6 but later on in the best combat version, the Mk 3, was to be done by a stocky, aggressive Scot with an absolutely fearless approach to throwing the big fighter around the sky. He was a genuine combat ace, with superb aircraft handling, combined with perfectly-controlled aggression in the air. The Mk 6 Hunter was acknowledged as the best low wing- loading type available for the trial. With extra engine power from the tweaked-up Avon and a reduced airframe weight, it promised to be a major headache as an opponent, whoever was flying it. To my delight the Hunter pilot was to be an old colleague from Gulf Hunter days, now on a tour at No. 2 Tactical Weapons unit at Brawdy as a QWI.

For the trial I was working-up against the Lightning and the Hunter in full combat down to 2,000 feet above ground, which didn't leave a lot of room for errors. In October we deployed to Valley to meet up with the full team of British and American scientists and technicians who gave us extensive briefings on the test procedures to be followed on the range. Both aircraft combating were to be tracked by a supremely accurate 3-D radar based at Aberporth, the missile test centre. This was an early version of the later instrumented air combat manoeuvring installations or ACMIs. There was a series of standard starting conditions for each combat and each Harrier pilot had to do one of each, to get sufficient test points to evaluate the results accurately. For example, one of the starts against the Lightning involved me flying XV277 straight and level at 5,000 feet at 550 knots (flat out) while my opponent pitched in on a supersonic quarter attack. Combat commenced when he was at one mile range. We were limited to a three minute engagement against the Lightning, with five minutes against the Hunter. During each test mission there would be up to six separate engagements and I would fly home literally drained and soaked in sweat.

XV277 was a dream to fly, this being my first experience of using an air-to-air missile. Additionally we had an audio angle-of-attack tone in the headset. Hence I never looked in the cockpit at all during the engagements, judging airspeed by aircraft feel, and power setting by engine noise. As usual, I judged g loading purely by the seat of my pants. Having trained myself this way I rarely looked at the g-meter and could concentrate on the opposition. The tweaked-up Pegasus gave considerably more thrust, even without using VIFF, and one of the main aims of the trial was to see how the Harrier got on both with, and without, VIFF. Hence, 50 per cent of all combats were flown using VIFF and 50 per cent without. Without VIFF the performance was spectacular anyway, there being a better than 1:1

thrust/weight ratio for most of the combats. This meant that I could enter a vertical fight against the Hunter and just keep on climbing until I got above him as he ran out of speed and lost control. I could then drop down behind him for a missile or guns shot. Against our Lightning opponent this didn't work so well as the Lightning's thrust/weight ratio was almost as good as the Harrier's. The pilot was also extremely canny about getting caught close in and was always extending and coming back into the fight at high speed with minimum risk to himself. Occasionally he would show off his low speed handling and drift the machine sedately around me in a beautifully-executed rolling scissors. Close in at low speed the Lightning looked huge and surreal, seemingly defying all the laws of aerodynamics to stay airborne. This was true piloting skill, the traditional stick-and-rudder stuff that was steadily going out of fashion as younger generations of pilots grew to regard the rudder pedals as mere footrests.

In contrast, against the Hunter pilot there was always a lot of close-in heavy breathing stuff, both aircraft gyrating about one another in a tight vertical rolling scissors with cockpits just yards apart until one pilot lost concentration momentarily and slipped in front of the other. Taking a shot with the Sidewinder was simple. All you needed was to aim roughly at the target's rear – the field of view of the IR seeker was quite generous – and listen for the 'growling' tone in the headset which showed that the missile had locked on. As soon as you got this – it took barely a second – you pressed the firing button. This was truly an idiot's weapon. Firing pulses gave a signal to the tracking radar and was recorded along with all the aircraft position and speed data to calculate if the kill was valid. You fought on anyway – missiles could go wrong. There was no immediate feedback of data from the ground monitoring stations; the scientists told us it would take months to reduce all the data and give accurate results. Hence we had to rely solely on the debriefs of the individual pilots concerned. We became quite good at it, leaving out all the bullshit in joint debriefs with the trial manager. Standard phrases were:

'I flew through like a herd of turds and we both pulled into a high speed yo-yo.'

'After the first couple of crosses we ended up in the standard vertical rolling scissors.'

'He fell out in front and I took a guns snapshot followed by a Fox 2 (Sidewinder shot) as he extended.'

Because of the excess power available with all participants, the fights usually degenerated into a vertical rolling scissors, both aircraft spiralling vertically upwards,, cockpit to cockpit, until one or other fell out in front, more or less out of control. In this manoeuvring the Harrier came into its own, even without using the nozzles. I found that I could manoeuvre XV277 down to almost zero airspeed to ensure that I usually came out on top of the opposition. When allowed to use the nozzles I could turn the aircraft through 180 degrees in a flash in the vertical, to end up facing the opponent no matter what advantage he started with. Additionally, at higher airspeeds the use of VIFF with very precise timing, gave quite spectacular short-term changes in flight path which could be used to foil an attack or get back the advantage. I flew the VIFF combats on the nozzle lever alone, leaving the throttle screwed down at full power (about 101 per cent rpm) all the time. Because we were allowed to use so much power both with, and without, VIFF, a completely unexpected result of the trial was the Harrier pilots' good performances during non-VIFF engagements. As always, use of the nozzles required a lot of concentration and care to avoid departures, and the hassle-free manoeuvring without VIFF allowed you to concentrate more on spatial positioning.

In November we flew the low level portion of the trial from RAF Brawdy. This was also to allow the Lightning more time in combat, Brawdy being closer to the range than Valley. Straight away all flying participants agreed that we needed to make a drastic change to the rules of engagement to get some useful results from the low level engagements, all of which had a base height of 2,000 feet. We demanded an upper height limit of 6,000 feet on all engagements, to restrict vertical manoeuvring. If we hadn't done this then all engagements would have ended up exactly the same as the medium altitude trials – we knew each other's tactics too well by now. As expected, the low level VIFF trials were even more spectacular than the medium altitude affairs. All starts were at high airspeeds (580 knots +) and so there was a lot of very high g manoeuvring before we ended up once more at minimum speed in the traditional vertical rolling scissors. Here VIFF came into its own. Because of the excess of thrust I actually had to reduce power in XV277 to avoid getting to the ceiling height too quickly. (I had more thrust than aircraft weight throughout.) The Hunter pilot and I would end up in an extremely slow vertical rolling scissors, barely yards apart and with me sitting 277 on its tail in the vertical with just enough nozzle deflection to give me full reaction controls. Then I merely had to use the roll reaction controls to keep my cockpit always facing the Hunter, my airspeed below 100 knots all the time. In the Lightning the pilot couldn't cope with such low speeds and was constantly breaking away to turn back for high speed slashing attacks. Whether the 6,000 feet height limit was realistic or not, we certainly found out a lot about low speed manoeuvring. The trials concluded in December at the MoD's research establishment at West Freugh, with us carrying out some simulated ground attack manoeuvres using VIFF to aid recovery. We found little advantage in using VIFF for ground attack.

The whole VIFF part 2 trial was extremely challenging and was by far the most fascinating flying I had ever done. By the end of the trial we were all working as a completely harmonized team with the scientists and technicians of RAE Bedford. Although it was to be months before the official results were released, we had all learned a lot about missile and gun combat, both with and without VIFF. In my individual report I was scathing about the current GR3's combat capability because of its lack of missile armament (The wiring and control panel for Sidewinder were quite cheap to fit), and appallingly bad air-to-air gunsight. My views on VIFF were mixed. Although it could produce spectacular results if used at precisely the right moment, if used carelessly it merely killed a lot of airspeed which you would need again very soon. I was asked to give various briefings to RAF Harrier pilots about the trial and I passed all of this on for what it was worth. However, in the end the money could not be found to fund the full suite of VIFF mods to service aircraft, and so RAF pilots were never able to capitalize fully on the results we did obtain.

Back permanently at Wittering the workload continued unabated. Ordinary OCU instruction seemed almost boring after the VIFF trial, however, we were about to lose several more pilots in accidents, with a third of the instructor staff being killed in the space of six months.

At Wittering morale had sunk low because of over-reaction to recent accidents. There had been a major tightening-up of all orders and restrictions. In my view this additional unwelcome pressure was counter-productive, and in frustration I wrote a letter to the RAF magazine *Air Clues* to that effect. At first the editor refused to publish my letter at all, saying that it was too controversial. Eventually he actually turned up at Wittering to interview me and see if I was some kind of dangerous radical, keen to overthrow the powers that be. After this the rag published my letter in full, with a scathing denunciation of my views in a comment by the editor, in the form of the mythical cartoon character Wing Commander Spry. Immediately all hell broke loose from the rest of the front-line RAF. I was literally deluged with copies of extremely aggressive letters of support from all over the RAF which had been fired off to *Air Clues*. All letters were entirely in support of my view that over-supervision was the curse of the RAF, and was leading to ever more accidents. Eventually Wing Commander Spry was forced to eat humble pie in public and, for the first and only time, was depicted standing in penance at the bottom of his symbolic column in the magazine. *Air Clues* then published a full and unreserved apology for its knee-jerk comments on my letter. Unfortunately, these minor theatricals were of little help to us in the front line, still trying to do the operational job and train students in the face of ever-increasing restrictions.

Our Aviation Medics had finally done some research on the effects of alcohol and were now publicizing just how long it took to get all the alcohol out of the bloodstream after a hard night on the booze. A famous RAF psychologist, had also done work on the infamous 'sinking trap door' theory of the way that alcohol affected the Otolith organ, the vitally important inner ear organ which controlled orientation in flight. There was still a lot of boozing and, in fairness, further measures to control drinking and flying were long overdue. A lot of this was due to the officially-sanctioned approach to social drinking, where it was deemed perfectly normal to drink large amounts of alcohol at a dinner night or squadron party for example, and then be woken early to fly on a no-notice exercise. The upshot of all this was that no one was legally fit to fly on the morning after any heavy booze-up. This put the dampers on a lot of social life for ever in the RAF.

The following February came the next disaster. Once again I was duty authorizer, having just taken over. My predecessor came back into the ops room looking worried. An hour before an 'A' Squadron four-ship (Green Section) of two instructors and two students had taken off for a formation attack mission to Wales.

'Are you ready for it, Win?'

'What's going on,' I asked.

'Drayton Centre have been on the phone. Green are on their way back; there's been a mid-air (collision) and two jets have crashed. We don't know any more detail yet.'

'Do you want to take over again?' I asked, partly in jest.

'No thanks mate – you're welcome to it!'

Eventually two very shaken students landed at Wittering and told the story. A pilot had been leading a rotate attack demonstration. At the conclusion of the attack, during the rejoin, the No. 4 had collided with the leader from underneath. The accident shook the whole station. Two more families were fatherless and the boss once again moved smoothly into funeral organization mode.

In early March there a was a further minor crisis as Guatemala threatened to invade Belize, a British protectorate in Central America. In line with a long-standing defence agreement, 1(F) were to be sent out there to defend the country, the first time they had actually deployed across the Atlantic. The new 330 gallon ferry tanks were essential for the deployment, and 1(F) had only just started flying with them. They had not practised any air-to-air refuelling with the big tanks on, and so a panic trial was set up at Boscombe Down with a test pilot (TP) trying it out for the first time. Because the squadron were due to start the deployment next day they were given an emergency clearance to try out tanking for themselves at the same time as Boscombe. At the end of the day a 1(F) flight commander rang Boscombe to see how the TP had got on, and see what clearance he was going to issue.

TP: 'Well, I didn't have too much problem on the port hose, but it was almost impossible on the starboard; I'm going to have to recommend a restricted clearance on the starboard hose.'

Flight Commander: 'What the hell are you talking about mate? I've had my most junior pilots on both hoses today with no problems at all!'

TP: 'Erm ... Let me think about this.'

They got the full clearance and deployed as planned.

With 1(F) enjoying the sun in Central America there was a need for a Harrier unit to take their place on the annual major NATO exercise 'Arctic Express', due to start in a couple of weeks. The RAFG squadrons were fully committed, so the OCU got the job. We ditched all our students for a month, did some work-up training, camouflaged the aircraft in 'snow cam' paint scheme and then set off in good order for the north of Norway. Initially masquerading as 1(F), we deployed via Gardermoen, Bodo and then flew direct to the island of Tromsø, the most northerly city in Europe. En route I bored the pants off the rest by telling war stories of my trip up here in the Jet Provost in the summer of '69. Northern Norway in March was a different ball game. Still deep in winter, the mountains were under tens of feet of snow and the temperature at Tromsø dropped to 20 degrees below overnight, staying below zero all day. Tromsø itself, optimistically described as the 'Paris of the North', was just a small fishing port with a couple of nice hotels and night clubs. We operated off packed snow at the civil airport on the island which lay in the middle of a fjord surrounded by high peaks. Flying at low level was like flying over a gigantic wedding cake, and your eyes soon wearied of the endless dazzle of snow, relieved only by the deep ultramarine of the icy cold fjords. We wore full Arctic flying kit, including immersion suits, which bulked out the tiny Harrier cockpit so that there was barely room to breathe.

After some local area familiarization flying (including some hair-raising TACAN letdown practice into the rocky valleys), we got stuck into the exercise proper. There was an abundance of ground, sea and air targets to attack, and we soon got the hang of flying tactically down the fjords and finding 'snow-cammed' tanks and troops playing in the snow. High tension lines strung across the fjords were a constant danger and not all of them were marked correctly on the map. There was constant air activity, with us being bounced by 'enemy' Norwegian fighters and Tromsø coming under regular attack by American F15s. After a fortnight of excellent flying we were well into the Arctic flying routine, and had ranged far and wide over the most northerly terrain in Europe, over the barren wastes of Finnmark towards the Soviet border. We learned the tricks of safe low flying over featureless snow, trying to have the sun behind you so that you could see your shadow on the snow in front. If your shadow came too close you were about to die. The girls were friendly and social life downtown was pretty good, although drink prices were horrific. We smuggled hip flasks into the clubs to ginger up the soft drinks a bit. Operating on sheet ice at the airport was not dull as we crept at sub-walking pace into our parking slots on the ice. Any use of brakes led to an immediate out-of-control skid.

Right at the end of the deployment there was further tragedy. One of our pilots landed back on at Tromsø and said that his wingman (recently arrived on the OCU from Wildenrath) had flown into the ground in perfect weather during a battle formation turn. There was no reason for the accident. I had known the unfortunate pilot since Cranwell days and my time at Leeming.

Four instructors out of twelve gone in under six months: it was beginning to look like a jinx. Who was next? I was flight safety officer and arranged details for the Board of Inquiry. It was a subdued group of Harrier instructors who arrived back at Wittering.

I had flown back early in a Hercules. For our 'morale' we got a visit from the AOC, who reassured us that he thought we were a good bunch who were just going through a bad patch, and we weren't to worry about it.

Our instructional task continued unabated at Wittering through a second long, hot summer in UK. The flight commander had been trying hard to persuade me to do my instructor's A2 re-categorization on the Harrier, but I resisted strongly. This would only reduce my chances of becoming a QWI. Looking around me in the Harrier force I saw old chums being promoted to squadron leader with far less experience than me. For the first time I began to be resentful of my lowly rank and decided to be a hypocrite and do something about it. After years of refusing to take the 'C' promotion exam, an essential requirement to be promoted squadron leader, I bit the bullet and entered for it. I passed the exam and went on the Officers' Junior Staff Course. My wife was by now heavily pregnant and I was commuting to and fro in freezing weather to RAF Henlow on a useless Jawa motorbike. On arrival after the eighty mile journey I would have to thaw out for half an hour in front of the fire.

The course was marginally interesting, the first time I had had anything to do with 'truckies' and bomber pilots at close quarters. They were a good bunch, but had no idea of how to get a ripple on and do things successfully at the run. At the end of the course a wing commander member of staff debriefed me:

'Jerry, eventually in the RAF you will learn that the secret of good administration is attention to detail.'

Needless to say I had not impressed them. I equated 'attention to detail' with getting bogged down in trivia, and I firmly believed that for the rest of my career.

At the end of January my daughter, Karen, was born and I began thinking really hard about my next posting. The boss promised me a QWI course if I was staying on Harriers next tour. In March I had an interesting formation landing with a new student. We had just done a formation take-off and pairs circuit in the T4 and – unknown to me – he had cycled the undercarriage selector button UP then DOWN in quick succession as we formated on another OCU two-seater for the exercise (I had told him to leave the wheels down). Crucially, he had also failed to ensure that the button was pushed all the way into the DOWN position after moving the buttons. All of this was entirely unknown to me in the back, as there was no way of knowing exactly what the stude had done with the buttons, apart from observing the gear indication lights. I checked that we had four greens showing all the way, and our pairs landing looked OK until we touched down in the briefed position, leaving a bit of nose-tail clearance between us and the leader, in case of loss of directional control on touchdown. I had always done it that way, and insisted that my student should do it also on this, his first Harrier formation landing. This saved our lives during what happened next. Straight after touchdown our wing dropped violently towards the leader, our T4 lurching across the runway out of control, just missing his tail by inches. The shock of touchdown had jolted the undercarriage solenoid valve to the UP position, causing the gear to retract on touchdown. The main wheel and outriggers collapsed rearwards, leaving us bicycling along on just the tail skid and nose wheel, which couldn't retract forwards against the drag of the grass. I had taken control from the back as soon as the wing dropped and with no directional control we immediately shot off the runway on to the grass. Instinctively I put more nozzle down and increased rpm to power up the reaction controls; with lots of stick and rudder I managed to keep us from rolling over. Eventually we slewed to a stop, balanced precariously on the partly-retracted nose wheel. I told the crash crews to stay clear in case of further gear collapse, and my student and I climbed out cautiously. I was dragged off unwillingly to the medical centre where, to my disgust, they found my blood pressure was off the clock. I was grounded for a couple of days, the medics muttering ominously about my hypertension. The subsequent unit inquiry discovered that there was a hitherto unknown technical glitch with the undercarriage solenoid valve which directed hydraulic fluid either to the UP or DOWN position, depending on electrical power. If the undercarriage button was left just slightly sticking out from the DOWN position then the solenoid remained un-powered, and it would flop either way on the shock of landing; in our case it went to the UP position. In future all Harrier pilots had to make certain that the DOWN button was fully in at all times gear was down.

Harrier instruction remained action-packed as the flow of new students continued unabated. In April I had a senior officer as a student. This officer was making rather heavy weather of the VSTOL aspects – like many mature pilots new to the machine. I got him through the initial duals and then sent him off for his initial hovering solo. I wasn't supervising this particular solo detail and sat nervously drinking coffee in the crew room, occasionally watching the Harriers hovering far down at the west end of the field. After a while I noticed the usual convoy of crash vehicles rushing towards the vertical landing area. The duty authorizer rushed in and shouted at me, a fierce grin on his face:

'Hey Jerry, your stude's just crashed!'

Shit. Here we go again. I piled into the Land Rover and rushed out to find my stude sitting disconsolately in the crash vehicle next to his severely-bent Harrier. He had suffered the infamous 'roll on vertical take-off' and broken off the outrigger. I tried to calm him down, explaining that he was in good company with many other distinguished pilots who had done exactly the same, but he remained wound up about it for some time afterwards. We all had to go through the tedium of yet another Board of Inquiry to investigate the accident, one of many during my time on the Harrier. The Board members got a bit excited about the fact that the crashed Harrier was described on our permanent aircraft state board as a 'Known Rumbler'. This note was in my handwriting and had been put there to inform other pilots in my capacity as unit air tester. It was my job to air test all of the OCU's jets, a time-consuming and occasionally action-packed job. This particular jet had been the cause of many student (and some staff) aborts, the pilots taxiing in without flying because they were nervous about the unusual rumble the engine made. To sort things out I had given the machine a full air test and reported that, yes – it did rumble slightly more than the average Harrier, but I could find absolutely nothing wrong with it, neither could the engineers, and in my opinion it was fine for training. The Board accepted that this had nothing to do with the accident, fortunately.

My best friend turned up at Wittering on several occasions to get some facts for a Harrier task he was working on at Boscombe. He had looked at the Harrier short take-off technique and had come up with an idea to simplify the VSTOL handling. Up to now we had used a variable setting for the nozzle stop, depending on aircraft weight. After checking on how Harrier pilots actually carried out a short strip take-off, my friend had worked out that it made cock-all difference whether you used a variable or fixed nozzle angle. In the teeth of hardened opposition from old Harrier hands, he persisted with his trials and demonstrated conclusively that he was right. Henceforth we used a fixed nozzle angle of 50 degrees for all short take-offs.

Another item the OCU was tasked with involved the evaluation of the Canadian CRV7 high velocity anti-tank rocket. The RAF was planning to buy this weapon and wanted to know if the Harrier force could make use of it. The boss picked a QFI to carry out this fascinating trial, much to the irritation of the QWIs, who automatically assumed they would be given the task. One of our QFIs got this plum job. He was an excellent character with tons of practical operational common sense. He was given several truckloads of rockets to fire on realistic tank targets at Bovington artillery range. After the trial he briefed the rest of us on the results. In the pilot's opinion the rocket was extremely accurate but not much use for anything except anti-shipping attacks (which we didn't do). The big problem was that it needed about a 5,000 feet minimum firing range to wind up to its maximum velocity. This meant that the pilot had to positively identify the target at about five to six kilometres' range – very difficult in the customary Central European hazy conditions. We all knew well just how difficult it was to positively identify real targets in the field, especially when pulling up close-in from an extreme low level target approach, which we would have to use in wartime. Once again weapon designers appeared to have had taken little account of the practical problems of operational weapon firing, a constant problem with RAF weapon procurement.

Quote: Comments on *Despatches on War Operations* by Sir Arthur Harris (1945) by Sebastian Cox, head of the RAF Air Historical Branch:

> Harris reserves some of his most choleric criticism for the armament design staffs of the Air Ministry and MAP, whom he charges with incompetence. The depressing regularity in the Appendix of phrases such as 'no improved design was received in the Command before the end of the war' suggests that there was much substance to Harris' complaints.

Not much had changed. Some of our weapon designers and procurers seemed to think that real battlefield targets had a gigantic Day-Glo arrow pointing towards them saying 'AIM HERE', visible from ten kilometres away. Failure to correctly identify friendly forces was a constant problem in ground attack operations, brought vividly to the public's attention by the press hysteria about so-called 'friendly fire' incidents in the Gulf War (we called it blue on blue). There was nothing unexpected about USAF A10s destroying friendly armoured vehicles in war: the only surprise to us in the business, was that it didn't happen more often – even though the vehicles concerned carried a Day-Glo cross on top. From five kilometres away a Day-Glo cross on a vehicle is invisible. CRV7 was not for us in the European theatre. We stuck with our old tried and tested SNEB rockets and cluster bombs, both of which could be delivered from much closer ranges to the target, making target identification easier.

I was one of the unit air testers. The Harrier air test was a very demanding exercise, involving a climb to 40,000 feet to test various engine functions, followed by a lot of wacky VSTOL manoeuvring at low level to test the engine to its limits. During the high level engine tests we had to do slam checks of acceleration, plus the measurement of various maximum rpm data to check out the pressure ratio limiter (PRL). This wretched device, set up by engine technicians on the ground, could only be tested at 40,000 feet and was often out of limits. In flight you had to use a complicated graph on your kneeboard to calculate exactly how it was controlling the rpm and, if it was wrong, radio the results back to the engineers who would have a technician waiting for you as you taxied in for adjustments. Then it was back up to 40,000 feet again, sometimes as much as four or five times on the trot to test it again. Only when the PRL was set up correctly could you do the slam checks. During these the engine would sometimes 'pop surge' with a thump, and you had to glide the aircraft back to Wittering for investigation for any damage. Pop surges also happened at lower altitudes, and also during VSTOL manoeuvring with these early Harriers. Then there would be a sheet of flame out of the nozzles and an ear-splitting bang like a field gun going off. In the cockpit the pilot would feel the jolt of intake disturbance like a collision with a 10-ton truck, his helmet banged violently against the canopy as the enormous airflow through the engine reversed direction for a fraction of a second. Amazingly, most 'pops' did no damage at all and the engine ran on perfectly afterwards. One particularly irksome T4 was continually 'popping' on me at 40,000 feet and the boss came along with me on the next air test to see what I was doing. After all the routine procedures in the thin blue stratosphere the engine 'popped' quite violently, giving him a bit of a jolt. I said little and glided back to Wittering in virtual silence with the engine idling. On one occasion there was fun in the Wittering circuit when ATC suffered a total power failure. As we didn't want to waste any sorties, the rest of the instructors and students who were airborne just used common sense to avoid each other and carried on our circuit work as if nothing had happened, radio chatter being at a blissful minimum. Afterwards the SATCO (Senior Air Traffic Controller) was furious.

Soon my posting turned up, as a Hunter instructor to 2 Tactical Weapons Unit at Brawdy. So my promised Harrier QWI course was scotched anyway. Resigned to a tour in south-west Wales I eased off down there for a recce, to find quite a few old Wildenrath hands on the staff. It seemed a reasonable set-up and I looked forward to flying the beautiful Hunter again. However, the posting was not to be. In April the postings department, rang to ask me if I was interested in an exchange tour in Holland with the Royal Netherlands Air Force. I jumped at the chance, discovering that it was on the RF104G Starfighter, and was tactical recce. There had been no RAF exchange pilot in Holland for over twelve years, and now there was a mad rush to sort out accommodation (I rented the house of a Dutch Air Force major), and language training, which involved six weeks in London, based at RAF Uxbridge. In early July we were en route to the lovely old Peel town of Uden in South Brabant, where we met up with the rest of No. 306 Squadron RNLAF.

Chapter 14

Flying the Starfighter

We were to be the only British family on base at RNLAF station Volkel. I arrived on the old Dutch Air Force Base, to be welcomed by the stocky, moustachioed squadron commander, plus most of the squadron pilots, who were rather curious as to exactly what they were getting from the RAF as an exchange officer. My six weeks' language training in London plus hours of listening to Linguaphone lessons had barely scratched the surface of the language problem. I calculated straight away that I would never fully understand how the Dutch Air Force worked unless I learnt Dutch as fast as possible, and I told the squadron pilots that I wanted them to speak only Dutch to me, regardless of any inconvenience this caused me. They were amenable to this, as they all spoke pretty fluent English anyway. However, the ground crew were more of a problem as their English was less good, and they were desperately keen to practise on their tame Englishman. I checked in at the Starfighter Training Flight, the CAV, based at Volkel and commanded by a lieutenant, who was an excellent instructor. For the first few months of training in Holland, life was pretty confusing. I attended the Starfighter ground school at Deelen and if it wasn't for the good old American Dash 1 technical manual, I would have found out very little about the machine. In the air, flying training was conducted nominally in English for me, but I soon began to use as much Dutch as possible and encouraged the instructors to risk using it on me in briefings. This led to one or two amusing incidents: during one briefing on a dual formation training mission with two TF104Gs, I was slightly nonplussed to hear the instructor briefing some extremely wacky manoeuvres, including a split-S (roll and pull through) at 0.9 Mach, I was wondering just how difficult this was going to be in close formation when it dawned on me that I had completely misunderstood the part of the briefing where we split up for individual manoeuvres.

I went through Starfighter training with just one other student who was an extremely funny extrovert. He spoke excellent English, having just finished an exchange tour with the Canadian Air Force, instructing on the CL41 Tutor. He had a wicked sense of humour and was constantly taking the Mickey out of my attempts to learn Dutch. Sample conversation:

'Hey pal, what's this comment I keep hearing when we sit down to eat in the canteen?'

'They're saying "Eet Smaaklijk"; it just means "Eat well".'

'OK, then what should I say in reply?'

'Well , you could say "Get Stuffed" if you like, but I don't think they'd appreciate it!'

And more in the same vein. The problem with Dutch, as demonstrated by my friend, was the sheer speed at which they rattled it out, running lots of words together in a series of machine-gun cadences which I had to write down and memorize verbatim. My friend was the worst example: he had a slight stutter and spoke even faster than the others.

Me: 'He jonge, langzaam effe – ik versta je niet!' (Hey lad, slow down, I don't understand you!)

My friend: 'Nee hoor, je luistert te langzaam!' (No mate, you're listening too slowly!)

You can see what I was up against.

The Starfighter was an exhilarating challenge to fly in the extremely demanding tactical recce role. Although I had flown recce before on both the Hunter and the Harrier, the RF104G presented one or two problems, and, at the same time, got rid of some others which I had been used to. The 'Zip' was an appropriate nickname for a manned missile designed uncompromisingly for sheer speed, out of the USAF's experiences of the Korean War. Lockheed's 'Skunk Works' had made a good job of it, although they had cut things a bit too fine in the early pure fighter versions of the machine. The heavier G-model was optimized for the low-level attack role, although also used for air defence by many NATO air forces. At the end of the '70s, this twenty-five year old design still held the world absolute airspeed record at over 850 knots in the extremely dangerous low altitude category, flown below 100 metres height. Even loaded down as she was with four external tanks and the centreline Orpheus camera pod, she could still outrun any other fighter with ease. Although given the affectionate nickname *De Ouwe Dame* (Old

Lady) by the Dutch pilots, with a take-off speed of about 220 knots and absolute minimum landing speed of 185 knots, she possessed some extremely unladylike handling qualities, a result of the many aerodynamic compromises necessary to achieve maximum speed at all costs. For the unwary pilot the fiercely powerful stall-prevention system could never eliminate the possibility of a super stall and uncontrollable pitch-up and departure (spin) if you overcooked it in a manoeuvre. The pitch rate kicker could drive you into uncontrollable pitch oscillations during any sharpish pull-out from a ground attack manoeuvre. However, at higher speed (550 knots plus) she was a honey – just like a cat peeing on glass – and the controls felt just right. This was just about the speed at which the Harrier ran out of steam, with overwhelming buffet and cockpit noise. The low speed regime was even more dramatic. When fully loaded and with flaps UP in the RF you were into pre-stall buffet at about 360 knots straight and level – if you were stupid enough to fly so slow with the flaps up. On the Starfighter conversion flight we had been brainwashed about engine handling after take-off:

'Out of A/B below 350 knots you're going nowhere but down – and fast!'

A Martin-Baker seat would have been a bit of a morale-booster as well, but the Dutch AF were still using the old Lockheed C2 rocket seat. At least Lockheed had abandoned the old downward-ejection seats which had been fitted because of the hazard presented by the tail. Engine-off, she glided nicely at 300 knots with mid flap. The mighty J79 engine had been through a long and painful development process to achieve its current excellent reliability. Although the German Air Force had lost over 200 Starfighters (out of a total buy of about 800), the RNLAF had a reasonably good record with the machine. There were only five fatal accidents during my time at Volkel, although there had been two just before I arrived. This compared reasonably with the RAF's Harrier GR3 accident record which I was used to.

The Starfighter came into its own at high speed. Even fully loaded with four tanks and a recce pod she could cruise at low level (without A/B) for an hour at 600 knots – and still land with 1,000lb of fuel. Our standard planned cruise speed over enemy territory was 510 knots for war missions. The strike squadrons used 540 knots. We 'pushed up' to 600 knots for target runs, even in routine peacetime training, and at night, in cloud. At slightly lower speeds the low level radius of action went up to about 360 nautical miles –

somewhat better than the Jaguar, whose pilots were constantly boasting about the great range capability of their machine. They had little else to boast about. The standard parrot-cry of RAF pilots who did not know the Starfighter was 'Ah, but it can't turn'. At those speeds you didn't need to turn to avoid enemy fighters. The Zip had sustainable high cruising speed and stunning acceleration to enable you to avoid combat in the first place. Just throw the tanks off and you could dial up 800 knots in just a few seconds.

This was the first aeroplane with afterburner (A/B) which I had flown. This was a very reliable system, with virtually no restrictions. I remember only two engine limitations: the first was a large red SLOW light on the instrument panel which came on when you reached the limiting compressor inlet temperature at either Mach 2 plus or about 750-800 knots at low level. The other factor was a maximum of thirty seconds running time on the ground in max A/B. This was somewhat academic: in max A/B you couldn't stay on the ground for more than thirty seconds unless the machine was chained down. The other splendid piece of kit was the NASARR radar. This was a multi-mode radar which we only used in the air-to-ground mode, although the TFs (two-seat trainers) still had the air-to-air mode working as well. The radar was great value for low-level orientation over the wide, flat areas of Holland and northern Germany. I soon learnt the difference in the radar image of the various towns and hill features, and was able to use this as an excellent navigation aid in poor weather. The radar image of German towns and cities varied on radar, depending on how old the town was. In more modern towns with lots of concrete tower blocks there was a strong image; with a concentration of older, wooden buildings the image was more diffuse. The maximum range of the radar was eighty miles, although we used it most often in the twenty and forty mile scales. We also had a radar altimeter, which was very accurate; you could set a 'bug' in the cockpit to put a light on if you went below a certain height. As our standard low flying height was 250 feet above ground, I would set the bug to about 180 feet, allowing for the standard NATO tree which we all knew was about seventy feet high. Over sea or flat terrain the rad alt was accurate down to less than fifty feet, and I flew comfortably at this height over the North Sea.

Although true dead-stick (i.e. engine-off) landings were prohibited by the RNLAF, we continued to practise the partial power pattern, simulating almost total loss of thrust if the afterburner nozzle should ever stick wide open. If that happened you would be left with about

1,200lb of thrust, not enough even to taxi. There was an excellent emergency manual override for nozzle closure, consisting of a black and yellow handle in the cockpit attached to a wire which operated the emergency closing gear. For the partial power pattern you started from about 12,000 feet overhead the airfield and came in on finals at 300 knots, dropping the gear as you flared to 250 knots over the fence (the gear went down very fast). Our tyre limiting speed was 240 knots. Stopping? No problem: the F104 had excellent brakes, a large brake parachute and also an arrester hook to take the cable. If you couldn't stop with that lot then you were in the wrong job.

One of the excellent things about RNLAF bases was the way that base operations worked. They actually controlled flying operations, instead of just monitoring (and sometimes hindering) them as in the RAF. The operations officers were all experienced and current Starfighter pilots, many of them ex-flight commanders, and they worked for an OC flying wing, ranked *Overste* (wing commander). The base commander, a full colonel, was an administrative figure-head. The RNLAF *Chef Vliegdienst*, literally chief of flying operations, was the squadron commanders' immediate superior (they were all junior to him in rank) and he took charge of all flying matters – including ops and ATC. His authority came straight out of an efficient and switched-on operations set-up.

The Dutch took instrument flying much more seriously than the RAF. For them it was the vital component of AWX, or all-weather operations. The squadrons at Volkel had a wartime IMC (instrument meteorological conditions) capability, (i.e. we could carry out our missions in cloud) – in war we were expected to launch regardless of the weather at base or en route to the target. This demanded a lot of peacetime training at low-level instrument flying, both day and night. On 306 Squadron we had no wartime AWX capability over target, simply because of the limitations of our camera system. However, there was always the likelihood of a transit to the target area in IMC in war and so we participated in all the peacetime AWX training along with the strike squadrons, and had to meet the same criteria. The only thing we didn't do was drop bombs on the ranges at the end of an AWX mission (we merely over flew the target). As operations controlled flying totally, as soon as the weather was deemed to have fallen below visual navigation limits the base switched over automatically into an AWX training programme, without any break in the flying programme. Aircraft flying on visual missions were told to land and ops would start issuing take-off times

at five-minute intervals for the chosen AWX route; from then on all
pilots had to fly this route on time and regardless of weather, on an
instrument flight plan. There were IFR AWX routes in Germany, and
we had some round Belgium and Holland. Because everyone had to
be capable of this kind of flying all the time, the RNLAF did a lot of
instrument flying training at low level in the TF 104Gs. This took
priority over all other peacetime flying – if necessary leaving single-
seaters on the ground to make sure that all the TF missions were
flown. They had a similarly professional approach to simulator
training. Anyone considered as 'inexperienced' on the F104G (less
than two years' flying on type) had to fly twenty-four training AWX
missions per year in the TF, or two per month. Experienced pilots
flew twelve. This compared with a total of only two mandatory
instrument flying missions per year on the average RAF squadron,
regardless of pilot experience. When I saw how much AWX training
the Dutch did, I realized why the RAF had a higher accident rate in
bad weather. In the RAF, operational squadrons were constantly
trying to avoid realistic instrument training. The prevailing RAF
attitude was that instrument flying was boring, of interest only to
'weeny' QFIs and IREs.

AWX was extremely demanding flying in the TF. First of all, the
pilot under training sat in the rear seat of the TF under a claustro-
phobic canvas blind flying hood, that cut off all outside view. Under
this *Kap*, the pilot would have the cockpit lights on to see the instruments, even in broad daylight. I was a bit like being in a submarine.
The safety pilot sat in the front. This was in contrast to all RAF I/F
training, where the pilot could always cheat fairly easily and see
some of the outside world. Some RAF aircraft, notably the Tornado,
had no provision for blind flying practice at all. The pilot sat in the
front with the usual view out of the cockpit. This made a farce of the
few so-called instrument training sorties that were flown. Only in
cloud or at night was there realistic practice.

A typical training AWX profile in the TF would start with a
standard low level instrument departure from Volkel, followed by
about an hour's low level navigation around Germany, using the
radar to navigate, with a radar prediction map on the pilot's knee.
Heights were calculated as 500 feet above the highest obstacle within
five miles of track on each leg. In hilly terrain we used contour-
shaded radar predictions and various hand-held gizmos in the
cockpit to stay on track. It was all too easy to get lost by misreading
the radar prediction. If you didn't stay pretty close to track then you

would fly into high ground. When you were obviously lost the safety pilot would take control only when you were about to fly into the ground. He would give no navigational assistance whatever, merely acting as a lookout for other aircraft. After the low level we would climb up to height for a bit of general handling, followed by a practice diversion to a RNLAF airfield. These were chosen because they had the most fiendishly complicated TACAN approach and departure procedures, all of which had to be followed precisely. Later on I became an instrument rating examiner (IRE) on the Starfighter, with responsibility for training new pilots in AWX techniques and for carrying out instrument rating tests on the other squadron pilots. In my RAF flying I had never worked so hard in an aeroplane as I had to on a typical AWX mission. At night or in IMC we also flew AWX routes solo. One thousand feet did not feel particularly high above ground on an initial point to target run at 600 knots at night in dirty weather over the north German plain. Every now and then the stratus would thin to give you a horrifyingly close glimpse of town lights flashing by underneath, leading to immediate doubts about your navigation: 'What the hell was THAT place? There shouldn't be a large town here.'

On clear nights with a bit of moon you could fly the machine visually at quite low level, the splendid forward view unencumbered by a HUD and the instruments giving just the faintest glow (they were properly designed for night flying). The main instruments were fluorescent, requiring no cockpit lighting at all; therefore your eyes could adapt fully to night conditions and see the ground pretty well if there was some moonlight. This was impossible in other RAF aircraft I flew, except for the Hunter. It would be totally impossible with a HUD. Most AWX missions over flew the Zuider Zee inbound Vliehors bombing range, where the target markers stood out clearly on radar. One strike pilot crashed and was killed on a night AWX and the whole of 306 was sent off to search for signs of wreckage in the sea, making use of our infra red scanners. We were also occasionally tasked by the Dutch Government to assist the police in searching for illicit alcohol stills, operated by gypsies in the extensive woodlands of the Biesbosch area of western Holland. Once again the IR scanner came into its own. Also, the Dutch Government required us to photograph and report all ships seen discharging waste oil at any time. The RNLAF took part in all the usual NATO alerts and TACEVALS, which were handled very professionally. In particular, the RNLAF did not skimp on spending on defensive weapons for their bases. For the Volkel/De Peel complex we had our own IHAWK SAM batteries, plus troops of CHEETAH mobile 35mm radar-laid guns. Additionally, all aircraft, ops and recce processing complexes were fully hardened against air attack, at a time when the RAF was still struggling to begin a hardening programme at its RAFG bases. RNLAF ops bunkers were palatial by RAF standards, with toilets (in RAF bunkers you used a bucket), showers and even sleeping compartments with camp beds. This was typical of the general Dutch attitude towards its armed forces. Within the RNLAF we had the concept of *Werkbezoek* (working visit) for most visits. *Werkbezoek* meant that the visitor saw the base operating exactly as it would normally. No one would put on best uniform except the officer hosting the visit, and no changes would be made to the normal daily working routine to accommodate the visitor. They saw what normally went on, and if they didn't like it that was tough.

On the Starfighter training flight we did a couple of Mach 2 runs with the tanks off and it was standard procedure for an air test. After take-off from Volkel we accelerated to the west in the climb in full A/B until the magic M = 2.0 appeared in the machmeter. By then we would be humming westward at 35,000 feet over the Scheldt Estuary in western Holland. A Mach 2 run would use up most of the internal fuel, and we would only have enough to return straight to Volkel. The air defence Starfighter squadrons practised supersonic air combat manoeuvring, the machine handling superbly above Mach 1. Every six months or so, 306 would take all the tanks and recce pods off and we would operate clean Starfighters for a couple of weeks, doing mostly air combat training (in which the main difficulty was staying subsonic), and some low level missions. This was real Zip flying: with 6,600lb internal fuel you could fly for an hour with no tanks, cruising comfortably at 600 knots with about ¾ throttle. In this configuration the g limit was 7.33, but we still wore no g-suit.

I managed to convince the other flight commanders of the value of a progressive air combat work-up programme, to sharpen up the younger pilots in the basics of formation manoeuvring and control. All of our new 'first tour' pilots had flown at least 500 hours on the Northrop F5, a slick little ground attack machine, as lead-in to Starfighter flying. The RNLAF still would not allow *ab initio* pilots to fly the machine. On my first day on the squadron, having just completed the Starfighter conversion course, I was given a brusque introduction to Dutch Air Force supervision. The duty authorizer, always one of the flight commanders, showed me my name on the night flying programme for that evening. I noticed that I was flying solo – 'Surely some mistake', I pointed out. Having just joined the squadron I expected something like the RAF system of a series of dual checkouts both day and night with various squadron supervisors to see if I was up to standard. Basically the standard RAF procedure was never to rely on the training reports from previous courses – you gave the newcomer a damn good check out first to see if he could cut it in the air before you let him loose on his own in a single-seater. None of that mollycoddling in the RNLAF: once you had completed the course you were qualified – and that was that.

'You completed the AWX syllabus didn't you?' said the authorizer.

'Er, yes.' (It consisted of just three duals: two day and one night.)

'Well then?'

I pointed out the attractive array of red and amber weather indication lights on the map of Germany where the route lay – clearly the weather was lousy for much of the route. The weather at Volkel wasn't too shiny either.

'Have we had any weather reports from round the route?' I asked feebly.

'Why do you need to know? That's the whole point of AWX: ALL WEATHER OPERATIONS,' he said testily from behind his newspaper.

'Don't forget to sign out and make sure you take-off on time.'

I saw that the whole night flying programme had already been authorized in advance by a signature from the duty authorizer. All I had to do was sign my initials, walk down the corridor to safety equipment and don my unwieldy back parachute and spurs before boarding the transport to the flight line. I was beginning to see the light. I had completed the course and was trained for the job. Now I had to go for it. What else did I expect – someone to hold my hand?

As I climbed awkwardly out of the crew bus I felt a momentary chill of apprehension, wishing that I had done a bit more night flying in my years of fighter-bomber flying with the RAF.

'But night flying's dangerous: – anyway, it keeps us out of the bar!'

That was the standard RAF reaction to any suggestions of a night flying programme. I hobbled towards the sergeant major crew chief, the parachute bouncing awkwardly on my back, spurs clinking hard against the still-warm concrete. The soft amber glow of the flight line lights picked out the sleek shapes of the Starfighters parked neatly wingtip to wingtip, a futuristically gleaming row of Buck Rogers star ships. The immaculately polished aircraft sparkled in the balmy evening air, suspended in a safe halo of light which isolated and protected them from the oppressive blackness beyond. Once again I was surprised at just how dark the moonless sky was over De Peel, the lonely fenland of south-east Holland.

'Dag Henk. Leuk weer, He!'

I conversed awkwardly with the sergeant major crew chief in faltering Dutch, wishing again that the RAF had given me more time to learn the language. I signed the aircraft servicing form and started the 'walk round' to check on the exterior of the machine. Now the sergeant major removed the red metal guards along the leading and trailing edges of the wings which prevented injury to the unwary. As I ducked under the wing to check the tyres he already had his forearm spread protectively along the inner wing leading edge, a standard ground crew drill designed to prevent the pilot from scalping himself on the keen blade. Even the gentlest bump against the equivalent of a 10-ton razor blade could cause serious injury. Strapping in, the aeroplane began to come alive. Impatient to put life into the machine, I was already busy with the pre-start checks; moving switches, checking gauges and aligning the inertial naviga-tion system as my body jerked intermittently with the effort of attaching myself to the ejection seat. In spite of the cool night breeze I soon felt the prickle of perspiration under the coarse Nomex flying suit. I could have worked more slowly, avoiding that extra stress and adrenalin which accompanies haste, but I knew I could never fly like that. My years of single-seat flying had conditioned me to move fast and cut corners wherever possible. I knew that I flew better under pressure, that the buzz of adrenalin gave me that edge of faster reactions and anticipation in flight, so often the difference between success and failure and, sometimes, life and death. If there was no pressure then I would generate a little of my own. Only in this way could I be confident that my reactions were tuned up to the highest pitch, my brain already moving ahead of anticipated problems and dangers.

'If it's not done fast, it's not worth doing!' – the unofficial motto of the RAF Harrier Force. I had often joked about this with the sprog pilots I had trained in the past, as I tried to persuade the slower ones to get a ripple on. There was a price to pay for this style of flying, and now on my fourth tour of single-seat flying I was paying it in spades. My blood pressure was on the limit for military flying, (I was a paranoid hypochondriac) and deep cynicism was a permanent condition. To stay alive there was a constant war against the vagaries of Sod's Law. I was always trying to work out what I would do in the worst case; 'What if?' was the question you always had to keep asking.

'What if the weather's a lot worse than the forecast?'

'What if my jet goes U/S? What if others go U/S in flight?'

'What do we do when the radios pack up?'

The number one variable in non-AWX aviation was always the weather. Because it was chaotic, pilots had to react and change plans on the spot to take account of variations in the weather. You always had a 'cascade' of options in your mind, running from 'weather fully suitable for the mission' down to 'pull up and go home at high altitude'.

Jets were constantly going U/S. The Harrier GR3 was always an appallingly unserviceable machine: the Starfighter much more reliable.

On the Starfighter I flew with the standard American bone dome and plug-in oxygen mask. Although a bit loose and floppy compared with British helmets, I cannot recall ever having a helmet or radio problem. Additionally, the double visor system was superior to the British type. In the RAF our aviation medicine experts insisted that our helmets should be capable of protecting against the most severe impact, regardless of how heavy this made the helmet. The Mk 3 helmet (which I wore for about twenty years on and off, weighed nearly 7lb. This meant that in air combat your head plus helmet weighed some 150lb under the force of 7g. This was not so bad if you had the luxury of being able to sit straight and keep your head permanently still until the g came off. I think that some of our aviation medics really imagined this was what we did in combat. Fat chance. In air combat you were constantly twisting your head around almost through 180 degrees under g to see what was going on, all the while with this huge load on your neck. Time after time we told the doctors that this was literally a pain in the neck and we wanted American-style lightweight helmets.

In the Harrier, radio problems occurred on about half of all sorties flown, because of the appalling radio installation. We had poor reception and transmission, receiver blocking, where you could talk to an aircraft several miles away but not to one in close formation on your wing and, most frustrating of all as far as I was concerned, constantly recurring problems with the helmet mic/tel wiring system. I was forever having an intermittent microphone in flight or losing reception because of poor connections to the ejection seat and in the helmet wiring. These intermittent problems, a result of our poor quality helmet wiring system, were notoriously difficult to trace on the ground. On one occasion, in Belize, I actually had the ground crew remove the wing of a Harrier to investigate a persistent radio problem. Only when they had sweated half a day to get the wing off did our embarrassed safety equipment workers finally manage to isolate the fault which, yet again, lay in my helmet wiring and was nothing to do with the aircraft.

By now the turbine air starter had breathed life into the J79 engine. I signalled the crew chief to shut down and disconnect the starter and now the two of us stepped up to a higher pace of operation. A dozen more switches came on simultaneously as the sergeant major moved ahead of the cockpit to check on the operation of the various services, using the famous Starfighter five-finger checks, familiar to crew chiefs in a dozen different air forces around the world. From Taiwan to Spain, from Italy to the north of Norway, there were technicians who knew the machine inside out. The Starfighter had been marketed worldwide extremely efficiently by Lockheed.

Flaps, airbrakes, engine nozzle etc., were selected according to a well-practised routine. After a brief radio call to the tower I was ready to taxi. Performing the last check, the sergeant major disappeared under the rear fuselage, reaching up into the engine compartment to light the pilot burner which would guarantee a snappy light-up of the afterburner on take-off. Years later I caused some amusement at an RAF base when a visiting Starfighter pilot reported that his pilot burner wasn't lit while taxiing past ATC. (His wingman had reported it). I was in ATC at the time and, after a brief radio conversation, walked out to the taxiway to light it for him. RAF ATC just couldn't compute: the idea of a fighter having a 'pilot burner' was too much for them.

Because the 20mm Gatling cannon had been removed from the RF104G to make room for extra fuel, on 306 Squadron we used to borrow 'F' models from the strike squadrons to do our range practice at Terschelling and Vliehors ranges on the Dutch coast. Skip or retard bombing (called glide bombing by the Americans and Dutch) was pretty straightforward and very similar to the Harrier and Hunter techniques, using the standard fixed gunsight with adjustable depression. Strafe using the 20mm Vulcan cannon was something else. The gun was powered by a huge electric motor and was capable of 4,800 rounds per minute. The muzzle of the gun lay just a few inches outboard of your left elbow and, when firing, there was a half-second delay as the Gatling mechanism wound up to maximum speed, followed by an extremely loud raspberry as it fired. One hundred rounds were fired off in just one and a half seconds. The gun was pinpoint accurate, and scores on the strafe panel were either very high or zero. Unlike the Harrier, the 'Zip' strafed on flight path. I was amazed at the minimum firing range, if I remember correctly it was something like 450 metres at 450 knots firing speed – much closer than the Harrier or even the Hunter. At that range it was almost impossible to miss. Dutch range safety officers (all current Starfighter pilots) exercised the strictest control on range work and were constantly harrying pilots about low pull-outs and too close firing. Their range safety officers had reason to be strict: just recently a Starfighter pilot had strafed what he thought was the correct target on an 'op' pass on Vliehors – unfortunately his target was a van parked near the targets which contained several civilian workers. The van was ripped to shreds and two of them had been killed. Fortunately he was firing ball ammunition and not high explosive.

The main 'gotcha' about strafing in the Starfighter was the aircraft's pitch control system. There was a stick shaker to warn you that you were pulling too hard, but the chief attention-getter was a powerful stick kicker which literally shoved the stick forward with 3,000lb of hydraulic pressure if you tried to pull out too sharply. At first I invoked rate kicker on quite a few strafe passes, the aircraft pulling out of the dive in a series of barely-controlled pitch-ups as the rate kicker came on and off with me pulling hard back on the stick. This was a bit off-putting for someone used to the simplicity of Hunter and Harrier controls.

I had settled into the routine of recce flying, and was enjoying myself immensely with the freedom to roam alone through vast areas of western Europe in the splendid Starfighter and find fascinating target systems little known to the short-range RAFG Harrier world. From Volkel you could easily get to Munich and back at low level, or cruise right up to the Danish border in Schleswig-Holstein. In south Germany our squadron recce experts picked interesting targets which were a real test of your recognition. Examples were old Mace and Bomarc missile sites, gigantic weapon storage areas completely overgrown with woodland, plus vast US Army training areas full of armoured vehicles. There was a wealth of recce experience on the squadron, many of the ex-NCO pilots having been in the role for all of their flying careers, with long experience of the top-class NATO recce competitions such as Royal Flush. I thought I knew a bit about low level navigation and planning, but my eyes were opened by the old hands of 306. My mentor was a typical example. Older than me, he had started flying the RF 84 Thunderflash as a sergeant pilot and was now a lieutenant. He was modest and self-effacing to a fault, although an absolute wizard at target planning and navigation. He showed me many tricks about map study and target run planning to guarantee finding the most difficult targets in awkward terrain. Some typical tips were:

"Never look on the 50,000 map as just a plan view. Study the contours and always try to visualize what you're going to see out of the cockpit at 250 feet agl."

"For every target there is usually only one good approach direction: MAKE SURE YOU USE IT"

'Never have a bend in your initial point run.'

'Always have a series of checkpoints over the last couple of miles to the target: if you can't find suitable ones, FIND ANOTHER initial point.'

'Always be prepared to ditch an initial point run and choose another if it gives better run-in – no matter how many extra maps you have to stick together.'

'Never lay two tracks over one another.'

'Never ever plan a large turn on to your initial point run: run straight over your initial point and on to your target.'

The Starfighter was very good for tactical recce. The view forward, unobstructed by a HUD, was splendid for ultra-low flying. The excellent inertial compass sat high in the cockpit, just below the pilot's sight line as in the Hunter FR10. The Orpheus camera pod held two obliques on each side, giving almost horizon to horizon cover, plus a forward oblique angled about 30 degrees down. We also had a first-class infra red scanner which we used mostly to plot exactly where the pilot had flown on his initial point run, the scanner being switched on at the initial point. From this you could accurately debrief every error in navigation on the target run; very useful for training up new pilots. The aircraft also had a very good autopilot which I used to engage after a target, while I wrote down my VISREP. With autopilot engaged, the aircraft would fly perfectly straight and level or even make a perfect 30 degree banked turn hands off. All of our en route navigation was planned using 30 degree banked turns. I was amazed at this, and even more amazed to discover that the strike squadrons in the RNLAF used the same bank angle, even at 540 knots. This meant gigantic turning circles, something we strove to avoid in the RAF by using 3-4g turns at all times. I found out the logic of the RNLAF's decision to use such a low angle of bank. Basically it fitted in with their American-style tactical formation, (called ingress formation); you could still interpret the radar at 30 degrees bank, and the radar altimeter still worked. At higher angles of bank these factors no longer applied. Most important, from an enemy fighter's point of view there was no difference in the side view of a Starfighter flying wings level and with 30 degrees bank on. At a stroke this avoided the great bugbear of RAF tactical formations – the constant 'wing flashing' that went on during any turn, so easily spotted by patrolling fighters. RNLAF pilots would actually map read around turns; because bank angle was so low this was easy (try map reading in a 4g turn). This led to more accurate rollouts on track.

One thing that was little different to my RAFG experience was the occasional burst of FAC tasking, in support of a NATO exercise. As always, the favourite 'Doom Country' was the Ardennes, where the gently folding terrain presented the pilot with a series of ridgelines which all looked exactly the same; a kind of European version of the Liwa Hollows of Arabia. There would be the usual preposterous choice of initial points and poor control by FACs, compounded by language difficulties. The 'sick joke' mission at Wildenrath had always been to lead a four-ship FAC mission in the Ardennes with a foreign FAC. Things hadn't changed. Quite often the FAC would misidentify the aircraft pulling up for the attack and start screaming at the wrong aircraft:

'I see you! I see you! Go Left! Go Right! Nose up! Nose down! The target is in front of you!'

All this in an impenetrable accent. You could only laugh, and sometimes I would be helpless with mirth in the cockpit at the shenanigans which went on (British FACs weren't much better). I remember a FAC mission with a young pilot of 20 Squadron when he was leading. Half way down the initial point run he had misgivings about the way he had allowed for magnetic variation. (NATO FACs were still dealing in magnetic headings; Harrier pilots had to add or subtract local variation to get the correct true heading.)

My friend: 'We should be on 086 shouldn't we Win? 090 minus 4 – is that right?'

Me: 'WRONG sport – you have to ADD the variation!'

'Shit!' followed by a huge overcorrection to starboard, followed by
total miss on the target; me laughing like a drain, the FAC screaming
blue in the face as we appeared from the wrong side of the target. All
good knockabout comedy and, as I suggested to a rather chastened
pilot afterwards, part of life's learning experience.

After some months of intensive work-up training, much of it
'chased' by my mentor, I completed my combat-ready check. This
included a full wartime planning exercise (to strict time limits) for
three recce targets in communist territory as far east as the Polish
border. You had to make allowance for all the known Warsaw Pact
defences, the extremely complex NATO wartime routing procedures,
and cater for all-weather options en route. We had some pretty heavy
targets as wartime options. I still remember the names of the airfields
in communist East Germany I would be going against in wartime:
Cottbus, Parchim, Juterbog, Grossenhain, Finsterwalde, etc. – all
very heavily defended. We knew that in wartime many of us would
not survive recce passes over these airfields. However, we were
confident in the machine and felt that we could get away with a lot
on our own because of our small size and high speed, plus the
excellent peacetime training we were getting in West Germany.
Fortunately from an AWX point of view our main wartime operating
area was particularly suited for periods of Rad Alt IMC cruising,
with extensive flat areas and good radar features.

In Uden we lived in a pretty suburb known as the Wijsthoek. Like
most Dutch housing estates, the whole area was attractively land-
scaped with trees, cycle ways and paths through shrubberies and
alongside artificial lakes and canals. The Dutch had an obsession
with water features, and included them in the most attractive way in
all their building projects. The housing layout was mixed, with quite
expensive split-level semis like our rented house, ranging down to
terraces of small but attractive council houses, each with an immaculate tiny garden. Dutch town councils controlled housing
developments rigidly, insisting on high standards of building and
integrated layouts of private and council housing everywhere, to
avoid ghettoes. As a family we became completely cycle-oriented and
went everywhere by bike along the splendid cycle ways, the children
on carriers on the back. Cycling in town was totally safe, and there
were well-signposted cycle tracks linking all the local villages and
beauty spots, sometimes running for miles into open countryside. We
were amused by the charming way 'lifts' were given by bike, each of
which had a stout metal carrier on the back. The etiquette required

Hunter 30mm Aden gun pack being changed by the armourers.

My Jodel DR 1050 Ambassadeur. I used it for commuting from Germany to Devon.

...rrier GR1 with ferry tanks. These were quite big compared to the size of the jet.

...ld War, RAF Germany. Harrier GR1s deployed at a field site in snow. Author shivering in ...eground.

...ding on a Mexe pad at a field site.

...t the Harrier! GR3 with snow camouflage in Northern Norway.

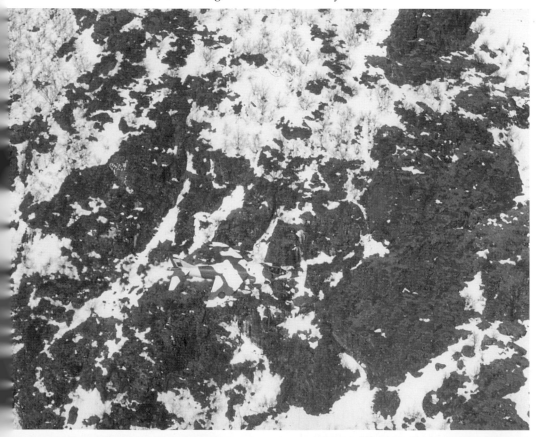

Author in cockpit of GR1 at a field site in Germany.

Communist East Berlin May Day parade. My brother and I checking out the opposition. East German anti-aircraft guns in the background.

elize Central America. A weekend trip to the Cayes from RAF Belize.

uthor plus kingfish, caught off Belize.

The author after first solo on RF-104G Starfighter, a mean machine!

Clean F 104. Sometimes we took the tanks off for training. The machine was then VERY fast.

A Starfighter formation. All 4 Volkel squadrons are represented here.

Frigate recce. This was a routine training task for us in the North sea.

alklands War images: an Argy 250kg bomb tail, found outside our tents in 1982.

ir Refuelling from a Vulcan.

Year 1982		AIRCRAFT		Captain or 1st Pilot	Co-pilot 2nd Pilot Pupil or Crew	DUTY (Including number of day or night landings as 1st Pilot or Dual)	Day Flying			Night Flying			Flight
Month	Date	Type and Mark	No.	—	—	—	1st Pilot (1)	2nd Pilot (2)	Dual (3)	1st Pilot (4)	2nd Pilot (5)	Dual (6)	Total Cols 1-6 (7)
—	—	—	—	—	—	Totals brought forward	3477.40	2.10	291.15	144.50		18.15	3934.10
Jun	2	HARRIER GR3	XZ989	SELF	—	1 RAPDAR/ASTRE — DACO WX	.40						.40
Jun	5	HARRIER GR3	XZ997	SELF	—	2 LL RECCE PORT STANLEY	1.00						1.00
Jun	7	HARRIER GR3	XZ997	SELF	—	2 2" AP ATTK SAPPER HILL ARTY	1.00						1.00
Jun	8	HARRIER GR3	XZ989	SELF	—	2 DACO u/s	.40						.40
Jun	9	HARRIER GR3	XZ992	SELF	—	½ HERMES — SAN CARLOS STBD	.40						.40
Jun	9	HARRIER GR3	XZ992	SELF	—	½ SAN CARLOS — HERMES (NO TGT)	.40						.40
Jun	10	HARRIER GR3	XZ992	SELF	—	2 A/R PORT HOWARD — STBD LOAD	.50						.50
Jun	10	HARRIER GR3	XZ992	SELF	—	½ SAN CARLOS — HERMES	.40						.40
Jun	11	HARRIER GR3	XV789	SELF	—	½ DACO u/s	.40						.40
Jun	11	HARRIER GR3	XZ997	SELF	—	2 ATTK MT HARRIET ARTY — CBU	1.10						1.10
Jun	13	HARRIER GR3	XZ997	SELF	—	½ 2xLGB MOODY BROOK ARTY — DH	1.10						1.10
		End of Hostilities 14 Jun 82 (for 1P Page)											
Jun	18	HARRIER GR3	XZ133	SELF	—	½ A1?	1.10						1.10
Jun	20	HARRIER GR3	XZ992	SELF	—	½ A1?	1.00						1.06
Jun	21	HARRIER GR3	XZ997	SELF	—	½ A1? + 1V1	1.00						1.00
Jun	21	HARRIER GR3	XZ997	SELF	—	½ A1? + 1V1	1.00						1.00
Jun	26	HARRIER GR3	XW919	SELF	—	½ A1? + 2V2	1.00						1.00
Jun	27	HARRIER GR3	XZ997	SELF	—	½ ADEX + 2V2 SHAR	.45						.45
						Totals carried forward	(1)	(2)	(3)	(4)	(5)	(6)	(7)

| Year 1982 | | Aircraft | | Captain or 1st Pilot | Co-pilot 2nd Pilot Pupil or Crew | Duty (Including number of day or night landings as 1st Pilot or Dual) | Day Flying | | | Night Flying | | | Fl... Tot Cos. |
Month	Date	Type and Mark	No.				1st Pilot (1)	2nd Pilot (2)	Dual (3)	1st Pilot (4)	2nd Pilot (5)	Dual (6)	(7)
		Operation Corporate			Sutton	— Totals brought forward	3438.25	2.10	291.15	1144.6		18.15	342
MAY	2	HARRIER GR3	XZ989	SELF	—	JITY - ST MARDON	1.00						1.01
MAY	3	HARRIER GR3	XZ989	SELF	—	AIR SPACE	.40						.4
MAY	4	HARRIER GR3	XZ989	SELF	—	ST MIDRIAN - ASCENSION	9.10						9.1
MAY	18	HARRIER GR3	XV789	SELF	—	ATLANTIC CONVEYOR - HERMES	.10						.1
MAY	19	HARRIER GR3	XZ963	SELF	—	2 V 1 ACM	.05						.0
MAY	19	HARRIER GR3	XZ963	SELF	—	2 V 1 ACM	.40						.0
MAY	20	HARRIER GR3	XZ963	SELF	—	CBU FOX BAY POL	1.00						1.0
MAY	21	HARRIER GR3	XZ988	SELF	—	A/R MT KENT (CBU+2x PUMA DEST)	.50						.5
MAY	21	HARRIER GR3	XZ989	SELF	—	A/R DUNNOSE HD A/F	1.00						1.0
MAY	22	HARRIER GR3	XZ997	SELF	—	ATTK GOOSE GREEN A/F-CBU	.50						.5
MAY	28	HARRIER GR3	XZ989	SELF	—	RECCE PT HOWARD	1.00						1.4
MAY	23	HARRIER GR3	XZ989	SELF	—	ATTK PEBBLE ISLAND A/F-CBU	1.05						1.
MAY	25	HARRIER GR3	XZ788	SELF	—	3xROUGH FE LAFF STANLEY AIR	.45						1.
MAY	26	HARRIER GR3	XZ788	SELF	—	A/R - MIL ACT - N/S	1.00						1.
MAY	26	HARRIER GR3	XZ989	SELF	—	A/R MT KENT 1xPUMA DEST	1.00						1.0
MAY	26	HARRIER GR3	XZ989	SELF	—	A12 DNCO u/s	.20						3
MAY	22	HARRIER GR3	XZ989	SELF	—	RECCE GOOSE GREEN	.55						.5
MAY	28	HARRIER GR3	XV789	SELF	—	A/R - MIL ACT - N/S	1.00						1.0
MAY	28	HARRIER GR3	XV789	SELF	—	2"RIP - GOOSE GREEN DUSK ATTK	1.00						1.
MAY	30	HARRIER GR3	XZ989	SELF	—	1000 LB RET + STR MT HOWARD	1.00						1.
MAY	30	HARRIER GR3	XZ963	SELF	—	2" RIP ARTY POSN (SHOT DOWN) WHILE MT (BY SEA FIRE)	.40						.4
						AC FLAMED OUT ON FSTB WITH SEVERE FUEL LEAK, MUD FAIL AND R/T FAILED. PICKED UP BY SEA KING 826 SQN.							
						Totals carried forward	(1)	(2)	(3)	(4)	(5)	(6)	

Author's Log book pages for Falklands War operations, 1982.

Harrier GR3 of 1(F) Squadron at Ascension, 1982.

Tornado GR1 formation at Cottesmore.

e author sailing *Would I* off Harwich (Elizabethan 29).

icet, a Nicholson 32, Mk 8.

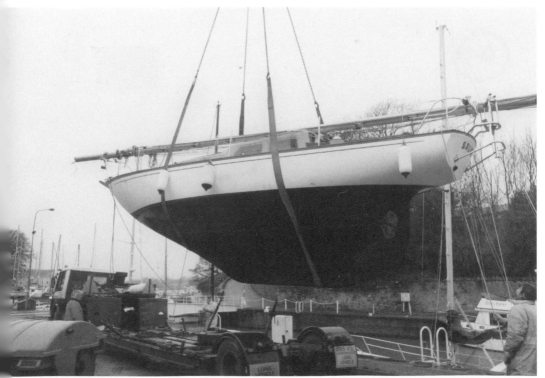

The author's DG600 glider.

A view of the Pyrenees from the author's cockpit at 10,000 feet.

the hitchhiker to trot alongside for a few steps and then hop tidily on to the carrier to cause minimum speed reduction for the lift-giver. Towards the end of our time in Holland my son Christopher was born.

In summer most of the base personnel cycled the five kilometres out to the base in uniform, the first social occasion of the day as hundreds of cyclists chatted while riding through the attractive Dutch farmland. There was no check on the main gate – we just cycled through en masse. Most of the RNLAF personnel lived in or around the town and we were invited to many pleasant evenings with various squadron members. Dutch social life had many subtle differences. You were never invited out to dinner at someone else's house unless you were 'family'. A normal social evening would start with coffee and sweet cakes, a sober half-hour period before there was any mention of alcohol. Then there would be a *Borreltje* (a tot of Jenever), followed by a *pilsje* (beer) or *glasje wijn* (glass of wine).

At Volkel the social life was of a different order to my RAF experience. The RNLAF was a very equal society. Relations between officers and non-commissioned ranks were very free compared with the RAF. The sergeants and corporals on the line wanted to know your first name straight away, and would use it freely.

Many of the soldiers were conscripts, doing just one year's service, but they were trained up to do certain aircraft work in that time, acting as the crew chief's helpmate. The crew chief was the lynchpin of the squadron engineers. Most of them were of sergeant major rank, and held total responsibility for the aircraft under their command. They kept the aircraft servicing Form 700 equivalent with them at the aircraft, and the pilot would sign the form at the aircraft steps. This was in total contrast to the rather bureaucratic RAF engineers' way of doing things, where all the senior ranking NCOs would lurk centrally in the line hut, leaving routine servicing and cleaning of the aircraft to junior corporals and airmen – the 'lineys'. In the RAF aircraft, no individual person, other than the squadron senior engineering officer, would take personal responsibility for the appearance of the squadron's aircraft. The superb crew chief system of the Dutch Air Force worked very well. I never once climbed into a Starfighter that wasn't in a pristine state of cleanliness.

Any technical snags were usually sorted out on the spot by the dual-trained crew chiefs. Some of these excellent characters had had the same aircraft on their charge for fifteen years or more, and took a fierce personal pride in its condition, in direct competition with the other chiefs. For 25-hour and 50-hour servicing, the chief would go with the machine to a central maintenance hangar. When major servicing came up the crew chief had a rest while the machine went into deep servicing at Ypenburg. Our Starfighters were Fokker-built.

Back with the RAF I spent a lot of time trying to find out what objections the RAF engineers had to this excellent system, with no satisfactory results. Dutch Air Force crew chiefs had a fierce pride in 'their' machine, and always went off with the recovery team in the event that the aircraft landed elsewhere – after a bird strike, for example. One newish crew chief actually went on strike because, mistakenly, he was not allowed to go with the recovery party to do an engine change on his machine which had landed U/S in Germany.

There were various trade unions in the Dutch Air Force. While no one was allowed to disobey an order, anyone was allowed to query it. The National Service *Dienstplichtige* soldiers, who spent a lot of time on tedious guard duty, sent union representatives for a monthly meeting with the base commander, to discuss terms of service and duties. Junior officers, including some of our pilots, belonged to an officers' union. Some of our pilots were National Service, flying the Starfighter for just one tour before having a choice to leave and join a Dutch National airline, either KLM or Martinair, or remain with the RNLAF. Unlike the RAF system, all initial flying training in Holland was joint civil/military, counting towards their civil licences, so their licences were valid as soon as they left the military.

More senior officers, in command posts, were quite formal in their relations with subordinate officers. I was always addressed as 'Pook' by the *Chef Vliegdienst* (CVD), who was the *Overste* (wing commander) in charge of all flying operations, even when I was made a flight commander, in the rank of flight lieutenant, and later promoted squadron leader. However, within the squadrons everything was on first-name terms, as in the British Army – a very comfortable arrangement. Additionally, the officers took great pains to make every soldier and NCO feel a worthwhile part of the squadron. We gave a farewell party in the line hut (with some of the wives) whenever a soldier or NCO was posted. The squadron boss would say a few words about even the most junior soldier. When there was any changeover of command, all personnel under command would have to parade with a band for a formal handover of authority. If CVD was posted, the whole Wing would be on parade in best uniform; for the base commander, the whole base. The outgoing commander would say a few words of thanks and then the incoming commander would introduce himself and state his intentions. Finally, each year there were several joint officer/NCO functions in Mess kit, where we socialized with NCOs and their wives.

After about six months on 306 I could pass the 'telephone test'. I could pick up the phone in ops and talk to a stranger without them immediately breaking into English. Eventually I could talk to staff officers in Den Haag and there would be several minutes of conversation before they would ask, 'Excuse me: are you Dutch?' This standard was achieved only after months of intense work at home and a lot of extra Dutch lessons at a language school in Uden. Eventually I was extremely proud when OC 306 Squadron appointed me a flight commander on the strength of my flying experience and the standard of my Dutch.

One RNLAF procedure I managed to influence was the formation weather abort. The Dutch still followed the inflexible American-style of formation leadership, where the leader was always responsible for his wingman who, in turn, was not allowed to use much initiative. For the abort their standard drill was to call the wingman into close formation and then make a controlled formation climb into cloud. This was a time wasting procedure, as – by definition – a real weather abort was an emergency, and speed in entering the climb was essential. The squadron had just had two pilots killed in Sardinia doing precisely this manoeuvre. Encountering a rapidly lowering cloud base, the wingman had taken rather too long to get into position. In the subsequent climb in cloud, they had hit the top of the only hill for miles around. I argued that the priority was to get away from the ground, using full power and regardless of formation integrity: in the RAF the manoeuvre was carried out individually and the formation was joined up in VMC (visual meteorological conditions), above cloud. Eventually I got through and they started to follow the new procedure.

Although we loved the *Ouwe Dame* as a first-class aircraft, it did have a couple of potentially lethal drawbacks. The worst of these could occur on landing in rain in a strong left crosswind. The Starfighter's powerful brakes and nose wheel steering system (NWS) were activated via a single micro switch on the left main gear oleo. On touchdown this oleo would compress and make the switch, enabling NWS and powered anti-skid brakes. With a left crosswind three factors combined to give the pilot a hard time: firstly, the left oleo would not compress because of the crosswind holding up the left wing, thus disabling both NWS and power brakes at once; the third item was the powerful rain remover, which operated only on the port quarter windscreen, hence in a left crosswind it was no use to the pilot. Because of this, the aircraft would crab down the runway at 180 knots, more or less out of control – no NWS, no power brakes, and the pilot unable to see forward through the rain because of the left crab angle. The only solution was to deploy the brake parachute and hope that the gear micro switch engaged before you got pulled off the side of the runway.

The oleo micro switch problem led to an accident during my time there. A pair of Volkel Starfighters made a stream landing at an RAF base and the wingman suffered a failure of the micro switch. With no brakes or steering he drifted across the runway and ran into the back of his leader.

One day one of the wing pilots speared in while running in to the initial point for Volkel. Eyewitnesses stated that his aircraft had just dived straight into the ground from 1,500 feet.

On 306 Squadron there were regular runs to Italy, flown at low level all the way down through eastern France and through the Alps to land either at Villa Franca or Grossetto. With full fuel we could just about make it at low level all the way in good weather.

One trip to Grossetto for me, was an epic demonstration of the long-range capability of the machine, although things got a bit tense as we approached the Mont Blanc area of the Alps and started to run into heavy snow showers. The terrain was spectacular but deadly and, realizing that we couldn't continue at low level, I called the boss into close formation and we climbed in full afterburner above the safety altitude of 15,000 feet, (the highest SA I had ever seen). We spent a chilly weekend in the Mess at Grossetto, Italian central heating not being up to much in the unseasonable cold that April. There were also lot of *Ample Gain* landaway exercises to NATO bases in Germany, Belgium, Denmark and Norway. The idea of these was to practise other bases in handling the turn round of the Starfighter. Trips to American bases in Germany were popular for one particular reason: the BX, or base exchange, where all kinds of high-quality goods were available at extremely low dollar prices. Visiting NATO pilots were entitled to use the BX, and all the Volkel squadrons had a number of standard AWX training routes terminating in the middle of the Eiffel – very convenient for landing at Hahn, Spangdahlem, Bitburg, Ramstein or Zweibrucken. Quite a lot of duty-free goods could be crammed into the Starfighter cockpit, and to make more space a few of the electronic 'black boxes' could be pulled from the E-compartment behind the pilot. I remember standing on the TF line at Volkel one bright, early Wednesday morning and seeing two strike pilots climbing into the TF next to ours:

'Morning: – off to the BX are we?' (the answer was obvious)

'Where are you landing?'

'Er, Bitburg.'

'Bitburg BX is closed Wednesdays – didn't you know?'

'Shit:- OK then, we'll re-file for Spangdahlem on the radio.'

Problem solved.

If the weather was totally un-flyable in Germany then we would fly long-range low level missions in pairs over France. The Dutch government had a private agreement with the French for this. We had quite a few standard routes, some of which took us far south of Paris and others as far as the Cotentin peninsula in the Channel. I had not flown much low level over France before and was impressed by the vast wide open spaces and endless vistas of smooth, rolling farmland.

TACEVALS and major NATO exercises continued at Volkel, with 306 Squadron packing up and deploying down the road to De Peel every time the alarm went. Departures and recoveries to the Volkel/De Peel complex were carefully integrated with the instrument patterns, to the confusion of many visiting recce pilots. De Peel was not well known to other air forces and visiting recce pilots were often totally surprised to find themselves on the ground at De Peel for a recce cross-servicing, having flight planned into Volkel. Once ops recognized an inbound recce mission the radar controllers automatically diverted the aircraft into De Peel. The climax of any major exercise or TACEVAL would be the vertical dispersal, when every serviceable aircraft would be sent airborne to 'lurk' in holding patterns for as long as possible. Returning low-level aircraft would also be diverted into these holding patterns. We had practised the same thing at Wildenrath and Wittering, but things were usually pretty fraught during the recovery of all these aircraft because, in my view, of the lack of experience of RAF ATC in controlling very large numbers of aircraft. Things were different at Volkel. During any major exercise or TACEVAL, all reserve officers would be called up for service, often from civilian jobs. This included ATC officers, the best of whom took over in the approach controller's position for the recovery from survival scramble, when up to sixty aircraft would be trying to get back on to the ground at Volkel and De Peel in poor weather with little fuel remaining.

This particular character was an absolute ace at controlling, and everything usually went like clockwork. He had been doing the job at Volkel for years. The main recovery aid was TACAN, feeding automatically into PAR (radar approach). If PAR failed then we all switched automatically to full TACAN runway approaches with minimum R/T. Only when the TACAN was off did things start to get a bit interesting. Dutch military ATC was always impressive, a breath of fresh air in comparison with the RAF.

Apart from NATO commitments, the only actual operational task we had on 306 was to keep two aircraft on permanent two-hour readiness for naval tasking in the North Sea. This was a Dutch national task, nothing to do with NATO. Their Navy wanted good photo coverage of all Soviet naval forces transiting the North Sea. For the duty pilots this meant carrying a 'bleeper' everywhere. I was only scrambled once, to look at a force including a Soviet Krivak-class destroyer. It happened at about 2000 on a Saturday night and soon I was airborne, sweating buckets in my immersion suit. (The RNLAF, like the GAF, used immersion suits whenever the sea was below 15 degrees C, as opposed to 10 degrees C in the RAF. This meant, in effect, that you were permanently in immersion suits over sea in summer, except for a few weeks in August. However, we didn't wear immersion suits for overland sorties in winter, unlike the RAF.) A long way out in the North Sea we were directed on to our target by a RNLAF Orion maritime patrol aircraft which had been shadowing the Soviets since they emerged from the Baltic. We made quite a few runs to get good photos down the funnel, which the Navy particularly wanted. The Soviet warships were absolutely bristling with armament and fired off flares at us in an aggressive fashion on each pass. This was the closest thing to 'operational' flying we did.

Next I went on a long-range landaway to Brindisi in southern Italy, via Villa Franca. After a fabulous night stop at Verona we set off down the spine of Italy for the long run through the mountains to the south. Brindisi was a bustling seaport and very attractive in places. In March the temperature was already steaming, and I was glad we weren't there in midsummer. Back at Villa the local Starfighter squadron showed us the splendid Italian Air Force way to get your flight plan clearance as comfortably as possible (usually a nightmare when trying to get into France). ATC expected us to call up before start up in the aircraft, after which they would keep us waiting for up to an hour in the heat before they gave us clearance. We merely requested our clearance via the squadron ops radio, using our call sign and pretending that we were already out in the aircraft. We then sat in the air-conditioned comfort of the crew room drinking coffee until ATC came through with the clearance. We then quickly zipped out to the jets and cranked up.

In June we went on squadron exchange to Eggebek, a German Navy Starfighter base in Schleswig-Holstein. We were taken on a joint formation with the Germans for some long-range maritime recce missions through the Baltic. Once we started operating on our own we determined to explore as far as we could in our longer-range RFs. We needed a bit of intelligence info about the attitude of the Warsaw Pact enemy forces – they had a lot of hardware available in the region. With our senior flight commander I went to the German Navy intelligence officer and we asked what we were likely to encounter. He said that there was no problem with the East German or Polish Air Force; they were very docile and would not give us any hassle. The Soviets also tended to stay out of things. In contrast, the Swedes were very aggressive and would intercept anything, no matter how low we flew. As for SAMs, the flight commander asked the maximum range of the coastal SAM 3 batteries which were scattered all along the southern Baltic coast of communist East Germany and Poland. Having got the answer, to my surprise the flight commander said that we would plan all our missions just outside this distance from the shore. I had expected him to stay much further away, as the Germans did. This was the typical Dutch Air Force attitude; they made up their own rules to suit the conditions on the spot. We flew some extremely long-range missions through the Baltic, almost as far as the Russian coastline. It was a slightly eerie feeling flying in a four-ship at low level in the Gulf of Gdynia, over 360 miles east of Eggebek and within sight of the Soviet coastline. If we had had to eject we would have been picked up by the communists. The weather got progressively hotter during our week at Eggebek and cockpit conditions grew almost intolerable in our bulky immersion suits. The Baltic was still below 15 degrees C. On one occasion I was sent off for a solo recce around Denmark at midday. I was so hot over the land that I just couldn't do anything except fly straight and level.

During my last year with 306 Squadron there were more trips to Italy and a lot of landaways, including one amusing trip to the air

defence Starfighter base at Leeuwaarden in Friesland. 'Fries' (pro-
nounced FREESSS), the language of Northern Holland, was a
notoriously garbled dialect, difficult to understand even for a non-
Fries Dutchman. At the squadron buildings I found the crew room
empty. It transpired that most of the squadron were on leave. Idly I
strolled across to the squawk box on the bar. The label on it said
OPS. Pressing the switch I asked,

'Dag: Is er iemand?' ('Morning: is anyone there?').

The reply was an unintelligible squawked phrase which I couldn't
make head or tail of. 'God, they were right about "Fries" – this is
gibberish', I thought. After further fruitless attempts to converse with
the person on the other end of the squawk box I gave up and walked
down the corridor to find the ops room. This too was empty, except
for a large, morose parrot whose cage was right next to the array of
squawk boxes. I had been talking to a parrot – this was its party
trick, apparently. It could do a passable imitation of a 'Fries' accent.
This was a famous bird – in fact the squadron claimed that it was the
only supersonic parrot in the world. The fools had taken it up for a
trip in a TF and flown it at Mach 2. A plaque on the cage recorded
this epic achievement. No wonder it was a nervous wreck.

I had just been promoted to squadron leader, with a welcome
increase in pay. By autumn I was already looking ahead to my next
posting. Although I was not looking forward to a return to the RAF.
I found out that I had a couple of choices of posting as a Harrier
flight commander, either back to RAFG or to 1(F) at Wittering. After
nearly six years of flying over Germany I felt I needed a change of
scenery. Additionally, as a family we could not face the prospect of
living in quarters in Germany. I opted for Wittering. I made a couple
of trips to Wittering in the Starfighter to make sure that our
Stamford house, which had been rented out, would be available for
us, and to check up on what was in store on 1(F) Squadron. 306 laid
on a tremendous going-away party which lasted most of the day. My
last day at work started with the most junior pilot on my flight
turning up at the Wijsthoek as my 'chauffeur' for the day in a vintage
Bentley. We packed up the house and, after a nightmare move by the
RAF's GFA removal agency, boarded the Hoek van Holland ferry.

I could have stayed on permanently in Holland. By now my family
and I were completely immersed in the Dutch lifestyle and my boss
had told me that the Dutch government would be quite happy for me
to stay on permanently in the RNLAF. Much as I appreciated the

honour that this implied, deep down I was starting to pine for the gentle green hills and beautiful coastline of England. I knew I couldn't live for ever in a country as flat as Holland, no matter how nice the people were.

I had mixed feelings about going back to the Harrier. I knew there had been little improvement in serviceability since I had last flown it; on the other hand, there were a lot of exciting new things to do on 1(F), including a lot of detachments to interesting places and also air-to-air refuelling, which I had never done before. It was going to be a hard slog, but I felt sure that I was about to start my most interesting tour in the RAF. I knew that I wouldn't be going anywhere after this: I had already decided to retire from the RAF after this tour to join a civil airline.

Chapter 15

Back to the Harrier

After my Starfighter flying, the RAF wisely decided that I should have the full forty-hour Harrier refresher course. I whistled through the course in three months, enjoying myself hugely as all the old techniques came back. There had been major improvements to weapon firing and the Harrier laser ranger and marked target seeker (LRMTS) had at last entered service. This – when it worked – could give pinpoint accurate ranging for all weapon events, and could be used in conjunction with a laser target marker (LTM) to show the position of targets on the ground. Basically a soldier would aim the LTM at the target and the Harrier's laser receiver would pick up the reflection and produce a marker cross in the HUD, exactly on the target position. At last a useful function of the HUD at low level, I thought. The system worked quite well, although there were severe limitations in training with it because of the RAF's strict attitude to laser safety. A direct consequence of this was that it took years before we were cleared to carry out laser-ranged strafe and rocket attacks at Holbeach range.

The staff of 233 OCU had changed completely since my time. I had not realized how much the enthusiasm for VIFF had taken hold of everyone. On my first instrument training trip the young QWI in the rear seat said he would show me a 'flop' manoeuvre; a back-flip in the vertical which I had heard about. I was dubious about the manoeuvre, partly because I could see little operational justification for it in wartime. Also the T4 was beset with tedious airframe and nozzle limitations because of its inferior VSTOL handling qualities and weaker airframe. In the vertical the speed fell through 120 knots as he braced himself for the application of full braking stop to make the aircraft flip over and reverse direction. In tight-lipped silence (I wasn't the aircraft captain) I noted that we were side slipping markedly already – not a good start to the manoeuvre. The QWI hadn't noticed the sideslip and was completely caught out when the aircraft instantly departed into a vicious spin as he applied braking stop. I saw it coming: with that amount of sideslip the departure was inevitable. I just let him sort it out, as a lot of heavy breathing came from the back seat while the jet tumbled wildly all over the place. Eventually he managed to recover and a very shaken QWI let me fly it back to base.

In March I went to London for my final civil service commission examination in Dutch and gained an interpreter first class qualification. Just what I was going to do with this I wasn't sure, but it was a satisfying end to my Dutch language training. In fact over the next few years I was occasionally called on by the civil service to examine candidates at colloquial level in London, a welcome excuse for an expenses-paid trip to the city.

I joined 1(F) in early June to commence three months' intensive combat ready work-up. I took over 'A' Flight. Straightaway I discovered that 1(F) and Wittering had a major problem. The station had 'blown' last year's TACEVAL and, in addition, the squadron had made a poor showing on the recent CFS standardization visit. This visit was known as the 'trappers' visit and involved a week's detailed evaluation of all squadron pilots by visiting Harrier QFIs. Everyone was put through their paces and had to demonstrate all the aircraft handling skills and appropriate technical knowledge. The trappers' visit struck fear into the hearts of all pilots. Any fall down would bring on the wrath of our superiors and leave the unit concerned in the doldrums until they had successfully passed the next check. Exactly the same situation prevailed in the event of a TACEVAL fall down, which was also taken most seriously at higher levels. As a result of all this misery, the squadron was under the most intense pressure to do well in the autumn TACEVAL, due to be carried out after deployment to Gutersloh (one of 1(F)'s many overseas deployment options).

'Here we are again, right back in it', I thought.

The pressure was on again in no small measure and I could tell from the generally 'twitched' attitude of all squadron personnel that everyone knew that we were firmly up against it. After the relaxed and easy lifestyle of the Dutch Air Force I knew there would be unremitting pressure from our commanders for the next year or so. It was like welcoming a bad-tempered old friend. In mid-July we deployed to Gutersloh in Germany to carry out a full-scale

MAXEVAL (TACEVAL practice), with evaluators from HQ Strike Command. Before we left Wittering the station commander gave us all (including the boss) an uncompromising warning, saying in effect that this was our last chance to prove ourselves and 'heads would roll' if we blew it again. A charming lead-in to a little continental holiday, I thought.

Gutersloh was sizzling in the midsummer heat and I was totally unimpressed with the cramped ops bunkers and hardened aircraft shelters. There wasn't even so much as a toilet inside the concrete ops bunker, and the air conditioning was totally inadequate.

The MAXEVAL was as tough as any I had experienced, and I came up against my bullshit tolerance limit on a couple of occasions. Late one evening we had just finished a hard debrief of a long day's flying when the evaluator's team came into the bunker and said they wanted me to carry out a planning exercise of an eight-ship attack over the border. This would take at least two hours. Looking at my watch I saw that we were on duty again in less than eight hours. As the evaluators refused to delay the morning start time I politely informed them that all my pilots were stacking to their pits, and they could shove their planning exercise. Luckily, I got away with it.

After the return from Gutersloh I was given my first air-to-air refuelling dual. The idea was to do a bit of low level in Wales, then climb up to join the tanker on the towline over Devon, with the instructor demonstrating all the tanker joining techniques etc. In the event he ran us a bit short of fuel and the join up was an undignified plunge straight at the starboard basket, which he plugged into with minimal style and a fair amount of heavy breathing. Needless to say there was a complete absence of instructional patter while this was going on which was understandable, bearing in mind the low reading on our fuel gauges. I was slated to become an AARI (air-to-air refuelling instructor) myself, and I resolved to make sure I always had sufficient fuel to carry out a satisfactory demonstration. Flight refuelling was great fun and reasonably straightforward once you got the idea. Unfortunately the Harrier's refuelling probe was a cheap-and-cheerful bolt-on job mounted above the port intake, which meant the probe tip was well aft and out of the field of view of the pilot. The Victor tankers' baskets jiggled and waved about in the slipstream, and had a tendency to move sideways as you got close to them. The technique was to line up on some formation reference points on the Victor's wing and slide forward gently without looking at the basket itself, hoping that the probe would slide in first time. Quite a trick, especially if you were short of fuel and tensed up. There were several problems with this, even in good weather. First of all the Victor was faster than the Harrier and the join-up required considerable judgement to get right. Without an on-board radar, just finding the Victor was a bit of a lottery. Too much overtake on hitting the basket could drive the probe tip through the metal spokes, the infamous 'spokes' contact which effectively destroyed the basket. In this case there was no alternative but to divert and land at the nearest airfield, in case of engine damage. You had to take great care manoeuvring around the tanker in formation, and there were strict rules as to how this was to be done in order to prevent accidents. A few years before a Buccaneer had collided with the tailplane of a tanker, causing it to crash. A 1(F) squadron pilot had recently managed to get the whole basket stuffed down his engine intake by mistake. This immediately surged the engine and he disappeared into the cloud tops over the North Sea, frantically trying to light up again. Fortunately he hacked it, but the tanker people were most unimpressed.

Having qualified on flight refuelling I enjoyed the long-range freedom of action it gave us on 1(F). We planned long-range low-level missions into the glorious Scottish low flying areas, pulling up to plug into the tanker above cloud before letting down again for another long low-level session on the way home. I was checked out again at freefall bombing, the first time since 1972, and we got plenty of practice in on Holbeach range. As an extra duty I took over as the squadron QFI because the pilot destined for that post did not have enough experience on type. This was a fairly heavy job on a Harrier squadron, as there were a lot of checkouts and re-familiarization duals to be done as pilots came and went on various detachments. On many detachments, Belize for example, our pilots got zero VSTOL practice and were badly in need of some extra dual training when they came home. I was to get heartily sick of the back seat of the 1(F) T4 during my tour – not the most serviceable machine.

As flight commander in charge of training, an immediate chore for me was to set up our pilot training procedures for the newly-introduced AR5 NBC aircrew kit – basically a gas mask to wear in the cockpit. Known cheerfully as the 'rapist's hood' by the shags, this long-awaited kit consisted of a rubber one-piece hood and integral face piece to be worn underneath the bone dome and lifejacket. I knew a little of the history of its development and was taken aback to discover that we were not equipped with the ejection seat blower pack (there had been no money for the modification), previously considered essential before we could use it in anger. For cockpit use we had the aircraft's normal oxygen supply which was originally intended only as a back-up in the event of failure of the seat blower pack primary ventilation system. I tried on the kit and discovered that it was impossible to remove in flight, leaving the pilot relying totally on a continuous oxygen supply to avoid immediate suffocation and to prevent misting of the face piece. With mounting unease I was also briefed on the water entry drill after ejection. The air intake for the mask was at waist level, guaranteeing instant drowning for any ejectee over water unless a complicated pre-water entry drill was carried out faultlessly, during the brief few seconds you might be hanging on your parachute. I was totally unimpressed with this device, especially after my first trip in the T4 wearing it, with a safety pilot. In only moderately warm weather I misted up completely only twenty minutes after take-off, and had to hand over control to the safety pilot. What it would be like in the expected heat and panic of genuine wartime flying did not bear thinking about. I started trying to find out more about why we were using what I saw as a dangerously degraded item of kit. Apart from the misting-up problem, which would create horrific problems in the air for solo pilots – there was absolutely no way to get the damn thing off once you were strapped into the cockpit. I was particularly concerned about the water entry procedure after ejection.

My first job on 1(F) was to take over as flight commander of No. 1417 (Harrier) Flight in Belize in August. This little outpost, in the wilds of Central America, was occupied in rotation with all the other flight commanders of the Harrier force and promised to be a splendid 'jolly'. The prospect of being away from the squadron for a tough TACEVAL added to the attraction of having my own little command far away from direct RAF interference. For the second time in my RAF career I drew tropical kit and stocked up with fishing gear, suntan oil and insect sprays.

Chapter 16

Belize, Central America

Belize, formerly the Protectorate of British Honduras, was a delightful oasis of ex-colonial civilization among the dangerously volatile states of Central America. The hinterland up to the Guatemalan border was mountainous, with sharp ridgelines covered in impenetrable scrub. In the east the terrain was boringly flat jungle, giving way to the Caribbean coastline which was marked by miles of dense mangrove swamp, permanently encroaching on crystal-clear shallow waters. Belize had a priceless and beautiful secret, known only to a few. Some ten miles offshore lay an unspoilt coral reef, the second longest in the world, and a paradise for diving and fishing from the numerous cays. Some of these tiny coral islands were barely a hundred yards long, supporting half a dozen palm trees. On my detachment there the secret was still largely undiscovered by the world's tourist trade. There were no cruise ships lurking offshore and, having been virtually wiped out in a recent hurricane, Belize 'City' was still a traditional Central American jumble of peeling wooden buildings and corrugated iron roofs. The few solid masonry buildings were the old-fashioned, non-airconditioned trading stores in the centre of town, full of dusty goods under shafts of hot sunlight.

The RAF VC10 landed at the optimistically-titled Belize International Airport in mid-August, the start of the rainy (hurricane) season. The temperature and humidity were almost unbearable as I stepped out into the fierce sunlight on the pan, to be met by the current OC 1417 Flight, from RAFG. The officers' Mess, a joint Army/RAF affair, consisted of single-storey tin-roofed buildings with separate accommodation huts. The dining room was a large, open-sided 'basha', quaintly thatched with palm leaves. Having been in the tropics before I asked for a room without air-conditioning, in order to get acclimatized quicker. On my first night I was unable to sleep much because of the heat and the virtually continuous thunderstorms which started up every night soon after midnight. For long periods I stood at the window watching non-stop lightning flashes which lit up the shrubbery for several minutes at a time. The sheets of rain hammering on the tin roof made sleep impossible until a brief lull just before dawn. Then, just as I dropped off to sleep I heard the pest control man approaching with his smoke gun. Every dawn and dusk this cove walked round the whole camp spraying insecticide in a thick smoke cloud from the gun which thundered away like a Doodlebug Pulse Jet engine. Just the thing to wake you up at 0600. The 'bug man' was a standing joke at sunset in the bar, when the visibility would drop to just a few feet for several minutes in choking clouds of insecticide smoke. Whiteout in DDT smoke was not considered a good enough reason to interrupt drinking, so we must have inhaled and imbibed a fair amount of DDT in our time there.

For a couple of days the flight commander showed me round as I became accustomed to the fierce heat and humidity. The storm drains around the camp area were infested with big, aggressive land crabs which would creep out in huge numbers when it was quiet. At the first sign of human activity they would scuttle away in reverse, waving their claws aggressively at any pursuer. They were great fun to squash on the dirt roads outside the base. At night they would be all over the place, like a Space Invaders game in your car headlights. There were also extremely large lizards, some over four feet long, that lived underneath the accommodation huts. They would stand motionless in the glare of the sun until you got within a few feet of them. I lost no time in getting acquainted with the NCOs and airmen of the Flight. Most were serving a six-month unaccompanied tour and living in airconditioned caravans next to the four aircraft hides at the eastern end of the airstrip. Ready-use weapon stocks were kept in dumps next to the hides, often submerged in several inches of monsoon floodwater. Morale seemed pretty good. It was my job to keep it that way. The flight commander briefed me on the various operational tasks of the unit in the tiny Flight offices. We were there to deter Guatemalan aggression, but the political situation had calmed down a lot since 1976 and there was little chance of any activity from the opposition. The flying programme consisted of FAC exercises in support of British troops in the border areas, live firing on a couple of jungle ranges and also splash firing on a sled towed by the resident Caribbean guardship. This was a Royal Navy frigate doing a couple of months' duty in the area. We also threw in some air combat training and regular airfield attacks for a bit of amusement, the latter also to train our resident Rapier SAM battery. I did some flying to get acclimatized to the local area before the flight commander handed over to me.

The Belizean coastal plain was fairly flat jungle with the occasional lightning-struck tree top sticking out well above the canopy. These were quite a hazard at low level, the bare white branches almost invisible against the sky. Further inland were the razor-sharp karst ridges of the Maya mountains. I flew on a four-ship splash firing detail out to the Caribbean guardship, where the flight commander rather unwisely insisted on leading a very low echelon flypast. All very well as long as you organize the run-in so that you don't have to turn against the echelon. I was on the outside of the echelon and did not appreciate the last minute jink towards me, my wing almost trailing in the sea. A couple of years later at Wittering I watched a formation leader almost write off a wingman making the same mistake during an air display: Soon the flight commander departed, thankfully leaving me alone with a good bunch of ground crew and three RAFG pilots.

As flight commander I made a point of insisting on HUD film being used at all times, and I personally debriefed all films of attacks flown. Ground attack manoeuvres were more challenging in the heat, particularly over the mountainous regions. We had the same IAS/TAS problem I remembered from desert flying days. At plus 40 degrees, the aircraft was doing over 450 knots true air speed when indicating 420. This led to more difficult pull-outs from dives – particularly dangerous in the jungle-filled ravines in which we often trained.

Range trips to New River Lagoon range were great value. This range was just an area of swamp next to the river in a remote jungle area. The rules were pretty free and easy and we helicoptered our duty FAC out there to act as range safety officer (RSO). One of our options was freefall bombing with 28lb smoke and flash practice bombs, which we used regularly on 1(F). The RAFG squadrons had not done any freefall, so I had to brief them up for the exercise and assess their film. On one occasion we got to the range to find that there was too much medium altitude cloud to allow attacks on the designated target, so I just flew down the river a bit and recced a suitably deserted patch of sandy beach which we then used as a target, plotting each others' bomb impacts. That was not the sort of thing you could get away with in the UK. On another occasion a troop of British soldiers also went out to the range under the command of a rather gung-ho young lieutenant, who wanted them to experience being fired on by air-to-ground rockets. I agreed that they could stand no closer than fifty yards to the side of the rocket target, but in the event our range safety officer told me that they had moved in quite a bit closer. Unfortunately our armourers had made a common error in arming my SNEB pods and had set the rockets to fire as a ripple rather than single shot. I had told the lieutenant to expect single shot firing, so they jumped a bit when all eighteen rockets arrived with an almighty supersonic bang just a few yards in front of them. Ideal training for them, I thought.

At weekends there were regular trips by RAF Puma helicopter to the resort island of Punta Gorda, although I preferred the cay trips in a locally-hired boat, a group of us setting off with beer and barbecue gear for a day of lazing in the sun and snorkelling over the magnificent coral reefs. Catfish were ridiculously easy to catch in the Belize River and I caught some very interesting stuff in a large lake in the RAF Belize bomb dump. I was there ostensibly to inspect our weapon stocks. Knowing about the lake, I took a fishing rod as a precaution. Our work routine was fairly relaxed, with early starts and an early finish to get down to the pool. Social life was fairly basic, with weekend trips downtown to rather dodgy eating houses and the odd poorly-lit drinking club, populated by more or less amiable locals. The music, typically Caribbean, was always red hot, the beer ice cold and pretty poor quality. There were few unattached girls. A bunch of us – Harrier pilots, an Army surgeon and the RAF dentist – hung around together and generally went out as a group.

The young surgeon was a very interesting type. He would clear off regularly on expeditions up-country to the dirt-poor villages near the border where he would act as a travelling jobbing surgeon, carrying out quite major operations on people's kitchen tables. For the local people this was just about the only opportunity to get operations done at this time. An Army intelligence officer was another interesting character. Among other 'pets' he led a wild puma around on a lead and was in the habit of carrying a large tarantula in his pocket which he would produce at parties, just to impress the girls.

Soon after taking over as OC 1417 the four of us in the flight went on a trip up to the border, ostensibly to get a close look at our likely wartime operating area on the ground. The main road westwards passed through mainly flat areas of swamp and savannah with occasional thick patches of jungle scrub. After the turn-off to Belmopan, a scruffy, nondescript village designated as the new capital, the road entered more hilly terrain and the grey mountains of the Maya range became visible in the south-west. Not long after passing the Army forward base of Holdfast we descended into a valley to cross the famous San Ignacio bridge, a vital target for any invading army. We had spent many sorties flying FAC missions in this area, attacking British Army units dispersed around the bridge. San Ignacio town – little more than a one-street hamlet – was even scruffier than Belmopan, and we wasted little time there. Further up towards the border we took a side track to visit the ancient Mayan ruin of Xunan Tunich; a classic stepped pyramid of massive stone blocks carved with mystic signs. It was eerie to stand atop the ruin and imagine the goings-on thousands of years ago in this ancient, barbaric 'civilization'. The border post itself was an anti-climax and we were disappointed that there were no Guatemalan armoured vehicles on view. We had seen them from the air, parked some distance down the road on the other side. It began to rain and I took a photo of us standing under umbrellas.

The trip back was uneventful, except for one incident on the only straight stretch of road where I had coaxed the Land Rover up to 70 mph. One of the passengers suddenly shouted out:

'Hey, stop Jerry – there's a spider in the road back there!'

A spider in the road? Visible from a Land Rover at 70 mph – how big is that going to be? I jammed on the brakes. With thick jungle overhanging the road on either side I started to reverse towards the ominous black lump in the middle of the road some fifty yards away. The lump was moving. We jumped out and cautiously surrounded the biggest tarantula we had ever seen, sluggishly making its way across the road. I got out my cine camera and filmed it crawling over my flying boot.

'They're sensitive to vibrations, you know', said one pilot knowledgeably. 'Watch this.'

He stamped his foot and the tarantula shot forward at maximum speed. In perfect formation four brave Harrier pilots jumped a foot in the air to land, magically, several feet further apart. The spider had stopped and was pawing the air menacingly with several of its legs.

'Let's go' I said. 'It'll be dark soon.'

The next event was for me to lead the first splash firing detail for our three pilots, none of whom had done it before. I briefed them on the technique and issued the solemn warning not to aim directly at the splash but just behind it. The Navy only had a couple of sleds available and once they had been shot off we couldn't do any more training. We launched to the ship in good order and found the smart-looking frigate cruising a brilliant turquoise sea, flecked with silver in the early morning sun. After the usual pantomime of making radio contact with the boat I set up the strafe pattern around the thin plume of water kicked up by the sled, trailing several hundred yards astern. I pitched in for the first hot pass and promptly shot the sled off the wire. Total embarrassment and egg all over my face. That was the last sled so we went home, my tail well between my legs.

Soon I learnt just how fickle the weather could be in the rainy season. One of our new guys was leading me on a FAC exercise way down south near Punta Gorda when I heard the CO of our local radar unit calling urgently on guard frequency for us to return to base. A huge thunderstorm was approaching the base and we had to get a ripple on. I took over the lead and we hammered back to base at maximum speed, to see an ominous black wall of water just off the western end of the field. The wind was a strong easterly (it's quite usual for thunderstorms to move rapidly upwind), and we had to pitch into the rain area to get on to finals. We were too heavy for vertical landings. I let my wingman go in ahead of me and nearly lost sight of the runway before landing. I called for the runway lights full on and touched down in a shower of spray just before the full force of the rain hit the airfield, all visual references vanishing in an instant in the torrent of rain and steam.

One weekend we took the Land Rover up the potholed jungle road to the Mexican border at Corozal, to stay the weekend at a very comfortable hotel. In the morning the manageress took us by boat across the estuary to the Mexican town of Chetumal, in Yucatan. This was typical non-tourist Mexico, the inhabitants poor but proud, their culture not yet overwhelmed by the requirements of the tourist industry. At a distance the proud Spanish architecture of the harbour area gleamed smartly in the searing sunlight; closer to, you could see the peeling facades and rotting woodwork. The locals were Indian in appearance, with colourful shawls and traditional hats. There was an all-pervading air of delicious boredom, as if the slow-moving inhabitants were waiting for something to happen, but couldn't really get worked up about it whatever it was. Being Englishmen we were visiting the town at midday and the few locals faded away into the shadows as the heat grew oppressive, the dusty streets shimmering chalk-white in the fierce glare of the sun. We found a drinks seller and bought bottles of dubiously-coloured soft drinks. The bottles looked recycled, i.e. it looked as if we weren't the first to drink out of them that day. Then after much searching we managed to buy some bottles of beer and retired to the relative cool of the jetty to await the return boat. The return trip to Belize was uneventful.

Back at Belize the Royal Navy's Caribbean duty guard ship frigate anchored inshore and the Navy threw a cocktail party for local bigwigs and selected officers. This was the usual glittering affair held on the quarterdeck under an enormous yellow tropical moon. The guests were ferried out to the ship, which was decked out from stem to stern in fairy lights. On board I noted the lack of armament on board. The thought struck me that the Royal Navy seemed to devote more money and space to fitting out their ships as comfortable cruise ships and travelling cocktail lounges rather than fighting vessels. Still, it was a nice party.

We were now in the middle of the hurricane season and I had already dusted off our contingency plans for hurricane evacuation, designed to safeguard the Harriers should a storm hit us. The basic plan was to fit the big 330 gallon ferry tanks and take the aircraft to Homestead AFB, nearly 1,000 miles away in Florida. The whole plan looked a bit dodgy to me: there were too many optimistic assumptions, the most glaringly obvious being the state of serviceability of our aircraft for such a long over-sea deployment. Our aircraft in Belize suffered constant radio problems and we could operate one of them only on its emergency radio on 243.0 MHZ, the international UHF distress frequency. This frequency was not used in the Caribbean: there was no emergency fixer/rescue service available at this time, south of 30 degrees north latitude. I hoped the weather would be kind to us: let it happen to the next OC 1417, I thought. Some hopes...

The late September day started dull and overcast with a threat of rain later. Having opted out of the cay trip, I had wandered across the deserted airfield to do a little fishing in the tributary of the Belize River behind the maintenance hangar. After an enjoyable couple of hours spent hooking catfish, I noticed that the wind was increasing markedly. There were a few ominous spots of rain. Abandoning fishing for the day I wandered back across the airfield and noticed with some concern that the ground crews were feverishly working on a couple of Puma helicopters outside their hangar. The response to my casual inquiry was curt:

'Hurricane warning, sir – we're flying out to Mexico this afternoon.'

The time was about 1230 local and I quickened my pace towards base operations, where I was informed that there was a tropical revolving storm approaching rapidly. Its track was straight at us and it would be on us within twenty-four hours. The winds were forecast as 40 knots straight across the runway by morning – well out of limits for us. In consultation with the duty ops officer, who was acting air commander, I decided to evacuate the Flight to US Naval Air Station Boca Chica, next to Key West in the Florida Keys. This was closer than Homestead Air Force Base. We had to get a ripple on and get airborne before dark. When I asked how soon we should be prepared to return to Belize the deputy air commander said, 'Don't call us, we'll call you!'

The engineers had already been alerted and were hard at work preparing our rather unserviceable Harriers for the long flight. The air commander, as usual at the weekend, was ensconced offshore at his island residence and did not appear as there was no RAF Puma available to pick him up. I already knew the serviceability state of our four aircraft. The biggest problem was a leaking canopy seal, which was hurriedly being glued back into place with non-standard glue – the correct stuff took ages to dry. The evacuation plan called for 330 gallon tanks on all aircraft, but there was no time for this. I told the troops to put the big tanks on the aircraft with the canopy seal problem, in case it failed and depressurized in flight. That would mean a 700-mile transit at a fuel-guzzling 18,000 feet, to avoid decompression sickness, instead of our planned 35,000 feet cruising altitude. I would take this aircraft myself. With 100 gallon tanks the other three jets could just make it to Key West. In spite of frantic efforts I was unable to get a proper weather forecast for either Key West or Homestead. The communications from Belize were hopeless and the civilian met officer had no idea of how to get a ripple on. I planned to lead in the aircraft with ferry tanks. I knew that the take-off from Belize was going to be dodgy, and I already suspected that we would be landing at night. Only my aircraft had a serviceable VHF radio to talk to Mexican ATC, the others would all have to stay on 243.0 MHZ, the emergency frequency. By now all four pilots were frantically at work planning the route, having already battened down our rooms in the Mess. The standard airways route ran up the eastern side of the Yucatan peninsula, entering the Havana flight information region as we crossed the Yucatan channel. Then we had to fly along 250 miles of hostile Cuban coastline to reach the tip of the Florida Keys, where Boca Chica lay. I had no illusions about the kind of assistance we were likely to get from Cuba. I had no intention of talking to them and during the briefing I emphasized the importance of monitoring the radar warning receivers to give warning of any attempt by the communists to intercept us with their air defence fighters in the event of the customary problems with the flight plan. We had to go regardless of clearance from Havana. During the brief I glossed over the question of what kind of evasive action we could take in the dark if a Cuban fighter chased us. My main concern was to get a weather forecast and just as we walked for the aircraft I was given a corrupt TAF (terminal area forecast) signal for the Key West area. This merely gave ... 2,000 feet BROKEN ... with no visibility or surface wind. There was still no acknowledgement of our flight plan. This was all we were going to get and I decided to go for it. It was 1700 hours – half an hour to sunset and the wind was moaning ominously. The sky looked bruised and threatening and I shook off the unpleasant thought that none of the others had done any night formation. I didn't dare ask about night currency. Later I found out that I was the only one night current and one pilot hadn't flown at night for two years.

After various last-minute delays in the cockpit and with darkness rapidly approaching we finally got airborne with two pairs rolling from opposite ends of the runway in opposition. This novel form of departure was forced on us by the constraints of the Belize taxiways – there weren't any. We still had not received clearance to enter the Havana airspace, but that was the least of our problems. I was concerned about joining up in the gathering gloom and keeping the flight together in the dark with our anticipated communications and lighting problems: the ground crew had had no time to carry out checks of our night flying lights. Having gathered the formation together in the rapidly-fading twilight we climbed on track to the north-east along the coastline. Once we were together in loose arrow formation, I switched to VHF as briefed, leaving the rest on 243.0. As expected, VHF comms with Mexican ATC were barely readable and I could get no sense out of them about our destination weather and clearance into the Havana airspace. Eventually I politely said goodnight and joined the rest of the formation on guard frequency, continuing the route as per the flight plan.

By now it was becoming uncomfortably black around us. The Harrier GR3 lighting – even when fully serviceable – was not designed for night formation, and even with the anti-collision beacons switched off, the section was finding it increasingly difficult to maintain station on me. Splitting up was not a viable option with our highly-unserviceable group of aircraft. By now one aircraft had lost its HUD and another had lost all radio reception. Finally, before we reached Boca Chica, my aircraft suffered complete pressurization failure. Additionally, because of the guaranteed effect of Sod's Law on our inertial navigation we needed a regular cross-check of position between aircraft to avoid a potentially disastrous navigation error. As the pitch black of the Caribbean night closed in on us I prayed that we would not encounter any cloud or, worse still, a thunderstorm. Soon we began to parallel the Cuban coastline and I was desperate for weather information from Boca Chica. With no acknowledgement to our flight plan there was not even a guarantee that they would be open. Fuel checks within the formation confirmed that things were getting tight: if Boca Chica was shut then we could barely make it to Homestead AFB.

During the last 200 miles I called Key West repeatedly on all frequencies, at the same time watching in frustration as the TACAN performed exactly according to expectations. None of us could get a lock on to the Key West beacon. Once again the lousy Harrier radio and avionics had let us down badly when we desperately needed them. At last, barely 100 miles away, I heard a faint acknowledgement of my R/T call. At last I was in contact with Key West and the weather at NAS Boca Chica was good. I was overwhelmed with relief as, by this time, we could already see the tiny blob of light marking Key West town at the extreme westernmost tip of the Florida Keys. After a brief consultation on R/T we split up for individual approaches. As last to land (I had most fuel) I nearly lost control on short finals. In my relief at having a 10,000 foot runway in front of me I momentarily forgot about the maximum power limitation when flying with ferry tanks. Drenched in sweat from the heat of the cockpit demist which had been full on for the last twenty minutes, I had to apply a handful of power to correct a sink on short finals. Instantly the aircraft began to pitch up out of control, even with full forward stick. Instinctively I pushed the nozzle lever forward a handful and regained sufficient control for a very untidy landing. As the cockpit depressurized on touchdown everything misted up in an instant in the hot and humid air. I had to open the canopy and raise my seat fully to look out over the windscreen arch to complete the landing roll. After the distinctly chilly temperatures at Belize the night air was like a sauna as we climbed wearily from the aircraft. Ahead was the promise of a 5-star night out on the town, and the prospect of at least a couple of days exploring the local area before our aircraft could be made sufficiently serviceable for the return flight.

There followed a truly epic night out in company with some US Navy RB66 aircrew who we met in the bar of the Officers' Club. Key West was a famous town of magnificent timber buildings redolent of the Old South. There were dozens of bars and clubs heaving with nightlife, with musicians and entertainers performing on the streets and in the veranda bars. After drinking in half a dozen bars, my recollection of events faded; next morning I found myself back in the Mess nursing a fair-sized hangover. I signalled Belize with a list of our unserviceabilities and requested technical support. It took just about the whole of the next day to put our sick aircraft to bed in a hangar. With every request came the standard American reply:

'I'm sorry, sir, I'm not authorized to do that; you'll have to speak to my superior.'

This went on and on and eventually I had to appeal direct to the base commander just to get our aircraft refuelled. I checked in at ops before we stacked; there were no signals for me so we hit the town for another splendid night out. Next morning a curt signal from Belize ordered us to return to base immediately. Clearly they hadn't received my signals. Now followed a nightmare couple of days for me as I tried to persuade the air commander to send me the spares and servicing personnel I needed. At every stage there were communication problems with Belize, the Americans not even knowing where it was initially. It was clear that Belize was in a panic to get us back regardless of our problems. Meanwhile, we Harrier pilots were spending our days sweating to do what we could to fix the jets.

My last weeks in Belize passed by comfortably under the relaxed regime of our new air commander. In November I boarded the VC10 for the trip back to the UK, shivering in the first chilly blast of winter. I settled into the hectic routine of 1(F) flight commander in charge of training, recce, flight refuelling and air combat. My Dutch Air Force habits were slow to fade and I was cycling five miles to and from work each day, much to the amusement of the rest of the station. I also found myself cursing in Dutch when things got out of hand.

Chapter 17

Harrier Flight Commander

Life on 1(F) seemed to be a permanent round of new training programmes, exercises, deployments, VIP visits and various crises, all directly stemming from the customary heavy tasking by our Group HQ, compounded by our general lack of serviceable aircraft. With the wide variety of flying carried out, there was constant requirement to keep a close watch on the daily planning of the programme, to make sure that we were getting the best out of our small numbers of available aircraft and not overstretching our less experienced pilots. The junior pilots were a good bunch, full of enthusiasm and keen to learn, needing the minimum amount of supervision, just the occasional tug on the reins to make sure they didn't go completely over the top. This was still the era of the bachelor junior pilot, living in the Mess and having a good time, so there were regular complaints from the president of the Mess committee and other senior officers to be dealt with.

Participation in exercises was constant on 1(F) and we were often tasked to run through fighter combat air patrol lines to give our air defenders practice at intercepting low level targets. In this we tried to make things as difficult as possible for the defenders, routeing our formations tactically through narrow valleys and hiding behind every geographical feature. Our radar warning receiver, not a particularly useful piece of kit, gave general warning that a fighter was looking at you with its radar, and a very rough direction of the threat. Among several tactical manoeuvres we used constantly in hilly terrain to foil a bounce, was the 'Wiggs manoeuvre', useful when you knew a fighter was approaching you from deep 6 o'clock. As you dived over a ridge line, temporarily un-sighting the bounce, the call was 'WIGGS STARBOARD, GO' and the formation would turn hard in place through 90 degrees, the bounce assuming you had continued straight ahead. With luck he would fly straight on and lose you; you could then reverse back on to a parallel track behind him. The smarter Phantom pilots learned what 'Wiggs Starboard' meant; they always listened in on our tactical frequency and would be expecting it. As soon as they heard the call they would turn to cut you off. To foil this we would brief on the ground that 'Wiggs Starboard' actually meant a PORT turn, thus throwing them well off track. The ultimate manoeuvre was the fiendishly cunning 'Silent Reverse Wiggs Manoeuvre', in which both aircraft would pull up ostentatiously at the ridge line and initiate a turn starboard while the bounce could still see them. Once safely down behind the ridgeline the turn would be reversed, without a radio call, to port, leaving the bounce searching for you in the wrong county.

Of course none of these visual contact fun-and-games would work against modern radar-guided missiles and different tactics were required. I was totally impressed with my first UK encounter with an American F15 in the middle of Wales, in distinctly unfriendly weather. Flying along as a singleton (we had only one serviceable jet), I had confidently assumed that the opposition – being American – would not dare to attempt to mix it in hilly terrain below the cloud – the combat air patrols were being flown at 5,000 feet, above the stratus. It was slightly worrying, therefore, to have a constant warning of F15 radar looking at me from the starboard side as I weaved my way up through the centre of the Welsh hills, heading for the deep valleys of Snowdonia. For several minutes the radar pulses followed me relentlessly, in spite of my weaving down the narrowest valleys as low as I could under the solid grey cloud base. He lost lock at times but every time I came out into flatter terrain the signal was back, and noticeably stronger.

'Wish he'd bugger off' I thought. 'Bet he'll claim a FOX 1 anyway – even if I never see him. Anyway, he'll never get down to get me visual in this muck – will he?'

I flashed around the end of a ridgeline and there was the signal again, much stronger than before. I cursed his persistence:

'Why doesn't he knock it off and chase someone else?'

Levelling the wings I looked up, and to the right, at the lowering cloud base. He was on me like a ton of bricks, the big grey fighter materializing out of the stratus like a ghost, turning hard already to convert to my 6 o'clock. I was flabbergasted that he had found me so precisely, to end up in the perfect attacking manoeuvre before I could even see him. At that moment I realized how out-of-date the

Harrier was, and how far ahead of us technologically were the Americans, with their incredibly accurate (and reliable) look-down, shoot-down radar systems.

In March we set off for the scheduled annual Arctic Express deployment to Tromsø, tanking all the way. Once again we had a brilliant joint service flying exercise in the Arctic wastes of northern Norway, my first visit there since 1976. We ran up against a problem with our flying orders, which were written for UK use, our staff officers taking no account of the vastly different weather patterns and availability of diversion airfields in northern Norway. This caused constant daily problems with our duty authorizers, who were being pressured into launching aircraft when weather and diversion conditions were clearly outside of the rules, as written.

Back at Wittering we were faced with a new tiresome requirement to provide jets for FAC exercises on Salisbury Plain every Sunday, as if we weren't working hard enough during the week. There was to be no time off in lieu during the week. We discovered that Coltishall, our sister ground attack station, was also tasked in the same way, flying afternoon slots when we flew mornings. As a gesture of common sense we asked Group HQ if each station could do all the slots on one weekend, so that Wittering and Coltishall could do the task on alternate weekends. Having got everyone in for a morning's flying, you might as well do the afternoon as well. This suggestion was dismissed. For the first Sunday's flying I briefed our pilots to make the maximum noise disturbance over RAF Upavon, where the HQ staff lived. Fortunately, one of the initial points for the FAC exercise was next to Upavon and I made sure that I made several passes at full power right over the staff married quarters. I was sure that our senior commanders would appreciate being reminded that their Harrier assets were fully occupied and working hard on a Sunday.

There were constant landaways for 1(F) pilots, often as theatre recces to give new pilots experience in our many European operating areas.

I soon became a bit fed up with these as I seemed to have permanent bad luck with aircraft serviceability. As soon as I landed away from Wittering my aircraft would go U/S and there would follow a major effort to get it serviceable to return to base, taking away all the enjoyment of the visit to foreign parts. In particular I suffered constant radio and intercom problems, about one a week on average. My helmets were constantly going U/S, leaving me unable to communicate with anyone in flight. This problem, combined with the never-ending Harrier radio problem, was steadily driving me mad, and relations with our flying clothing workers sank to an all-time low as I kept on bringing back U/S kit which would usually work perfectly on the ground. This was one of the main reasons that caused me to leave the Harrier for good in 1984.

With Karen and Christopher growing rapidly I was becoming much more of a home-lover anyway, and I was looking forward to a more relaxed job, hopefully in civil aviation. However, there were already rumblings of a big recession in the air transport industry, which would mean problems for me in getting a job. I would have to keep my options open and see if there was any flying job within the RAF which would get me away from the constant running around with hair on fire, of the Harrier force.

By now we had moved to a new house on Casterton Road in Stamford, a larger pre-war property with an extensive and overgrown garden which I was determined to turn into something worthwhile. Jobs for me as a Dutch interpreter turned up now and then and I was still occasionally called down to London to examine candidates in Dutch colloquial examinations. I volunteered to go to Gleneagles hotel for a major NATO nuclear weapons conference, as a hosting officer and interpreter for the Netherlands Government deputation. This turned out to be a fascinating experience, not just for seeing the no-expenses-barred treatment doled out at this level, but also to sit in on the conversations of the Dutch delegation. The final dinner was a sumptuous affair with our Minister of Defence, John Knott, as guest speaker.

Throughout the summer we worked up to a peak of performance at Wittering and on various detachments for our TACEVAL, and I grew heartily sick of the acrid smell of CS gas, which our training evaluators sprayed around liberally to simulate a nerve gas attack. As soon as we smelled it we all had to get into gas kit immediately and rush around like that for the rest of the exercise – very sweaty in the heat of summer.

In September the TACEVAL itself started. A 1(F) TACEVAL was, if anything, harder than the ones I was used to in Germany or Holland, because we had to fit a full air deployment to Denmark into the programme, as well as all the other practice bleeding. While the RAF's Jaguar squadrons stayed in comfortable hotels on exercise overseas, 1(F) had to set up a full dispersed site at our deployment airfield, complete with hides, Mexe pads, tents, etc. We weren't supposed to use any of the host airfield's facilities except the runway. At Vandel the evaluation team really put us through it and, by the end of a week, we had all been through the wringer. The exercise was nearly over and I was duty commander as we sweated in the foetid atmosphere of the concrete ops bunker, preparing for the climactic survival scramble. I had called all aircraft to two minutes readiness as a series of incoming signals warned of imminent simulated nuclear attack. The duty evaluator was an old acquaintance, ex- 88 Entry, at Cranwell, and I was trying to watch him all the time for a clue as to when we would get the inevitable gas attack. I knew he would throw his oar in at the most difficult time for me, to test my control of operations at the critical moment.

With a dozen occupants, the bunker was fully closed-up for an air raid and sealed off from the outside world as the evaluator passed me a note saying that a bomb had blocked the main entrance, and we were trapped inside. I called all our aircraft to scramble while I still had communications, and was relieved to hear everyone check in with an acknowledgement. The evaluators could do their worst now; at least our aircraft would be safely airborne. Donning his gas mask, the evaluator ducked behind a pillar and I shouted 'Gas, gas, gas!' as I saw him pull the canister out of his pocket. Within seconds the bunker was full of CS gas and I was shouting to the ops clerks to get tools to break-out through the emergency exit, our only way to get out. This was a bricked-up part of the bunker wall which led out to a vertical concrete shaft, leading up to the open air. It took several minutes of hammering with crowbars to make a hole big enough to get through. I was first man out, as planned, running with a spare copy of the mission order and the essential bookwork to resume operations immediately from our standby operations location several hundred metres away. Our efforts were rewarded and we passed the TACEVAL with a pretty good result. Afterwards I was pleased to take a couple of days off to unwind on a walking holiday through the pretty Silverborg area.

Back at Vandel we carried on with an enjoyable programme of air combat missions against the F16s of the Danish Air Force. We had already run up against them during the TACEVAL missions, acting as low level CAPs, along with the ubiquitous American F15s. The Danes were a pretty competent and aggressive mob and gave us a pretty sound going-over in the air. Against them we were totally up against it, the F16 being able to outturn, outrun and generally outmanoeuvre us in all areas – except one. I found out that the Harrier could outmanoeuvre the F16 in a vertical rolling scissors, once airspeed of both aircraft was below 100 knots – a pretty extreme corner of the envelope.

In November we flew some air combat missions against the USAF aggressor squadrons at Alconbury. They were pretty sharp and fairly took us to the cleaners in medium altitude combat over the North Sea. They were flying the F5E Tiger 2, a very much hotted-up version of the F5 ground attack machine. They used ground-based radar units to direct them into the optimum position to bounce us, appearing out of the high blue in a supersonic dive – very similar to desert tactics we had used on 208 Squadron. During the debrief the pilots we flew against were uncharacteristically modest about the exercise. They admitted that they achieved their good results simply because they did nothing else with their flying time, training constantly with the same radar operators to get the best results. They readily acknowledged that if they had our diverse roles, of which air combat was only a part, then they wouldn't do as well. They also admitted that they would do much worse against us in unrestricted low level engagements, where their radar controllers couldn't help them.

Next came one of the regular mallet blow exercises, where we attacked live targets on the huge Otterburn ranges in Northumberland with rockets and cannon. No live 1,000lb drops were permitted on Otterburn any longer after relentless environmental protests and some aircrew errors in targeting. On one occasion a star American F111 crew had dropped a hefty practice bomb fifteen miles away from the correct target. This was a not-uncommon theme of live firing exercises on tactical ranges. Unless you were very familiar with the range terrain, which was unlikely as we weren't allowed to fly there outside of the exercise periods, then it was all too easy to get a bit lost and attack the wrong target. A colleague had discovered this the hard way when observing some USAF A10 pilots attacking vehicles under FAC 'control' with their powerful 30mm GAU8 cannon. My friend was ensconced in an observation hut with the FAC and several other observers as the first A10 ran in to attack. The target was some distance away to the left. My friend saw the American pilot pull up and roll out, pointing precisely at the observation hut, in spite of the increasingly agitated calls by the FAC. Just as the FAC screamed 'Stop, stop, stop!' my friend decided not to hang around to see if the pilot responded and joined the rest of the scrum diving out of the hut and running for their lives.

Another colleague had an even better tale of a splendidly screwed-up firepower demonstration organized by the USMC in the States. Apparently the spectators, a large group of senior Marine officers, were accommodated in a wooden stand, in front of which was a foxhole with the ubiquitous 'grunt' peering tactically over a sandbag, his laser target marker (LTM) aimed at a group of tanks half a mile away. A box of aircraft were running in at medium altitude, armed with 500lb high explosive bombs. Marines were not renowned for lateral thinking and this grunt had failed to appreciate that the laser transmitter of his LTM was several inches below the sighting telescope. Hence, in his efforts to be extremely tactical and expose not one inch more of his helmet than was necessary, he ended up with the laser beam reflecting nicely off the sandbag just a few inches in front of his face instead of the target. The laser target seeker operator aboard the lead A6, 20,000 feet above, was blissfully unaware that he was locked on to a foxhole just a few yards away from the spectators as he cleared the pilots to drop. Fortuitously, some sharp-eyed bright spark among the spectators spotted the bomb release way above and obviously aimed dangerously close. To the traditional Marines' cry of 'incoming!' the stand was evacuated in seconds and a horde of super-fit Marine officers sprinted away for the safety of the foxholes nearby. Many of them – veterans of Khe San, Da Nang and other Vietnam battles – felt it was just like old times as the stick pounded the stand to matchwood behind them. Amazingly no one was injured – not even the grunt in his foxhole right on the aiming point.

The definitive episode of ballsed-up firepower demonstrations has to be one related to me at Chivenor in 1969 by an old colleague. In the late '50s he had been a junior pilot flying ground attack Venoms in the Middle East. Apparently the squadron had been tasked for a firepower demonstration using 60lb head high explosive rockets on a wooden mock-up fort near Muscat; a fairly routine event. The spectators were various Arab military bods, attaches, Sheiks etc., and four Venoms ran in, in 'pansy' echelon formation, aiming straight at the spectators' stand before pulling up and turning through 90 degrees to attack the fort way off to the left. Recently the squadron had started a modification programme on the weapon firing controls, whereby on some aircraft the rocket firing button – tradi-tionally located on the throttle – had been moved to the stick to replace the radio transmit button, which had been moved to the throttle, where the rocket button used to be. Unfortunately the lead pilot was unaware that he was flying a modified aircraft – he thought the transmit button was still on the stick. The inevitable happened. As the lead pilot pulled up he tried to call 'in hot' on the radio, and promptly rippled off two rockets which whistled uncomfortably close over the top of the stand. Unaware that the reason the rockets had fired was because what he thought was the radio transmit button was, in fact, the rocket firing button, he then called 'sorry!' and fired two more rockets in error. The firepower demonstration ended in pandemonium as the formation split all over the sky, the deputy lead shouting at the leader not to press the stick top button, while the leader sprayed the rest of his rockets at random around the scenery as he tried to answer.

Mallet blow exercises turned up about every three months as a regular commitment, and were usually good value if we could also get some action against our Phantom CAPs en route to the target. To cut down noise complaints the CAPs usually operated over the sea, but we were also used to taking on the Phantoms over land in our routine daily operations. Their usual initial tactic was the head-on attack, simulating launch of the big Skyflash missile from about three miles in front. Before this they would fly past us for a visual identification, often head-on and uncomfortably close. This tactic was basically flawed because they were never really sure of what they were shooting at until it was too late. I surmised that there would be a lot of 'own goals' in war with this lot. In a turning match they were less than impressive, the machine too big and unwieldy to survive long against determinedly-flown Harriers. One area of constant ridicule on our part was the 11 Group (to which the fighters belonged) attitude to weather. On several occasions we would find no CAPs, having expended much fuel over the North Sea looking for them in dodgy weather. After landing we would discover that 11 Group had cancelled the CAPs because of the weather. This was pretty rich coming from our much-trumpeted all-weather fighter force.

Training up our new pilots was never dull. On arrival on the squadron I had begun a training programme of night formation and regular night air refuelling to cater for our operational option to carry out long-range deployments at night. This had not gone down well with the squadron pilots. Many single seat ground attack pilots were against night flying on principle, simply because it kept them out of the bar. I had no sympathy with this attitude. There were no squadron standard operating procedures for this exercise, and I had to write them myself, having first tried them out in the air. As squadron QFI I ended up doing all of the dual checkouts of our pilots on night formation and night air refuelling. We had only the standard night navigation lights, completely inadequate for formation. Only one of our pilots had any experience of night tanking, having been tasked by 38 Group for a night deployment to Cyprus just before I joined the squadron. This was with no previous experience of night formation or night air refuelling.

Night formation was never dull in the Harrier. The best bet was to take-off in formation and stay in close, the probe light lighting up the leader reasonably well as long as it kept working. For recoveries, in really dark and dirty conditions, I worked out that it was best to put the gear down and landing lights on above cloud, before the descent. Flying tactical formation and joining up into close, was a bit more challenging. I worked out a system for the wingman to fly 500 feet below the lead, on altimeter, and about 45 degrees stepped down. By simple trigonometry this put the wingman about 200-300 yards from the leader – accurate enough. Joining into close, the wingman would move forward and up until he could clearly identify the triangle of the leader's navigation lights, when he would call 'anti-colls off'. (The anti-collision beacon was too bright for close formation). He could then slide gently into close. I checked out all new pilots on this technique and it seemed to work reasonably well. Joining a tanker at night was fraught with problems, even with ground radar assistance, and on one occasion I wasted quite a bit of fuel chasing the planet Jupiter by mistake.

Day flying with some of our young pilots also kept you on your toes. On one occasion I was led by one of our young pilots on a low level west departure, in close formation in really bad conditions, the low cloud scudding the ground in places and with in-flight visibility only a couple of miles at best. I knew the leader had planned our departure track uncomfortably close to the gigantic antenna farm at Rugby, and my sixth sense was warning me that he was drifting off track. Suddenly the leader just pulled up into the murk without a word, leaving me staring straight at the entire array of masts and cables right in front of me.

Dual checkouts of squadron shags were equally entertaining, and I was regularly taken aback at the indifferent standard of VSTOL handling of guys who had been away on detachment for some time, with little opportunity to practise the manoeuvres. There were also many firepower demonstrations and live FAC exercises on various weapon ranges, firing full pods of HE SNEB rockets, plus HE 30mm ammunition. The only chance to drop live 'crackers' (1,000lb HE bombs) was on Garvie Island range, right at the northern tip of Scotland. This involved a tedious deployment exercise via RAF Lossiemouth, who always made the most almighty fuss about handling armed aircraft. The whole of Garvie Island was the target, some 200 metres long, so it was just about impossible to miss. The 'crump' as the bomb went off behind you was pretty insignificant, although the seagulls were not too happy about it. As my wingman dropped his bomb I flew in a close battle formation to see the impact. The tiny speck of the bomb with its white parachute tail seemed to fly for ages before it impacted the beach, followed by an instantaneous mushroom of smoke and debris before the delayed concussion caught me up.

We also carried out regular automatic bombing and laser ranging exercises on Holbeach, using a LTM to illuminate the target. Unusually, the LRMTS (laser ranger and marked target seeker), was a fairly user-friendly piece of British kit. One brilliant new weapon event which turned up was level SNEB rocket firing, with level break-out. At last our commanders had taken note of our request to use a more tactical weapon profile than the academic 10 degrees dive pattern. Actually there was nothing new in level SNEB: many years ago the RAF had discovered, during Hunter rocket trials, that level-fired SNEB rockets would level off about three feet above ground and ride on their Mach wave until target impact – an ideal tactic against tanks and ships. The profile had been approved for live firing on Holbeach range and they had built a special 'tank target' consisting of an arrangement of 50 gallon oil drums in the shape of a tank hull. By good luck I was the first pilot to fire on this target. I let the rockets go in level flight at about 100 feet above ground and every one I fired was a direct hit. After four single rockets the target was scattered all over the range and I had nothing left to fire at. In disgust the range workers rebuilt the target on a 6 feet high embankment, to make sure that any level-fired SNEB would impact slightly short and preserve their precious target.

We had also introduced a programme of so-called ultra Low level training for all combat ready pilots. I had to get 'checked out' in a Jaguar, as we had no radar altimeter in the Harrier, then I checked out other squadron pilots in the T4. Ultra low level was basically a bit of a con, really not much lower than we had flown in the '60s and '70s when the limit was 250 feet above ground level.

Early in the New Year I did a re-categorization trip with the charming and talented new OC 'B' Squadron on 233 OCU and I was upgraded to A2 category. At the beginning of March we deployed to northern Norway again for another enjoyable 'Arctic Express' exercise. I had to ferry a U/S jet home at the end of the detachment on my own. This machine couldn't carry ferry tanks, so I had to do it in two long hops via Bergen in southern Norway. At Bergen I had to do a TACAN letdown through some pretty thick weather as there was no radar available. All the way down I was uncomfortably aware of the rocky peaks all round me in the cloud, only my interpretation of the twitchy, unreliable TACAN indicator standing between me and a terminal collision with a mountain. After landing I was marshalled away along miles of tree-lined taxiway until I came to the entrance to a mountain hangar. The entrance was a gaping hole in the rock, flanked by camouflaged steel doors barely visible through the trees from more than a few yards away. The Norwegian ground crew appeared out of the bowels of the earth to refuel me and send me on my way on my lonely trek across the North Sea to Wittering.

In the back of my mind was the uncomfortable realization that retirement was less than two years away, if I followed my plan to leave and join civil aviation.

In this my growing disillusionment with the RAF was fuelled by the never-ending 'injects' (unplanned tasks unrelated to operational training), to which we were subject at Wittering. As the only operational Harrier squadron in UK we were constantly being called on for tactical demonstrations to visiting MPs, foreign statesmen, diplomats etc., all in the name of marketing the Harrier and other items of defence equipment. A typical routine for such a demonstration would start with the dreaded tasking signal, or a direct call from the station commander, giving the date of the 'demo' and the number of aircraft required. This was usually no more than four but we knew that we would end up having to use the entire squadron's resources to achieve the task. Then the planning would start. Because of the AOC's inevitable involvement, the station commander would demand a pre-final rehearsal, several days before the AOC's, to make sure that things were OK. As a squadron we would rehearse the routine in Vigo wood, usually consisting of a strip take-off, followed by an airfield attack and pad landing, until there were no mistakes. All in all there would be several weeks of work involved and four or five flying days written off, not including the immense effort to wash down and polish all the aircraft involved, including ground and airborne spares, for each demo watched by a senior officer. Everything had to go right, from the way the ground crew worked on the aircraft through to the precise timing of the landings.

Unfortunately, in the early '80s, the jobs situation outside had become distinctly chilly and many ex-RAF colleagues were languishing in dead-end civil flying jobs, unable to get a decent post with an airline. I had no intention of getting stuck like that and began to think of the alternatives. One obvious choice was to go specialist aircrew at age 38. This would mean no more promotion (that didn't bother me), but the chance of continuing flying until age 55. As more news came in about the lousy employment situation outside, I started to look for a likely place to spend my next few years flying as spec aircrew. I had no intention of staying on Harriers any longer. Apart from never-ending radio problems I knew that I was getting too over-confident and slapdash in my approach to flying the jet, and this could only lead to disaster in the long run. I checked out various service flying options not too far from Stamford. At RAF Finningley I had a trip in a Jetstream multi-engine trainer to see what the job was like training 'truckie' aircrew. Although the machine seemed quite pleasant to fly I realized that the job would eventually be far too boring for me. Next I had a trip in a Tucano basic trainer, which was fun to fly, but having thought it over I wasn't impressed with the idea of returning to the world of basic flying instruction.

One obvious choice was the tri-national Tornado GR1 training establishment at RAF Cottesmore, just a few miles up the road from Stamford. This would be my first two-seat aircraft, and I went up there on a recce to see what was going on. I was shown round the jet by an old colleague (ex-Bahrain 208 Squadron and Phantoms), and was most impressed by the new 'electric jet', which was very much a high-tech aeroplane. I liked the cockpit a lot and was impressed by this pilot's views on the machine. The job would be OCU instruction of British, German and Italian student pilots and navigators. Within a few days my mind was made up and I wrote to our personnel department asking to be transferred to specialist aircrew at age 38. OC 1(F) and the new station commander were dismayed at my choice and tried their best to talk me out of it. I got the old line about 'career' and 'should get your own squadron in time' etc. but they couldn't change my mind. In the eyes of a conventional career officer, what I was asking for was unthinkable, a negation of all the officer training I had ever had. The transfer to the spec aircrew system was intended for un-promotable flight lieutenants who could fly well and do not much else. It was never intended for use by squadron leaders already in executive posts – I was about to become deputy squadron commander. I didn't give a damn about this: if the RAF wouldn't let me go spec aircrew then I would leave and take my chances outside.

The next exercise lined up for 1982 was the annual Green Flag exercise in Canada. This promised to be a great event and we were already into a heavy work-up programme. An important part of the exercise would be our reaction to attack by the many fighter combat air patrols and, on joining 1(F), I had discovered to my dismay that our squadron en route formation tactics were geared solely to the peacetime rules of engagement of this exercise. The squadron had been on the previous Green Flag, which I had missed, and current Harrier force doctrine was that we should always operate large formations in what I saw as the tactically-flawed pairs trail formation. In this, individual battle pairs of aircraft flew in trail, about one minute apart, and targets were attacked in the same way. Remembering my desert and Germany experiences I thought this a pretty un-tactical way to operate, and asked why the squadron no longer operated in more compact and manoeuvrable formations, such as the well-tried battle four and escort, where you could get a larger formation through the target and away in just a few seconds. This is a vital factor in wartime when everyone is shooting at you from the ground. When it came down to it, the answer was that our young pilots were no longer trained to fly as wingman – 'welded wing' as they contemptuously called it. In our new non-hierarchical formations everyone was a potential leader or deputy lead – an unrealistic prospect in war in my view.

The squadron's workload increased to fever pitch as the date of departure for Canada approached. I was heavily involved in planning the cross-Atlantic ferry operation, as we had to ferry all of the RAF's Harriers. The participating Germany squadrons weren't qualified at air refuelling. Departure date was 13 April 1982, a fateful date for 1(F) Squadron.

On 3 April Argentina invaded the Falklands. At first we were sure it would not affect us but that's not how it turned out. Robin rang

me from Warminster singing *Don't Cry for me Argentina*, and asking
if we were going to get involved in operations in the South Atlantic.
'Don't be silly', I had replied, without really thinking about it. The
whole thing looked like a busted flush to me. I couldn't see how we
could get enough forces down there to retake the islands. Anyway, I
was familiar with our wartime options and there wasn't a single one
aimed at that kind of seaborne operation – none of us had ever flown
off an aircraft carrier. Straight after the long weekend was the start
of the cross-Atlantic ferry, and my mind was full of routeing details
and contingency plans for the deployment. There had been no hint
of the adventures to come as we stood down wearily for a well-
deserved Easter break; the events in the South Atlantic pushed to the
back of our minds.

Chapter 18

Back to the Harrier OCU

The unexpected commitment of 1(F) Squadron to the Falklands War was a major event in my life, not least because it came as a total surprise. As a flight commander I was well aware of our squadron wartime deployment options and not one of them involved operations off a carrier. Indeed there had been no RAF Harrier flying off carriers since a brief early trial at the beginning of the 1970s. Fortunately for us our peacetime training in finding and attacking difficult targets at low level was to serve us well in the chaotic situation we were to find down south. The full story of 1(F)'s involvement in the war is contained in *RAF Harrier Ground Attack Falklands* which I wrote immediately after the event and finally had published in 2007.

By the end of the momentous year of 1982 I realized that the Falklands War had left me quite seriously disturbed. I was withdrawn, moody and nervous and suffered sleep problems. Some of the other guys who had been with me down south were in a similar state. My marriage was not in too good as state either. However, there was no room for self-pity and, as a frantically busy flight commander, I just had to get on with my job and put my personal problems aside.

Wearily, in the spring of 1983 I completed a memorable tour on 1(F). I had hoped to start Tornado training in April, but there was a backlog of students at Cottesmore and 233 OCU was, as always, short of experienced Harrier QFIs. I would have to do some more instructing on the OCU as a holding posting until a slot became available at Cottesmore. Before I left the squadron there were more accidents involving old colleagues as a final demonstration that you couldn't afford to relax for one instant flying the jet. From Germany came sad news of the death of an old colleague from Wildenrath days, killed in a mid-air collision with a Starfighter. He had been in the back of a T4 and the front-seater, who survived, said that they never even saw the Starfighter until the collision. Yet another funeral at the tiny church in Wittering village; yet another grieving widow and children. The funeral was an epic event, with old colleagues turning up from all over the globe. Not long after this I was the duty flight commander on standby in 1(F)'s crew room when the crash alarm sounded. The Tannoy said something about a 'mid-air collision', so I rang the duty pilot straight away. The story was confused but reports were coming in of a mid-air collision somewhere nearby. I quickly checked our flying programme and saw that it couldn't be a 1(F) jet, so I put in a quick call to my wife at home. Officially you weren't supposed to make phone calls off base after an accident, until it was firmly established who was dead, but I had always ignored this as it put an intolerable pressure on the wives, hearing the news of the disaster within an hour, on the relentless media news broadcasts. Starved of any real news for their hourly 'updates', the media would go into a feeding frenzy whenever there was a hint of an air accident, speculating wildly about what might have happened and who might be dead.

This media overreaction was an agonizingly painful experience for wives and families as they waited patiently to be told if they would see their man again. My solution was to ring home immediately and get my wife to pass on the message as soon as I knew that 1(F) pilots weren't involved. If a 1(F) pilot was dead then the station commander or the boss would go immediately to see the widow. My wife would start off the 'bush telegraph' and pass the message that there would be a news item soon 'but it didn't involve a 1(F) pilot'. I had done this already in the past, both on 233 OCU and on 1(F), and the efficient wives' 'bush telegraph' had done the rest. I hurried to the ATC tower to be told that search and rescue helicopters were already airborne and that an explosion and parachutes had been seen just north of Peterborough. The story was confused, and conflicting information was coming in from all sides, at one stage the USAF chipping in after someone on the ground claimed to have found an 'American' flying helmet on one of the bodies. After checking the OCU's flying programme it looked ominously as if their pilots were involved. In the tower we listened patiently as the story filtered in from the airborne rescue agencies on the emergency frequencies. Only one pilot had survived and two bodies had been found. My temper was sorely tried by the usual half-wits who rang the tower to ask 'what was going on'. This was strictly forbidden during any emergency, and they all got a flea in the ear in reply, no matter what the rank. After two hours we still weren't 100 per cent sure who was alive and who was dead, but a helicopter was inbound with the survivor. It transpired that two out of the three pilots had not survived. Later on I was called in by the Board of Inquiry to give independent expert advice on VIFF manoeuvring, because of my experience on the VIFF trial. I was also given an RAF 'trick cyclist' to brief on the subject. This character was to provide a report on the 'human factors' of the accident, a modish buzzword and a new procedure for all Boards of Inquiry. I started off with the basics of how air combat was flown, but it was rather a waste of time because of his lack of knowledge of even the basics of flying an aeroplane. He had his own fixed ideas on how pilots appreciated parameters such as range, aspect, closing rate, roll rate etc. and wasn't interested in my descriptions of how we did these things in practice in the heat of combat. The 'trick cyclists' were gaining an increasingly strong hold on all aspects of piloting and flight safety and their views were being given more emphasis, a retrograde step in my view. In my opinion they were merely another class of specialist adviser like the met man, whose reports could be accepted or disregarded if they conflicted with professional piloting common sense.

This was a sad ending to my time on 1(F). In April I was posted back to the OCU for a year of the old QFI routine while waiting for my Tornado course. We were still training a lot of Royal Navy pilots and the main effort was aimed at a batch of Indian Navy students. They were about to buy the Sea Harrier, plus HMS *Hermes*, to set them up with an up-to-date Naval Air Arm. The Indian students were a charming bunch overall, although a bit of a challenge to instruct at times. All of them were experienced on other operational types back in India . In June I received formal notification that I was now specialist aircrew, in a curt note from our personnel department.

The constant travelling of 1(F) had left me with itchy feet and I managed to wangle my way on to one or two interesting trips, including 'babysitting' for the SASO (Senior Air Staff Officer) on a short Harrier work-up and visit to a 1(F) deployment at Vandel. I had first met the SASO when he was a Phantom squadron commander at Bruggen. I had been 'volunteered' to give him some dual training and sit in the back of a T4 while he flew some front-seat tactical sorties in Denmark. After the deployment flight from Wittering to Vandel we carried out some cockpit tasking on arrival and during the exercise joined in with 1(F) squadron attack missions. In the two-seater we had several entertaining exercise missions during which we were bounced by F16s and F15s. I only had to take over control a couple of times, and the air commodore took all of my instruction with good grace, including my grabbing the stick off him in the middle of an almighty punch-up with a mob of F16s at low level.

I was almost beginning to enjoy my OCU job again when a Part 1 TACEVAL reminded me forcibly of the never-ending balls-ache of the front-line Harrier world. It occurred to me that I had been in front-line single-seat flying for fourteen years without a break. Also, if I counted each week of the Falklands War as a TACEVAL, then I calculated idly that I had done the equivalent of at least twenty years' worth of TACEVALs since 1972. Although nominally an OCU, 233 had always been very much an operational outfit, practising many of the normal routines of a front-line squadron. I longed for a routine flying job without all the tedious ground training niff-naff and practice bleeding that was an unavoidable consequence of all RAF front-line flying. I was also weary of the ingrained Harrier force habit of doing everything at the run. I had done my share and it was time to move on to a more relaxed job. After the customary sea survival course at good old RAF Mountbatten, soon to be handed over to the Navy, I began training for the Tornado GR1.

Chapter 19

Tornado Instructor

The Tri-National Tornado Training Establishment (TTTE) had commenced training operations in 1981, with the variable-geometry Tornado GR1 just introduced into service. The TOCU (Tornado Operational Conversion Unit) was a big operation, at this time by far the largest operational conversion unit in the UK. There were three instructional squadrons, A,B and C, each commanded by a boss of different nationality, plus Standards Squadron. There were over fifty aircraft on base, and the engineers put out twenty-eight per day on the line, intending to fly them all at least twice. Flying went on year-round on five days a week, with night flying every night from Monday to Thursday. This was definitely an all-weather OCU. After the extremely complex ground school and simulator phase I joined 'B' (RAF) Squadron in May . The joy – and confusion – of TTTE was that the instructors and students were all divided up between the squadrons. Thus it was quite feasible to be instructed by an Italian navigator instructor in a German Tornado, or by a German pilot instructor in an Italian Tornado. The numbers of staff, students and airframes were provided according to each member nation's financial stake in the operation.

The Germans put in nearly 50 per cent of the money, followed by the Brits, with the Italians providing about 10 per cent. Hence the Germans were the senior partners, in spite of the fact that we had a Brit station commander. His function was paralleled by equivalent-ranked German and Italian officers, there to make sure that the RAF didn't try to put over too much unnecessary stuff that would interfere with the flying and social life. This was a good arrangement as far as I was concerned, with the three nations adopting the most liberal and convenient rules to make our job easier and the social life more agreeable. Thus, for example, we stuck to the extremely liberal

RAF rules on flying in weather, which allowed for maximum flexibility in the air. In the Mess, and on the squadrons, the Germans refused to put up with the stuffy and restrictive RAF drinking regulations. In Germany, service personnel had a right to have alcohol at their workplace and so each squadron was well-equipped with a cosy bar serving cold beer or wine at the official end of duty time for that squadron – strictly forbidden on 'normal' RAF stations. This cosy arrangement was not popular with senior RAF officers outside the TTTE as the RAF was now committed to the 'minimum alcohol at the flight line' culture. The four squadrons flew a shift system of early, middle and late take-offs, with appropriately staggered working days. The squadron boss's definition of 'cease work' was his and his alone: this usually meant last landing time for that squadron. That's when the bar opened. The early shift would start with a 6 o'clock met (painful in midwinter), while the late (night flying) squadron's last landing would be around midnight. Hence the frenetic social life every day.

The Tornado course proceeded at a leisurely pace, characteristic of the 'What's the rush?' attitude of the medium bomber force. I found the machine straightforward to fly from the front seat and very comfortable in the spacious cockpit. After my years of instruction on the Harrier I found no problems in getting on with the navigators, who were generally a good-hearted bunch, just as keen as the pilots to get good results in the air. Getting on with the other nationalities presented more problems occasionally, and I fell back on my Dutch Air Force experience to remind me of how a continental Air Force worked. The Germans, in particular, were a problem. Traditionally, German Air Forces (we had German Navy aircrew as well) had relied on other nations to carry out most of their training for them, either the Brits or the Americans. As a result they had no real tradition or experience of the problems of training aircrew. My favourite German image is of the German Army *Oberst* (played by Gert Frobe) in *Those Magnificent Men in Their Flying Machines* being asked how he will learn to fly an aircraft.

'From the book!' he splutters. 'The same way we do EVERYTHING in the German Army!'

In my view that just about sums it up for the Germans; as long as it is written down they are happy. In general they could see no reason for the kind of interpretive and individual style of instruction practised by RAF instructors, which is adapted as required to suit different types of student. Like the Dutch, the Germans' permit to fly was a written licence handed out on completion of training, requiring a process of law (sometimes in the civil courts), to take it away.

My interest in cycling was rekindled with the more relaxed pace of life in the medium bomber force. I had bought a Claude Butler touring bike and was getting into some more long-distance stuff, cycling to and from Cottesmore on two or three days a week; about thirteen miles each way. I started going on longer distance trips, by train first, then cycling back. One magnificent run was up to Darlington then cycling all the way down the Pennines to Sheffield, while another trip was all over the Lake District.

Towards the end of the course we started training in automatic terrain following (ATF). This was completely new to me. The machine had a very sophisticated autopilot that could be used in conjunction with the terrain following radar to fly 'hands-off' down to 200 feet above ground. The system was well-proven by 1984, after years of trials. Characteristically, because of limited understanding of the technology, RAF senior commanders insisted on writing extremely restrictive clearances to use the equipment under actual conditions (i.e. in the dark), in spite of our claims that the system was perfectly safe to use as designed. There was no clearance at all to fly in cloud at low level, for which the system had been specifically designed, simply because of the UK low flying regulations, which stated that low flying could only take place in visibility of five kilometres or more. That regulation had hardly changed since the Second World War. This was the modern equivalent of legislation requiring someone to carry a red flag to walk in front of all motor vehicles. One of the night terrain following flying orders required us to calculate minimum en route altitudes (MEAs) for each block of every leg of our night low level routes and write them on our maps. In flight, as well as monitoring the TF system you were supposed to check continuously that your Baro altimeter never went below the MEA for that block. If it did, you were supposed to disengage the autopilot and manually fly the aircraft above the MEA before re-engaging. Tornado aircrew tried to point out to senior officers that constantly engaging and disengaging the autopilot was the most dangerous thing you could do during TF in IMC or at night – far more dangerous than just trusting the system to work as advertised. The terrain following engagement and monitoring procedures were complex but effective and, in over 100,000 hours of terrain following flying so far, no crew had been flown into the ground by the terrain following system.

This was a situation which cried out for the selective interpretation of orders, and that is what happened. Fortunately, at TTTE, we had a fair quota of experienced aircrew on the staff; hence, many of us quietly ignored the regulations and – even as students – happily TF'd along at night and in cloud as the system was designed to do. TF training by day in good weather was no problem, but the first time I used it at night was a genuine attention-getter for me. For the first time I was sitting in an aircraft below safety altitude, unable to see the ground, and totally relying on the avionics to avoid death. That first press of the autopilot ENGAGE button at night was a memorable experience and there followed a teeth-sucking few seconds as the aircraft dived down into the black hole below. Tensing up on the stick had to be avoided at all costs. We were supposed to rest the hand lightly on the stick in case of any problems. However, any undue pressure would trigger the stick force cut out (SFCO) and disengage the autopilot.

Although night terrain following was challenging, daytime terrain following in cloud in hilly terrain was totally ball-grabbing the first time you tried it. Approaching a range of cloud-covered hills there would be an overwhelming instinct to turn away or climb quickly to safety altitude, the only option for non-Tornado aircrew. However, a quick engagement of the terrain following system and you dropped quickly into the TF monitoring mode, calling out the indications on the E-scope (TF radar display) to the navigator. As you reached the rising ground the 'Ski-Toe' on the E-scope penetrated the ridgeline painted on the screen and you felt the first pull of the autopilot as it commanded a climb to maintain a precise 300 feet clearance over the top of the ridge ahead. If you had any sense as you approached the cloud you would have your head firmly buried in the cockpit, ignoring the awful reality of what was about to happen immediately in front. You were about to fly serenely into cloud in a shallow climb with high ground dead ahead. How many of your colleagues had been killed doing just this in conventional aircraft in the past? Every piloting instinct screamed out at you ' Pull up, pull up!'

Just relax Sunshine – relax and trust the system.

Jesus Christ! There's got to be a more relaxed way to die!

But it works.

The autopilot commands a gentle climb into cloud, you see on the E-scope that you have crossed the first ridge and then the system commands a stomach-churning pushover: 'Down, for Christ's Sake! We're only 300 feet in total IMC and there's more hills ahead – why can't we go up?'

But the system keeps working perfectly: you see the 'Ski Toe' touch the next hill and the autopilot deftly flies a pull-out to hold the height at 300 feet on the radar altimeter before beginning the next smooth pull-up. Flying in a turn was the worst time. Cloud over hilly terrain is seldom continuous, no matter how bad the weather, and you get occasional terrifying glimpses of rocks and trees flashing past, seemingly just a few feet away, before you plunge once more into the white stuff. You don't get that problem in the dark. After a bit of practice at this kind of thing you can get 'TF-happy', willing to trust the system in the most difficult of circumstances. This was exactly what TTTE needed to achieve, in spite of our senior commanders restricting the value of the training by smothering it with unnecessary restrictions. In just a few years' time many of our students would be going to war at night at low level, and it was vital that they should have absolute confidence in the terrain following system to be able to do the job and hit their targets.

At the end of the course I went to Standards Squadron to complete the brief competent to instruct (C2I) course. In just fifteen sorties the C2I student had to learn to fly the Tornado from the back seat, operate the navigation kit and the radar like a navigator, and also learn all of the instructional sequences for pilot and navigator students. Even with my previous instructional experience I found this a tall order. Unfortunately the three nations would not fund any more training for new instructors: this was typical of the Germans' attitude to instructional technique – they couldn't see what all the fuss was about. As far as they were concerned if you were capable of flying an aircraft yourself then you could instruct on it from the book. As they had the major financial input they had had a lot of say in how the training was set up initially. First of all the aircraft was fairly easy to fly when fully serviceable, and even with one engine failed it was straightforward to bring home and land. Secondly, all low flying by student pilots was at 500 feet, allowing plenty of margin for error when the student's head was buried in the cockpit. Finally, very few sorties were 'crew solo', when a student pilot and student navigator flew together.

The staff navs were a phlegmatic and long-suffering bunch, with even less instructor training than the pilots. In my view they did a fantastic job flying in the back seat of the strike Tornados (which had no flying controls in the rear seat), keeping the student pilots out of trouble. The majority of aircraft at TTTE were dual-control trainers, and staff navs preferred to fly in these, although they were given no formal pilot training. On one memorable occasion a student pilot became seriously disorientated on a GCA at night in a trainer. The aircraft was almost out of control when the British nav took control in the back and flew the aircraft safely back on to the glidepath. There were times when you were completely out of the loop as an instructor pilot (IP). If the wing-sweep mechanism jammed fully swept back then the landing speed was horrific and the landing had to be done by the student pilot in the front, it being impossible to see the runway from the back seat because of the huge angle of attack on finals. The first ever genuine fully swept-wing landing demonstrated the problem graphically. The instructor pilot reported the wings stuck fully swept and the newish station commander turned up in the tower to watch the landing with the other senior national commanders. Because it was a staff call sign they weren't too bunched as no-one twigged that the student would have to land it. They watched a very high-speed touchdown and the 'wheels' all drove out to congratulate the instructor pilot on the runway as the crew shut the aircraft down with smoking brakes.

'Good landing,' called the station commander, addressing the instructor pilot .

'Nothing to do with me, Sir – the stude did it all: I could see fuck all from back here!'

Only at this stage did the assembled 'wheels' appreciate that the extremely tricky landing of the £17 million aircraft had been entirely in the hands of the nervous, barely-qualified student in the front seat.

After the all-too-short competent to instruct course, I was posted to 'C' Squadron, where I spent several enjoyable years under three different Italian bosses. The instruction of student pilots was pretty straightforward, there being a lot of dual time for them before we would risk letting them loose with a staff nav. Rather like the Starfighter course, we usually got in some instrument sorties and close formation before their final solo clearance check ride. Student navigators were an unknown quantity for me. The main aim of the course was to teach the student navs to use the 'kit' and the radar properly and, in this, we were greatly helped by having a majority of German and Italian aircraft on the flight line. These aircraft, unlike the British models, had a repeater radar display in the front cockpit and the instructor pilot could easily see what the stude was doing with the radar. My Starfighter radar experience was useful, as the Tornado radar picture was similar at the longer ranges. At closer ranges the Tornado radar (an excellent American-designed piece of kit) was an order of magnitude better than the Starfighter's, with a crystal-clear picture of close-range objects, down to hedges and individual buildings.

As always there was plenty of staff continuation flying, and I usually asked to fly in the back seat where you had the challenge of finding and marking offsets and targets on radar, plus the much more difficult problems of circuit work and instrument flying. Just like my flying training days I still enjoyed doing the difficult things when possible. From the back seat, landings were much more difficult: only with the seat fully raised and your helmet hard up against the canopy was there a good enough view of the runway. There was no HUD in the back seat, only a rather cheap and nasty set of standby instruments. A particular challenge which I enjoyed was flying accurate steep turns from the back seat at low level at night in the black out over the North Sea, where we did a lot of our night low level general handling training. Formation staff continuation training on 'C' was always brilliant. There were always air combat opportunities during the many long-range low levels. The clean machine was very 'zippy', like the Starfighter for high speed chases and run-outs, and you could go supersonic at low level within just few seconds of selecting reheat. If forced to mix it at low speed then with wings fully swept forward and the excellent full-span manoeuvre flaps, you could manoeuvre like a Hawk trainer. If you kept your eyes open there were always Phantoms, Harriers, Jaguars or Hawks willing to chance their arm and 'mix it' with you.

Later on we came across the more adventurous Tornado ADV pilots cruising over the North Sea. The ADV was a prettier aeroplane than our stubby GR1. The ADV was heavier, with more fuel in a longer airframe; it didn't seem much cop in close manoeuvring against our lightly-loaded GR1s.

The flying and general atmosphere at Cottesmore was unbelievably laid-back in comparison with my previous RAF experience. In particular it took me a long time to 'wind-down' to the speed of operation of the medium bomber force. I was often frustrated at the generous amount of time allocated for everything to do with flying, and the general lack of pressure involved. As an example, during atack missions the squadrons would plan to attack just two targets in a low level mission lasting eighty minutes. I got nowhere by pointing out that on the Harrier we would often be attacking twice that number of targets in just a fifty minute sortie. The night flying routine was very pleasant: with most of the day free we would turn up for work late in the afternoon to fly an evening wave and then one night wave. We never flew more than twice per day.

Although straightforward to fly, there were one or two handling quirks which made the Tornado an interesting challenge for more experienced student pilots who had flown other high-performance types before. One instant put-down for the many ex-Starfighter pilots we trained was the Tornado reheat system. In the Starfighter you rocked the throttle outboard to select reheat. In the Tornado this same action selected thrust reverse, so instead of rolling for take-off the aircraft would lurch backwards instead – a mortifying experience. No matter how many times you reminded them of this there were always some clowns who fell into the trap on their first take-off.

As a bit of relaxation my instincts were turning towards sailing again and I went on an RAF dinghy sailing course in gorgeously hot weather in September '85. With the laid-back and routine nature of Tornado flying, I developed a hankering for a bit more adventure and my thoughts turned towards offshore sailing. I decided to buy a small trailer-sailer. After a fateful visit to the Boat Show at Earl's Court I was much impressed by the Chinese Junk Rig and started looking for a second-hand Newbridge Coromandel. The children were still too young for sailing and I knew that my wife would never consider boating as a sport, so it was to be single-handed sailing for me from the start. In spite of my general lack of experience I was quite happy with the thought of single-handing, my years of single-seat flying being a good preparation. I did the theoretical day skipper course and booked a week's day skipper practical course with a one-man outfit based at Poole. Our first-class instructor was an ex-Royal Navy lieutenant with a beautiful cutter-rigged Rival 36. On the first day of sailing – with snow showers blasting horizontally across Poole harbour – two of our fellow students chickened out and abandoned the course, leaving just myself and a young schoolteacher as students. We then had a glorious week of sailing with lots of hands-on practice in winds up to Force 8. On Rutland Water I started teaching myself to sail a junk-rig cruiser. No engines were permitted on the water and so I had one or two interesting departures and arrivals before I settled down and learned the ropes. After a couple of weeks practice I felt ready for the open sea and started trailing down to the south coast for some solo offshore sailing. After exploring all the creeks and harbours of the Solent I ventured out into the open sea, eventually completing passages from Plymouth to Falmouth and back, one of which was at night. I enjoyed night sailing particularly. Like all professional aviators I had a good understanding of met and a sober appreciation of what the weather and sea could do. From my time spent carrying out open-sea dinghy survival drills with the RAF, I knew that my chances of survival alone in the water were minimal.

From Cottesmore we flew occasional landaways to the well-known RAF stations of Lossiemouth and Leuchars and the TOCU started regular winter deployments to Machrihanish, one of the most remote outposts of the RAF, at the tip of the Mull of Kintyre. Their weather factor was better than Cottesmore's, and operating from there gave access to the superb low flying territory of north-west Scotland. The airfield, bleak and forbidding, lay across the end of the Mull with high ground just to the north. The primitive domestic site had hardly changed since my visit there by Jet Provost to play squash in 1967, in fact from the air the station looked as if it was stuck in a time warp since 1945. Going U/S there was a major problem – it could take up to twenty-four hours for spares to arrive by road from Cottesmore. However, the scenery was the compensation. I loved to fly up the west coast past Jura, Mull and Skye, dodging around the brilliant white snow showers which contrasted so vividly with the deep blue/black of the sea. Inland, we boomed through the sealochs and glens at high speed, leaving dense wingtip condensation trails as we hurtled around the crags. Conditions were dangerous where there was thick snow cover. We briefed the students on the dangers of 'white-out' and the foolhardiness of pressing on into snow showers.

On these landaways a greater than average proportion of sorties were flown back seat. This was because whenever the weather was below student pilot's minimums, the only way to get the student pilots airborne was with a staff pilot instead of nav in the back, much to the disgust of our nav instructors. On these sorties you were working pretty hard because you had to keep a careful eye on the stude and, at the same time, operate all the back seat gear and the radar in a professional manner. Some of the most demanding missions were the supposed student-led attack sorties in formation, when you were back-seating and had to take responsibility for the formation and your student, and find all the fix points, offsets and targets on the radar. Other sorties I enjoyed included the back-seat night TF missions in poor weather. Up to the end of 1987 the UK low flying system was the same by night as by day, and you could plan routes where you wanted, to all the interesting areas. There was a system of roundabouts all over the country, and you often met up with other aircraft en route. Hence there was a need to keep your night vision at top level, turning all unnecessary cockpit lights down to a minimum.

Later on I was appalled to hear of a proposed new policy of the RAF's personnel department (PMC) to immediately ground pilots who asked to retire. This was intended both as a deterrent and punishment for the increasing numbers of RAF pilots baling out as the civil airline employment situation improved. As a protest I decided to offer my resignation straight away, in case they tried the same trick on me. After a while a group captain arrived at Cottesmore on a routine PMC visit, and he asked to interview me about my decision to retire. I explained that I felt the proposed new policy was grossly unfair, especially in the case of people like me who had flown for over twenty years already in the RAF. My view was that it was a lousy way to treat people, punishing them just because they wanted to retire. He was completely unsympathetic to my view and announced with some relish that, 'We're going to ground people like you in future'. The interview became very frosty and I said little more before leaving in disgust.

By the following year the civil air transport employment situation was looking good so I decided to go for the airline transport pilot's licence (ATPL). Time off for study and exams had to be begged from sympathetic superiors; if they wouldn't cooperate you were stuffed. I booked into a training school at Hurn and obtained my full ATPL-A in the summer after four hours flying on the Piper Aztec F, including night rating and full instrument rating. Although I was still enjoying the flying at Cottesmore I realized that financially I would be much better off with an airline. I hadn't really considered the other aspects of leaving the RAF after twenty-four years' service.

I got a job with Monarch airlines and set off confidently to Luton in early December to begin ground school for the Boeing 757. After barely three weeks' training at Luton, I was totally disenchanted with civilian life and desperate to return to the RAF. I had realized – almost too late – what a gigantic mistake I had made. I just hadn't considered the likely effect on me of the separation from the service that I had joined straight from school, the everyday banter with like-minded colleagues at work, the comradeship and professional pride of flying and instructing on high-performance aircraft. I realized how much I owed the RAF. It was as if someone had pulled out the plug that kept me sane. The RAF wasn't something of my own that I could take or leave – rather the RAF owned me as the Aborigine is owned by 'his' land. I was desolate and demoralized by my stupidity. Suffering from an attack of 'flu I decided to tell Monarch to shove it and try to return to the RAF. To my utter relief the RAF took me back without a qualm and I joined Standards Squadron of TTTE at Cottesmore in the New Year. My precious ATPL, which had cost me over £4,000, I have never used.

I kept my head down for a while on Standards Squadron as I went through the short conversion course to become an instrument rating examiner on the Tornado. Unlike a Standards Squadron on an RAF training unit, we had no remit to carry out regular checks of the competency of the rest of the staff – something that was routine on normal RAF training units. Some checks were done, but only a proportion of the annual requirement across the wing. The remainder were done by squadron bosses or other supervisors of the pilot's own squadron.

In my first year on Standards Squadron, the chief instructor asked me if I was interested in leading a three-ship Tornado GR1 display team. I had got over my post-Gemini aversion to display work and agreed. I collected a young, punchy nav and we set about working out a routine with the other two crews, one of which was Italian, the other German; all first-class guys. We briefly thought of doing a routine involving lots of smart close formation, to show off our technical skill, and naturally enough after a moment's consideration we rejected the idea in favour of lots of low-level flying with maximum noise and speed that would involve minimum skill on our part, knowing from experience that this was what Joe Public really appreciated. After some intense practice we had a reasonable show, involving just a little close formation but a lot of high-speed stuff in fully-swept wing configuration, which looked nice from the ground. We also split at the end of the display to carry out a coordinated attack on the airfield – lots of speed and reheat to make maximum impression for the kiddies. Just before landing I would do an individual flypast very low in fully-swept wing with gear up (with a huge angle of attack), then select full reheat right in front of the crowd, just a few yards away. This seemed to go down well and left eardrums ringing. It always amused me that Joe Public equated lots of noise and high speed with piloting skill in fighter aeroplanes. We did a few shows in the local area, which was sufficient for me. I didn't really fancy getting into the full-time display nausea of travelling all over the place all summer long. What we did was fun and we had a good time.

Like any other Standards Squadron there was a big workload of administration and paperwork to be done by the instructors, involving constant updating and rewriting of our extensive briefing guides, syllabi and instructional technique books. Naturally enough the majority of the tasks fell to the Brits, and I was soon to get deeply involved in rewriting a lot of our training guides and instructional material. I was able to get paperwork sorted out fairly smartly and I worked out how to get new ideas through the TTTE bureaucracy reasonable fast.

Training instructors on the too-short competent to instruct (C2I) course was hard work. Most of our trade was with young German Air Force (GAF) aircrew, many of whom had barely eighteen months' experience of flying the jet. For the pilots, the first few sorties were aimed at teaching them to fly from the back seat by day and night, the latter a particular problem as the GAF never flew 'visual' circuits at night back in Germany for noise abatement reasons. As an instructor you had to use every trick in the book to get them to fly a safe 'demo' circuit at night from the back seat. All the basic night flying problems were there: inability to estimate distance out downwind (use the moving map, say I); failure to appreciate sink rate in the finals turn (use the bloody vertical speed indicator); inability to judge drift on finals (keep your head moving). The occasional bit of encouragement didn't go amiss. This was basic instructional technique – encourage your student if he's doing well:

'Not bad mate, I have control. I'll just demo a single-engine circuit while you relax for a bit.'

Next we were into practice of instructional routines. This could end up being quite tedious for the Standards Squadron instructor. First of all you had to brief the stude carefully on what the requirements were, including tips on good instructional technique. Then, after some preparation by the stude, you went into 'student mode' yourself and sat down in a briefing room to listen to the student instructor's attempts at briefing. I would make mental notes of the errors made and not comment at this stage. After this I would brief the student about the 'student on/student off' procedure. Basically, I would be playing at being a student (student on) once we started to taxi. I would then allow the student to get on with his instructional practice for as long as I could bear it (usually about twenty minutes) before taking control and saying:

'OK mate; relax – student off!"

Now I was the instructor again and attempted to debrief him on his techniques so far; maybe I would re-demonstrate some aspects of instructional technique, using him as the student. Then I would hand over control and say 'Student on!' so he could try being the instructor again. Naturally, too many changes 'student on and student off' could throw the student instructor completely, never allowing him to get into his stride. Any fool of an instructor could destroy a student's confidence in the air, so you had to be positive and helpful, no matter how badly he was doing. Towards the end of the mission I would usually simulate a major emergency during which I would remain 'student on' i.e. the student instructor had to make allowances for the kind of stupid mistakes real students would make when dealing with an emergency. This you could easily take too far; you had to judge it carefully or things would start to get too dangerous. As captain of the aircraft you always had the dilemma of judging precisely how far you could let things go before you intervened, which was doubly difficult if you were training an instructor as opposed to a student, because you were trying to train the student instructor to recognize a developing dangerous situation and intervene at the right time. Nevertheless, it had to be done and occasionally some risks had to be taken to achieve the training aim. This was our professional duty on Standards Squadron.

Although hard work, training instructors was not all serious, dedicated stuff. As with all flying instruction I encouraged the student instructors to enjoy the flying and try to pass on that attitude to their students. No matter how badly a student was doing it was always possible to think of some light-hearted banter or a joke to cheer them up. The TTTE itself was a wonderful example of this. It was the only flying course I had ever attended when, as a student, you were ordered to enjoy the course. This was in stark contrast to our students' next phase of training, the Tornado weapons conversion course, which was entirely RAF-run, containing little humour or fun factor for the students.

One particular interest of mine was the Tornado automatic terrain following (ATF) system and the way we trained our students in its use. It seemed vitally important to continue to develop a complete trust in the integrity of the system because using it in anger was not at all natural. One particular problem area involved flying over calm water surfaces, when the TF radar would not pick up any returns. This would lead to the system dropping into a degraded, although still safe, mode. I discovered that few pilots or navs on the staff fully understood this aspect of the system and it was not uncommon for crews to come back from a mission claiming that 'The terrain following system just tried to kill me!' In that case I would ask for a description of exactly what had happened and in each case it was obvious that the terrain following system had dropped into the degraded mode without the crew realizing. To publicize this more, I used to make a point of demonstrating the problem to our trainee instructors by finding an area of calm water and carrying out a 'TF letdown', in which you allowed the terrain following system to take over and initiate a descent on autopilot. The resulting manoeuvre – the machine would always level out safely – would demonstrate clearly that the system was safe to use as briefed.

All in all I found the flying on Standards Squadron challenging and interesting, even the check rides we carried out on students and staff. We worked harder and flew more hours than the other 'waterfront' squadrons. They took no account of the extra admin and paperwork we had to do on standards, for which the extra flying was some compensation. A pleasant duty on Standards Squadron was giving short Tornado training courses to senior officers, many of whom were old colleagues from many years back. New staff posted into TOCU had to complete a short refresher C2I course and many of them I had trained twice before; once as main course students on their initial Tornado training, and once again as C2I students a couple of years later. In spite of its obvious organizational defects, there was always a pleasant international club atmosphere among the aircrew of the three nations; a unique military example of a successful multinational cooperation.

My Dad had not been well for some time and there had been a couple of scares when Robin and I had rushed to Dawlish to find him in hospital. The end came on 25 November 1988 when Mum rang to say he had been taken into hospital again. Because of previous false alarms I set off in slow time for Dawlish, to be immediately caught up in a disastrous four-lane traffic jam on the M69, caused by a thirty-vehicle pileup and fire on the M6. After three hours of zero movement I found a phone box and rang Mum. Dad was already dead and I was grateful for the fog as the floods of tears refused to dry up. There had been no tears since I was a teenager, not even for my best friend, so hardened had I become to the loss of friends and colleagues. For Dad it was different.

The protracted work-up to the Gulf War in 1990 brought back memories of the Falklands, as tension increased steadily throughout the autumn. Many of the Tornado pilots I had helped to train would be going to war and would be feeling the way we did in 1982. There were tiresome reruns of the same problems that we had suffered in '82, and which still had not been solved: inadequate equipment (we still hadn't got the IFF sorted out); crazy ideas on tactics by people who didn't know what they were talking about; inadequate weapons; blue-on-blue cock-ups and the usual indecision at all levels about who was going to war, etc.

At TTTE we continued our normal training routine while some of our staff with GR1 operational experience were sent to Saudi Arabia on ops/plans ground jobs. This was to be an ongoing theme for the next few years and, as I had never flown the GR1 operationally, I managed to avoid it. The limit of my contribution was lending out some of my old Bahrain slides to the operational squadrons, plus some advice on the problems of operating over deserts. Having done my bit in the Falklands I was happy to take a back seat and we all watched with bated breath as the balloon went up in the middle of January '91. Knowing the strength of the Iraqi defences we could all predict the problems the guys would experience at low level, the only tactical option with the runway-busting JP233 weapon. As we had predicted back in the mid-70s when the Tornado/JP233 combination was first proposed, there were to be a lot of problems with low-level over-flights of heavily defended targets.

The rest is history. The lads did their bit at night low level in magnificent style, although they lost an aeroplane per night with almost half the shot-down crews killed during the first week of the war. Like the Falklands, some day an RAF pilot or navigator who was there, will write the full story of what went on in the Gulf War: the day-to-day bravery of ordinary squadron shags, the unbelievable stress both at squadron and high command level, the cock-ups, the reported equipment inadequacies that had been complained about for so long, etc.

Later on some of the stories filtered back to Cottesmore. Fortunately, in the best RAF traditions, the vast majority of aircrew just got on with it and tried to avoid the media frenzy, doing a thoroughly professional job night after night without complaint or advertisement. Personally I was disappointed at the way TV cameras were shoved in the face of exhausted crews as they climbed out of cockpits. This was done in order to milk every last drop of good publicity from the war. Apparently this was approved by the RAF's top brass, remembering the experience of the Falklands War, where the Royal Navy ran a slick media operation that tried to claim exclusive credit for the British success.

As well as the lives lost in action, several fatal accidents marred the intense work-up training for the war. One old colleague, an absolute gentleman, crashed at night in the North Sea and was killed with his nav while practising routine loft-bombing attacks. Another crew flew into a sand dune and died while training in Oman.

In the New Year I was delighted to find I had been awarded the MBE, Military Division, for my work on Standards Squadron. For me this was, if anything, more important than the DFC, because that was for just a short period of flying. The MBE was for a long period of training Tornado instructors and had been recommended by all three national commanders.

I was beginning to relax more on Standards Squadron. Having taken up golf again I was enjoying membership of the lovely Luffenham Heath Club, a gorse-strewn environmental paradise amidst heavily agricultural Rutland. However, by the end of '91 I was starting to suffer from an indefinable sense of weariness. I just didn't seem to have the same energy as before. I couldn't work it out, and put the thought behind me as we entered 1992. I was still enjoying flying very much and had, at last, given in to my increasing short-sightedness. I had managed to cover this up in the air by sometime using the radar to pick up other aircraft before the hawk-eyed students saw them.

'Bogey right One-o'clock, range about 7 miles, Hans,' I would call to the front-seat stude.

'No contact' says Hans, thinking 'Shit, this old bugger's got good eyesight!' Meanwhile I continued to call the bogey, which I was plotting on radar, until my student finally saw it. Eventually I realized that this was no way to carry on and went to the Doc. Wearing my brand-new pair of aircrew specs for the first time, I was absolutely amazed at how much more I could see in flight.

The weariness increased. I could no longer cycle uphill back from town. One day I walked downtown and had to get a taxi back. Still I refused to accept the obvious; the thought was too terrible to contemplate – don't even think about what it means. I tried to push it to the back of my mind. Flying was fine, I felt fine all the time. It was just when I exercised: on the golf course I got slower and slower up the hills: Jesus Christ! You know what this means. Anything but that – anything. It couldn't be, it was impossible – there must be some other explanation.

The cruncher was a routine trip when I got a fire warning in cloud after take-off. Absolutely no big deal: shut down the engine, open the cross-drive, make a brief emergency call and set up for the single engine recovery. My Nav was splendid – totally relaxed, helping out when I needed it, shutting up when not. Easy single engine GCA and landing and turn off the runway.

Just a minute – what was that strange feeling, the slight tightness in the chest? Barely noticeable but I'd never had that before, even after much bigger emergencies. I went home in a dark mood, fearing the worst. If the old pink body couldn't cope with a simple engine fire warning then what? Still I refused to accept the inevitable.

By the end of March I could no longer ignore the symptoms. Thus began the most tiresome eighteen months of my life. In early April I flew what I knew might well be my last ever flight, before taking two weeks' leave. My GP suggested a heart condition, issued pills, and booked me in privately with a cardiologist in Peterborough. I had to have an answer as soon as possible and I wanted nothing to do with RAF medics at this stage. Before the end of my leave I had been tested on the treadmill and the cardio confirmed the problem and booked an angiogram at Oxford. I came home from the appointment and told my wife that it was all over, as far as flying was concerned. I was totally numb: I felt dead already. I returned from leave and paid a visit to the RAF Senior Medical Officer. Ironically, she had in her hand the ECG report from my recent RAF medical and gave me a clean bill of health. Not surprisingly: a non-exercise ECG is useless at predicting blocked arteries. Grim-faced, I handed her the cardiologist's report.

So, at 47, this was the end of my flying career. From the pinnacle I fell to absolutely nothing overnight. I had hoped to continue until I was at least 60. Idly I scanned back through my flying log books to 1964, the year I had begun flying with the RAF. In the twenty-eight years I had flown some 5,500 hours, mostly fast jet and single-seat, single engine. I had been on four operational squadrons: 208 Hunter, 20(AC) Harrier, 306 Starfighter (RNLAF) and 1(F) Harrier. I had instructed on two operational conversion units: No. 233 Harrier and TOCU Tornado. Most of this flying had taken place in the context of the Cold War, plus war flying in the Falklands. From my log book I saw that there were only nine individual months between January 1964 and April 1992 when I did not fly at all. At least six of those were taken up with ground school on various aeroplanes, so I had only had about three complete months off flying for other reasons in twenty-eight years. This included my abortive attempt to join the airlines in 1987. I had done no ground tours at all – extremely unusual for an RAF pilot. I had taken a lot of chances and expended a fair amount of adrenalin over the years – that was my style of flying and I could do nothing about that. Perhaps, on reflection, it was time for a rest. I had no regrets and would have done the same again, except for going to Cranwell and CFS. I had been extremely lucky in spending most of my flying career on four different types of high-performance aircraft: the Hunter, the Harrier, the F104G Starfighter and the Tornado GR1. Many of my contemporaries had been bored flying the same type for most of their careers. Unlike many of my Cranwell colleagues, my bag of luck had lasted until the end.

There followed a summer and autumn of ground jobs on Standards Squadron while I awaited the operation, the unpleasant angiogram procedure having confirmed what I already suspected – I needed open-heart surgery. Because I was only 47 and had youngish children, I had a good chance of getting it done within a year; for an older man the chances recede. Eventually the operation was carried out by the excellent team at the John Radcliffe Infirmary in Oxford and I was overwhelmed with admiration for the dedication and humanity of the nursing staff in the heart surgery department. Unfortunately I was then forced to go to RAF Halton hospital for several more days of recuperation which, in retrospect, I would rather have spent at home. The operation was pretty revolting and left me feeling totally steamrollered, as well as causing short-term psychological problems. I found I had to learn to carry out every physical activity again like a child. First it was a great adventure to walk to the bottom of the garden, then a walk across the road was like crossing the Sahara.

After about six weeks, my customary impatience nearly did for me. I went back to work and rode a bike for a while. Big error. The next day began a series of severe anxiety attacks which were to plague me for the next eighteen months on and off. This was the most terrifying time of my life and I have no wish to repeat it. I ended up a nervous wreck on sleeping pills and my recuperation from the operation was set back a long time. Some time later I read in *New Scientist* magazine what the problem was. On the heart/lung machine your blood is cooled for the operation and your brain expands for some reason, causing pressure on the grey matter. This was known to cause short-term psychological damage to some people, affecting them in different ways. It seemed I had drawn the short straw.

An anxiety attack would start with a vague feeling of unease, rapidly developing into a feeling of dread, a deep-seated terror of something so appalling you could not imagine it. Soon the shakes would start, and within a few minutes my whole body would be trembling violently, my heart (my sub-standard heart), racing out of control. The fear would develop and intensify, but there would be no clue as to what I was afraid of. Because the fear had no name and no face there was no way that I could exorcise it or come to terms with it. The only cure was oblivion, by means of a rapid-acting powerful sleeping pill. Without a pill the attack could go on for an hour or more, leaving me totally drained.

Everyone at Cottesmore was very understanding and I joined the staff of ground school as a flight simulator instructor. Later in the year I took over as officer I/C simulators. There were regular trips to London to MOD meetings on the RAF's Tornado GR1 simulator fleet (there were five of them) and I found I enjoyed the simulator instructional sorties for the new crews and also regular training for TOCU staff aircrew.

I was setting out on a long, hard road to full recovery.

Chapter 20

Recuperation

For the next few years I was to be plagued by self-doubts and lack of confidence to do things, especially anything new, much to the frustration of the family. After a long flying career, characterized by calculated risk-taking and sublime (if unjustified) self-confidence, this feeling of uselessness was a pain in the ass all round, and was now compounded by a sinister addition to my customary hypochondria. The quacks had warned me about giving in to cardiac neurosis (an irrational fear of heart problems), which I should have fought off once the op was successfully completed. Unfortunately, I soon became convinced that the op had not fully succeeded and I was still operating with a sub-standard heart. This grisly feeling affected everything I did as I tried desperately to rehabilitate myself.

Eventually things began to improve and over the next few years I was able to suppress my cardiac neurosis sufficiently to be a bit more adventurous. I realized that I would have to forcibly drag myself back to a normal lifestyle by doing the kind of things I had enjoyed before the problem began. I bought a small fishing dory and trailer, and began trailering to the east coast, usually Brancaster, for some very gentle sea-fishing expeditions. Unfortunately, my old preference for doing things solo was still there, despite my medical problems. Irrationally, if I had a medical problem I felt that I would rather be on my own, so there would be no witnesses to what I saw as a physical weakness. My greatest horror was of dying of a heart attack in public. It would be so embarrassing. My solo expeditions slowly built up my self-confidence, though doing nothing for my relations with the family, who still could not understand what I was going through. This was sad as it would have been nice to go more often with the family, especially with Christopher. Unfortunately I was not getting on at all well with Chris, as he was going through that intense phase of adolescent rebellion, which was quietly driving me mad.

Within a couple of years my confidence had returned sufficiently to
buy a yacht to start solo sailing again, from the River Orwell. For me
this was quite a challenge as the 2½ tons of Elizabethan 29 were a
bit of a handful, bearing in mind that my only previous solo experience was with the junk rig. I stuck with it and eventually was able to
sail out into the Thames estuary with confidence. and explore some
of the east coast rivers. I particularly enjoyed night sailing off
Harwich, although the weather was always much more unpredictable. My aim was to sail solo across to Ramsgate. This would
involve about forty miles of difficult navigation through the
dangerous sandbanks and shipping lanes of the outer Thames
Estuary. I had been warned that the 'sand' banks, were more like
concrete banks, and if you were so foolish as to run aground then
your yacht would be pounded to bits on the hard surface. The trip
would be a preparation for an eventual cross-Channel trip to France.

In 1997 I retired from the RAF and took up a post as Harrier
simulator instructor at RAF Wittering, having been 'headhunted' by
their boss. It was good to be back with the old firm again. Not much
had changed, although the 'jet' was now much more complicated.
The young pilots were still running around with their hair on fire,
just like the old days. As I had been away from the force for thirteen
years, a whole generation of Harrier pilots had entered the system
who were completely unknown to me, although there were still a few
old hands I remembered who were now quite senior officers. The
'jet' had by now evolved into a very high-tech machine in comparison with my day, and the new generations of Harrier pilots were
much more into button-pushing than the simple stick-and-rudder
techniques of the old days. Gone were the bad old days of getting
lost at low level and using unsuitable old-fashioned weapons; during
my first ten years in the flight simulator the Harrier, in its GR9 form,
was to evolve into the most potent and efficient ground attack
machine the RAF had ever possessed.

The cross-estuary trip to Ramsgate in the Elizabethan 29 never
came off. I always chickened out before the half-way point. Basically
I was finding the 29 just a bit too skittish in the choppy estuary
waters and was looking for something a bit heavier, now that I had
more confidence in my solo sailing with the Bermuda rig. On one
occasion I was about five miles offshore when I took a heavy fall
during a tack with a bit of a sea running. I fell hard against the angle
of the cockpit seat, cracking a couple of ribs and totally winding
myself. Somehow I managed to hold together long enough to get

back to my berth up the river. If this had happened further out, or at night, the outcome would have been much worse. I realized then that if I was to continue solo sailing I needed a bigger yacht.

I found *Salicet* in a marina in north Wales on a cold late November day. She was beautiful; a Nicholson 32 Mk 8, 32 feet long and over 7 tons of long keel hull – classic lines and as solid and stable as anyone could wish. You could sail round the world in her. Her engine was almost new and she had £3,000 worth of Monitor wind vane – essential for solo sailing. Her owner was almost in tears at the sale and I could see why. By mid January she was safely transported cross-country to Suffolk yacht harbour and I put her straight in the water. By the end of spring I was confident enough to be tacking her up the river on busy days and was able to make the trip to Ramsgate in style by midsummer. Shortly afterwards I sailed from Harwich to Calais, a distance of about seventy nautical miles via Long Sand Head, Fisherman's Gap and the run outside the Goodwin Sands. After sixteen hours' sailing, I arrived at Calais feeling as if I had crossed the Atlantic. After a couple of weeks I sailed Harwich – Boulogne in about the same time. On the return trip I felt confident enough to sail into Ramsgate in the dark via the Downs. *Salicet* was magnificent. There was no better feeling than clinging to the forestay and watching as she pounded along at 7 knots, close-hauled in a stiff breeze, everything sheeted in hard and the spray flying free. I began to make plans for the next great sailing event: a solo trip to the Scilly Isles. However, my rambling imagination was already going several steps further.

As my self-confidence had returned with a vengeance I began to think the unthinkable. If I could sail across the channel solo then why shouldn't I start flying again? My only option was gliding, of which my only experience was the gliding camp in 1961 at St Eval. I had no interest in powered flying; anyway, I knew that that would involved more contact with the medics and the Civil Aviation Authority, and I had had enough of them to last a lifetime while gaining my ATPL.

On a beautiful late summer afternoon fate drove me to Buckminster Gliding Club at Saltby airfield, just south-west of Grantham. Here I introduced myself as a hopeful new member and was delighted to be offered an introductory flight in the Puchatz trainer. My instructor, who was to send me solo after half a dozen duals was a bluff, down-to-earth ex-mines inspector and long-time glider pilot. Amazingly, he was the elder brother of an old Harrier colleague who had been killed in the early '70s. I felt an immediate kinship with him and realized that this was a sign to me that I was doing the right thing in taking up gliding again. I was soon to find out that gliding, like offshore sailing, was an extremely free-and-easy sport under the excellent light-handed regulation of the British Gliding Association.

After nearly forty years' break, the technology had progressed a bit. Although the club had some old metal and fabric gliders, the majority of my flying was to be on the more modern fibreglass/carbon fibre machines, with much higher performance. I was keen to get on to cross-country flying, which proved to be a fascinating challenge, unlike any kind of flying I had done before. By the following summer I had my Silver C cross-country badge and was looking for a glider syndicate to buy into. After a frustrating time trying to fly my 300 kilometres Gold Distance challenge in the club's Astir, I bought into a dream syndicate at the end of the season. The glider was a German-built DG 600, a beautiful high-performance machine with full-span flaps, which handled almost like a jet. The other two syndicate members rarely flew, so I had the machine almost to myself. Over the winter I practised hard and managed to fly the 300 kilometres Gold Distance and complete the Gold Badge award. The 3,000 metre Gold Height climb I completed while wave flying in the Cairngorms on my first flight out of Aboyne on Deeside.

Before achieving my Gold Badge I got myself on to a Soaring Club trip to Cerdanya in the Pyrenees. I fancied the idea of gliding in the mountains and the two weeks included some of the most enjoyable and exciting flying I have ever done. After one dual checkout the chief instructor sent me solo mountain flying using the club's single-seaters. I enjoyed the flying so much that I determined to go back again the following year, this time taking my own DG600 along.

I wrote the following report for Buckminster Gliding Club's magazine on my return; it gives a flavour of what mountain flying is like:

La Cerdanya is a small Spanish airfield lying in the centre of the 20 mile long valley of the river Segre, in the eastern Pyrenees right next to the tiny state of Andorra. The airfield is at about 3,500 feet above sea level, with snow-capped peaks just a few miles to north and south rising to 10,000 feet. You can be soaring among the peaks at 10,000 feet just 5 miles from the airfield, so it is ideal for initial mountain soaring training. The valley has its own micro climate, protected by the mountain ranges, and it is often warm and sunny even when both Spain and France lie under thick clag. The Soaring Club have been using it for about 10 years in springtime. There has been little Spanish interest in the airfield. I flew here last year for the first time and determined to return this year with the DG600.

Monday, Cerdanya airfield. Briefing at 1100. All Brits present, plus several Spanish pilots, to my surprise. (there were none last year). According to the Chief Instructor there are only about 40 Spanish cross-country glider pilots – amazing in a country famous for its soaring weather. Gliding is just not a traditional Spanish sport. This will be the routine for the next couple of weeks: a leisurely breakfast at the farmhouse, an excellent briefing by the Chief Instructor about the day's conditions and procedures, rigging gliders then first take-off about 1300. I receive a characteristic initial brief as follows:

'You've flown here before haven't you Jerry?'

'Yes.'

'Well, you can sort yourself out, OK?'

'Fine by me.'

For those new to the mountains there will be a programme of hard-working duals, followed by solo when (if) the Chief Instructor thinks you are safe.

For the first week we have progressively stronger westerlies down the valley. This is not the best wind direction to produce waves. The aerotows are character-forming , and the basic rules apply: never pull off in sink and you must be within gliding range of the field when you release (allowing for strong sink). On a tip from an old hand I wedge a block of wood behind the hook, to prevent back-release on tow in heavy turbulence. For the first couple of days ridge soaring is possible and the Chief Instructor gives the basic rules of flying figures-of-8 near the rocks:

'Whenever you point at the mountain always check 3 things: AIRSPEED, DISTANCE OUT and ESCAPE ROUTE."

These are vital safety elements as there are major differences from flatland soaring. Firstly, you can no longer use attitude relative to the horizon to achieve correct airspeed. When pointing at the mountain the horizon is miles above you, and vice versa when turning away you just have to monitor and fly airspeed constantly. The common instinctive error is to raise the nose as you turn towards the hard stuff. This is when you invariably encounter monster sink as well, hence the need always for an escape flight path towards lower ground. The shallower slopes are more dangerous than vertical faces.

Another gem from the oracle:

'Listen to the aeroplane: if it's going quiet, you're running out of airspeed.'

I always fly with the vent partly open to hear the airflow. Another hazard is the rapid-forming cloud cover over the high peaks . If climbing below it you need to be aware of an escape vector through cloud back into the valley in case it all goes white suddenly. I am glad of the new Ferranti Mk6 artificial horizon I had fitted to the DG over winter. This means that cloud flying is as comfortable as any other military jet I've flown.

Everyone pays the closest attention to these excellent morning briefings, as the dangers of getting it wrong are all too obvious. With the stronger winds later in the week there will be severe turbulence near the mountains and no question of gentle ridge soaring. As usual in mountain flying the majority of lift will come from different kinds of thermals in among the high ground and all over the valley area. You can climb in thermals triggered by ridgelines, from hot-spots, wind shadows, convergence and rotors under wave etc., etc. On the third day wave flying is on the cards. In the brief the Chief Instructor describes Rotor Thermals (which I've never heard of), and gives the technique:

'Get into the rotor and hang on until you pop out of the top into the wave.'

Can't believe this. Sure enough it works. It's bumpy all over the valley and eventually I jump into what must be a rotor thermal. After a roller-coaster climb of several thousand feet at 12+ knots, suddenly it all goes quiet and I'm in the wave at 10,000 feet, climbing smoothly at 2 knots. It's so smooth that it's surreal – I could be sitting on the ground in a flat calm. I follow the brief and don't stay too long as the aim is to improve your technique, not just build hours. Anyway it's not good enough for Gold Height as I can hear other pilots at a maximum of 14,000 feet. I drop back down into the Tumble Dryer for another attempt at a climb.

This kind of flying is extremely exhilarating and hard work at the same time. At times you hit turbulence which can throw you to 90 degrees of bank with no airspeed, your head pounded against the canopy. The DG's legendary lack of stall warning is no problem here. You just fall away ballistic – as long as you've got room below. Average sortie lengths for me are about 2.5 – 3 hrs.

By the end of the first week 2 things happen: the wind moderates and a heap of new people arrive, including a large contingent from Dunstable, a few from the Borders Club, plus a heap more Spanish pilots with their own tug. Life on the tiny airstrip is about to get much more interesting as the Spanish speak no English on the radio. Amazingly, everything works well under the firm control of our senior instructors. We have Spanish and Brit tugs launching alternately and the Spanish co-operating fully with the briefed procedures. One or two of them are real mountain pilots, flying 100 kilometres up into the highest peaks of the Pyrenees and back. That is A-level stuff: – away from our valley there are just a handful of tiny fields for outlanding in which you will probably be uninjured. Your glider may or may not be recoverable with a JCB. Maybe I'll be more adventurous next year, but for this I'm happy to stay in the valley again.

There are no major cock-ups, except for one visiting 2 -seater landing half a mile short of the runway in the cabbages. (no damage). After 10 days the weather deteriorates and I set off for home, having had my fill of excellent flying. I chickened out on just one day, when the wind was a bit too sporty for me.

Afterthoughts

This story began in the aftermath of the Second World War and I feel a need to refer back to those times. Our post-war RAF flying – mainly peacetime – involved adventure and sacrifice, duty and sheer love of aviation for its own sake, as in all periods of aviation history. But like the post – First World War aviators who looked back, we had an almost unreachable standard of courage and endurance to live up to.

We must remember the incredible hardiness and sacrifice of those young men, particularly of those 55,000 Bomber Command aircrew who lost their lives during those momentous years 1939-45. These were ordinary, hopeful young men, lacking the guile and world-weariness of later generations, who merely 'did their bit' with aircraft and weapons that they thought of as up-to-date and reasonably capable. There were no 'risk assessments', 'performance appraisals' or PR flannelers, and flight safety was still a vague ideal, totally subordinated to the desperately dangerous business of fighting through the defences and getting bombs on to the enemy's heads.

With our hindsight we can see how vulnerable those slow old machines were to enemy fire, with not so much as a scrap of armour to protect the majority of the crew, and with only rudimentary and unreliable navigation aids and inadequate weapons. Bad weather and darkness also took their grim toll, with pilots receiving barely adequate instrument flying training.

These problems were addressed gradually as the war progressed, but the enemy's capabilities improved also and, right into the final few months of the war, enemy guns and fighters were still able to take a bloody toll of our bombers and fighter-bombers trying to finish the job off. For too many of those young men the standard bomber tour of thirty operations was to be unattainable, their lives snuffed out in a burning wreck with no hope of escape, or freezing to death in the unforgiving winter seas.

In our time we too reached for the stars in modern high-performance jets, but our chances of survival were infinitely better. There were casualties along the way, but these caused few second thoughts to those of us who survived – because we were doing what we had always dreamed of, reaching for the skies and taking the risks willingly and without complaint.

No, our post-war achievements in the air were meagre in comparison with those of the heroes of the Second World War, those 55,000 dead of Bomber Command and all the other fallen aviators of that unique period of history.

May this be their epitaph:

> Let them in Peter, they are very tired;
> Give them the couches where the Angels sleep.
> Let them wake whole again to new dawns fired
> With sun, not war. And may their peace be deep
> Remember where the broken bodies lie...
> And give them things they like. Let them make noise.
> God knows how young they were to have to die!
> Give swing bands, not harps, to those our boys.
> Let them love, Peter – they have had no time -
> Girls sweet as meadow wind, with flowering hair.
> They should have trees and bird song, hills to climb -
> The taste of summer in a ripened pear.
> Tell them how they are all missed. Say not to fear;
> It's going to be all right with us down here.

Anonymous

Index